Praise for *The Optimistic Environmentalist*

We hope you enjoy this book. Please return or renew it by the due date.You can renew it at **www.norfolk.gov.uk/libraries** or by using our free library app. Otherwise you can phone **0344 800 8020** - please have your library card and PIN ready.You can sign up for email reminders too.

NORFOLK COUNTY COUNCIL
LIBRARY AND INFORMATION SERVICE

NORFOLK ITEM

D1428545

"In *The Optimistic Environmentalist*, Boyd inspires hopefulness, particularly for young people." —*BC BookWorld*

"For anyone who is starting to feel beaten down and defeated by the magnitude of our planet's green problems, this book definitely provides a much-needed fillip." —Green Spirit

"Boyd offers hope and inspiration with *The Optimistic Environmentalist*, outlining progress that has been and is being made on the environmental front." —David Suzuki Foundation

"*The Optimistic Environmentalist* is a breath of fresh air . . . an accessible book that is interesting, well researched, and always hopeful."
—*Vancouver Sun*

"Nowhere will you find a clearer explanation of the extraordinary growth of renewable energy and its implications for addressing climate change." —*The Georgia Straight*

"*The Optimistic Environmentalist: Progressing Towards a Greener Future* is a book with an abundance of hope. Author David Boyd's enthusiasm is palpable." —*National Observer*

"As the title suggests, [it] is a paean to the amazing progress we have made on the environment globally and the possibility of solving our major environmental problems, even the most difficult ones such as climate change, in our lifetimes." —*Literary Review of Canada*

"A timely and important book." —*Australian Book Review*

"David Boyd has given us all a great gift—a book to lift our spirits. As story after story is recounted by one of Canada's leading environmental lawyers, we catch some of his contagious enthusiasm. We must all be optimistic environmentalists." —Elizabeth May, Canada's first Green Party Member of Parliament

The
RIGHTS *of* NATURE

The
RIGHTS *of* NATURE

A LEGAL REVOLUTION
THAT COULD SAVE THE WORLD

David R. Boyd

Also by David R. Boyd

~

The Optimistic Environmentalist: Progressing Towards a Greener Future (2015)

Cleaner, Greener, Healthier:
A Prescription for Stronger Canadian Environmental Laws and Policies (2015)

The Right to a Healthy Environment: Revitalizing Canada's Constitution (2012)

The Environmental Rights Revolution:
A Global Study of Constitutions, Human Rights, and the Environment (2011)

Dodging the Toxic Bullet:
How to Protect Yourself from Everyday Environmental Health Hazards (2010)

David Suzuki's Green Guide (with David Suzuki, 2008)

Unnatural Law: Rethinking Canadian Environmental Law and Policy (2003)

~

For Meredith, Margot, Neko,
and the Southern Resident Killer Whales

"A human being is part of a whole, called by us the 'Universe'—a part limited in time and space. He experiences himself, his thoughts, and feelings, as something separated from the rest—a kind of optical delusion of his consciousness. This delusion is a kind of prison for us, restricting us to our personal desires and to affection for a few persons nearest us. Our task must be to free ourselves from this prison by widening our circles of compassion to embrace all living creatures and the whole of nature in its beauty."

ALBERT EINSTEIN, 1950 letter

"Throughout legal history, each successive extension of rights to some new entity has been, theretofore, a bit unthinkable."

PROFESSOR CHRISTOPHER STONE,
Should Trees Have Standing?

"As the crickets' soft autumn hum
is to us
so are we to the trees
as are they
to the rocks and the hills."

GARY SNYDER, "They're Listening"

CONTENTS

PREFACE

Not surprisingly, this book about the rights of nature is inspired by my love of the natural world. It's a passion that was ignited when I was a kid roaming the Rocky Mountains, and I still fan the flames by sharing the wonders of Canada's West Coast with my daughter, Meredith, and my partner, Margot.

In 2000, I went on a sailing trip in British Columbia's Great Bear Rainforest with friends working for the Raincoast Conservation Society. One morning, at the crack of dawn, Captain Brian Falconer spotted a pod of killer whales. Soon we were all on deck, watching dorsal fins emerge from the sea and listening to orcas' explosive exhalations break the morning silence. Brian tossed an underwater microphone over the side, set up a battery-powered speaker, and we were suddenly eavesdropping on cetacean conversations. We could distinguish different voices, some deep and booming, some squeaky and almost soprano. It was both alien and familiar. As the whales communicated with each other, tears streamed down our faces. We were awed and privileged to hear the whales' conversations, intimately connected for this moment to these remarkable and complex, social, intelligent animals.

In 2004, on the evening before Margot and I were married on Pender Island (in the Salish Sea between Victoria and Vancouver), at least fifty killer whales passed by our house, interrupting their regular circuit to put on an amazing display. Orcas leapt from the sea, spy-hopped, tail-slapped, and generally carried on as though they were having a blast. Maybe they were hunting salmon. Maybe they were celebrating something. Maybe they were playing a game or engaging in some ritual we don't have the slightest inkling about. In any event, it was spectacular, and our visiting friends and relatives were astounded.

Since then, we have crossed paths with pods of orcas on many occasions as we kayaked around our island home. These are the Southern Resident killer whales who spend most of their time in the waters surrounding America's San Juan Islands and Canada's Southern Gulf Islands. It can be unnerving, to put it mildly, to see a dorsal fin almost two metres tall slicing through the water toward you in *Jaws*-like fashion as you sit in a plastic kayak. Your vessel suddenly seems kind of flimsy. Once I was paddling into a strong headwind, unaware that orcas were approaching from behind. I nearly lost control of my paddle and my bladder when a large male surfaced right in front of me, so close that I could see individual beads of water rolling off his massive back. An adult orca can be nine metres long and weigh more than 5,000 kilograms—abstract numbers until they're suddenly within reach.

The Southern Residents occasionally interrupted the writing of this book. Sitting at my desk in our solar-powered writing cabin, I can hear them approach through Swanson Channel from the southeast. Even though I've observed these creatures hundreds of times, I still tingle with excitement when they appear. I'll leave my desk and run down to the ocean to watch until they've all passed out of sight. Sometimes I'll jump into my kayak, tailing them from a respectful distance for a few minutes.

Scientists have only scratched the surface of the mysteries of these animals, but what their research has uncovered is fascinating. Orcas live in matrilineal societies, meaning that their social structure is based on units comprised of adult females and their offspring. They spend their entire lives—over 100 years in some cases—in close-knit family units called pods. The whole pod contributes to raising the young ones, sharing food, and teaching them to hunt. Older females go through menopause, one of only two non-human species known to do so. (The other is the short-finned pilot whale.) Scientists believe that older female orcas play vital roles in helping raise the calves of younger females and in identifying bountiful feeding areas. Different populations have different dialects, food preferences, and mating patterns, essentially reflecting cultural differences. Scientists and keen observers can identify each individual whale through differences in their size, dorsal fins, and colour patterns. Orcas have large brains and use echolocation for navigating, locating prey, and communicating. Their voices can travel across many kilometres of ocean. We can only speculate about what they are saying to each other, why they live in such close-knit societies, and what kind of culture they have developed.

These killer whales are listed as endangered species in both Canada and the U.S. In the late 1960s and early 1970s, about fifty individuals from the Southern Resident population were captured for display in aquariums. Another dozen or so were killed in the process. The stories of these abductions and deaths, and the desperate efforts of the adult orcas to protect their calves, are heartbreaking. It must have shattered those tight-knit killer whale communities to be torn apart, and they have yet to recover.

Today there are only about eighty orcas left in the Southern Resident population. The main threats to their survival are a shortage of Chinook salmon (the cornerstone of their diet), the accumulation of toxic industrial chemicals in their bodies (harming their health and interfering with their ability to reproduce), military exercises, and the noise from boat traffic, which causes stress and impedes their ability to hunt. Under the weight of this multipronged assault, the Southern Residents are perilously close to the point where recovery may be impossible.

But there is always hope. During the year that I spent writing this book, females in the Southern Resident population gave birth to several new calves. Although there is a high mortality rate for these youngsters, there are few sights as joyful and optimism-inducing as seeing the tiny dorsal fin of a newborn calf slicing in and out of the ocean, swimming snugly beside its mother.

There are moments in life, rare and fleeting in my case, when you get a flash of insight. Several years ago, I was attending a gathering of activists from across the Americas at a retreat center nestled in the redwood forests outside San Francisco. I awoke early one morning with ideas whirring through my head at hyper-speed, and I thought I'd better go for a run to try and calm my mind. Alas, it was pitch black outside, and I didn't have a headlight or know the terrain.

I needed a Plan B, and luckily there was a small swimming pool, perhaps eight metres long and six metres wide. It was too short to swim lengths, but there was no one else in it so I thought I'd try swimming around the perimeter. At first it was kind of fun, but the novelty soon wore off. It was physically uncomfortable contorting my body into a ninety-degree turn every few seconds.

Doing it for more than a few minutes not only would be painful but would drive anyone crazy. And that's when the lightning struck.

If this was uncomfortable for me, what was it like for captive killer whales? Living in a small pool, day after day, week after week, year after year, separated from their families, their communities, and their homes has been the plight of hundreds of orcas in aquariums around the world. The life expectancy of orcas in captivity is far shorter than in the wild. Wild orcas have an average life expectancy of fifty years, although they have been known to live over 100 years. In captivity, the lifespan is twenty-five, with some living to forty years. Despite the array of harms we've inflicted upon them, killer whales in the wild have never attacked or harmed a human being. Yet orcas in aquariums have killed several people, including their trainers, and injured others.

Floating in the tiny swimming pool, I realized that I had a responsibility to contribute to efforts to protect these magnificent animals. It was the least I could do in light of the joy and wonder that they had gifted me.

Governments in Canada and the U.S. are in the early stages of implementing actions intended to foster the recovery of the Southern Resident orca population. Despite the protection of the U.S. Endangered Species Act, the U.S. Marine Mammal Protection Act, and Canada's Species at Risk Act, the population of Southern Resident killer whales continues to decline. Would their future be brighter if they had legal rights?

The second creature that interrupted my efforts to complete this book is a calico cat called Neko, who joined our family two years ago after a lengthy debate. Meredith was enthusiastically pro-feline and was aided and abetted by Margot. I've never been a cat person and was genuinely worried about the catastrophic impact of domestic cats on wild bird populations. Eventually we compromised on getting a kitten that would be largely house-bound and closely supervised when outside. Neko turned out to be a scaredy cat who likes to watch the birds come and go at our feeders from the safety and comfort of our living room. Neko often sat on my lap purring during the cold winter months when I was writing this book, and my affection for her has grown. But, more importantly, she has made me reflect on the relationship between people and pets. What are the rights and responsibilities that define our relationship?

My writing was also interrupted by our efforts to re-wild the land we live on. Our Pender Island home is on a south-facing acre of land within a Garry oak ecosystem. Early explorers described Garry oak meadows as "a perfect Eden" surrounded by unkempt wilderness. This landscape features gnarled oak trees and dazzling arbutus trees (a unique bark-shedding evergreen with leaves and red berries). The trees are surrounded by luscious wildflower mead-ows featuring camas, chocolate lilies, and pretty shooting stars. At least that's the theory. In practice, this is an acutely endangered ecosystem, decimated by urban/suburban development and the conversion of meadows into farmland. The only oak tree and all the chocolate lilies at our place are ones we planted after ripping out thousands of invasive Scotch broom bushes. Regional efforts are underway to restore this once-spectacular ecosystem, but it's an uphill struggle. As I wandered around, pulling up baby broom plants, I wondered, *Would it help if the Garry oak ecosystem had legal rights?*

A growing number of people around the world believe that today's environmental laws are not strong enough to protect nature. I've practised and taught environmental law in Canada and internationally for more than twenty years, and in that time there have been many victories, but the overall prognosis is still grim. We need new approaches if we are going to successfully change course. Much of my work in recent years has involved studying, analyzing, and ultimately promoting recognition of the human right to live in a healthy environment. This promising approach has spread widely in the past forty years, contributing to substantial environmental progress around the world. While writing a book about environmental protection and human rights a number of years ago, I was amazed to learn that Ecuador had created a revolutionary constitution that extended rights to nature itself, including all the species and ecosystems in that biologically rich country.

Change is in the air, and not just in Ecuador. Just fifty years ago, nobody blinked when SeaWorld used speedboats and spotting planes to locate, trap, and take killer whales from the oceans and hold them in small pools for human entertainment. Today in most countries, such an act would be widely condemned. A growing number of places, from California to Costa Rica, have passed laws prohibiting the capture, public display, or breeding of orcas. With climate change, extinction, and pollution in the headlines, people are growing more aware and are looking for creative solutions to our ecological dilemmas.

To what extent do existing laws recognize the rights of nature? Do captive killer whales living in aquariums have any legal rights? Do wild orcas like the Southern Residents have any rights, as individuals or as a species? Do the ecosystems in which orcas live have any rights? Would rights help to "save the whales" and prevent other species from toppling over the precipice into extinction? Do domestic animals like Neko have rights? Could recognizing nature's rights help push human society toward a reconciliation with the rest of the community of life on Earth? These are the questions I set out to answer in this book. The answers surprised me, energized me, and hopefully will prove interesting to you.

Introduction
THREE DAMAGING IDEAS
AND A POTENTIAL SOLUTION

"There is a hue and cry for human rights, they said, for all people, and the Indigenous people said: What of the rights of the natural world? Where is the seat for the buffalo or the eagle? Who is representing them at this forum? Who is speaking for the water of the earth? Who is speaking for the trees and the forests? Who is speaking for the fish—for the whales, for the beavers, for our children?"

CHIEF OREN LYONS JR., Faithkeeper of the

Onondaga tribe of the Haudenosaunee (Iroquois) Nation

Humans today have a deeply troubled relationship with other animals and species, and with the ecosystems upon which all life on Earth depends. We purport to love animals but regularly inflict pain and suffering upon them. Every year, according to the UN's Food and Agriculture Organization, humans kill over 100 billion animals—fish, chickens, ducks, pigs, rabbits, turkeys, geese, sheep, goats, cattle, dogs, whales, wolves, elephants, lions, dolphins, and more. Scientists are in agreement that human actions are causing the sixth mass extinction in the 4.5-billion-year history of the planet. Species are being declared extinct every year, and we are pushing thousands more to the brink of oblivion. Humans are damaging, destroying, or eliminating entire ecosystems, including native forests, grasslands, coral reefs, and wetlands. Ancient, complex, and vital planetary systems—the climate, water, and nitrogen cycles—are being disrupted by our actions.

Homo sapiens emerged from Africa less than 200,000 years ago. Thanks to their fertility, adaptability, and ability to use technology, our ancestors colonized the entire Earth around 12,000 years ago, including the continents we now call Europe, Asia, Australia, North America, and South America. Over the course of the past two centuries, our population has exploded, growing from one billion in 1800 to 7.5 billion today. While birth rates are falling the world over, the latest UN estimates indicate that increased longevity and improved health are pushing us toward a population of ten billion people by 2050.

To meet the needs and desires of this booming population, the global economy has also exploded, from a worldwide GDP of about one trillion dollars a century ago to more than 100 trillion dollars today. Much of this economic growth has been driven by ever-increasing human appropriation of land, forests, water, wildlife, and other "natural resources."

Our environmental impact has grown exponentially because of population and economic growth. Humanity's collective ecological footprint is estimated to be 1.6 Earths, meaning we are using natural goods and services 1.6 times faster than they are being replenished. This is largely the result of high levels of consumption in wealthy nations. Geologists, a group hardly known for hyperbole, have named this geological era the Anthropocene because of the scope and scale of human impacts on the Earth.

Our ongoing use and misuse of other animals, species, and nature is rooted in three entrenched and related ideas. The first is anthropocentrism—the widespread human belief that we are separate from, and superior to, the rest of the natural world. Through this superiority complex, humans see ourselves as the pinnacle of evolution. The second is that everything in nature, animate and inanimate, constitutes our property, which we have the right to use as we see fit. The third idea is that we can and should pursue limitless economic growth as the paramount objective of modern society. Anthropocentrism and property "rights" provide the foundations of contemporary industrial society, underpinning everything from law and economics to education and religion. Economic growth is the principal objective for governments and businesses, and it consistently trumps concerns about the environment.

These ideas have a long history. The ancient Greek philosopher Aristotle believed that animals lacked souls and reason and therefore, as inferior creatures, were appropriately used as resources by man. As he wrote in *Politics*, "Plants exist for the sake of animals, and animals for the sake of man—domestic animals for his use and food, wild ones for food and other accessories of life, such as clothing and various tools. Since nature makes nothing purposeless or in vain, it is undeniably true that she has made all animals for the sake of man." Aristotle also worked with Plato to develop the concept of a hierarchical ladder of existence that ranked animals and plants. Later Christian philosophers built upon this, devising the Great Chain of Being that placed humans near the top of the ladder, just below God and the angels. Nonhuman animals languished below us, while snakes, insects, and creatures incapable of movement occupied even lower rungs. The chain imposed a strict hierarchy on all life forms.

Genesis, the Christian creation story, states that God made humans in his image and granted us "dominion over the fish of the sea, and over the fowl of the air, and over the cattle, and over all the earth, and over every creeping thing that creepeth upon the earth." Humans were given clear instructions: "Be fruitful, and multiply, and replenish the earth, and subdue it." Not all Christians viewed the rest of creation as subject to human dominion. St. Francis of Assisi advocated for the equality of all creatures, referring to the sun, the Earth, the water, and the wind as his brothers and sisters. St. Francis, however, was an outlier.

During the seventeenth and eighteenth centuries, some of history's most influential thinkers reinforced the anthropocentric perspective, and the place of animals in human society took a turn for the worse. Non-human animals were deemed unable to speak, reason, or even feel. French philosopher René Descartes forcefully expressed the idea that "animals are mere machines" and wrote, "The reason animals do not speak as we do is not that they lack the organs, but that they have no thoughts." Descartes concluded, "Man stands alone." Similarly, German philosopher Immanuel Kant wrote, "Animals are not self-conscious and are merely a means to an end. That end is man . . . our duties toward animals are merely indirect duties toward humanity."

A contrary and more progressive attitude toward animals was suggested by nineteenth-century British philosopher Jeremy Bentham. He concluded that the critical moral question for how we should treat animals "is not Can they reason? nor, Can they talk? but, Can they suffer?" In his view, some animals could indeed feel pain, and therefore had the right not to be harmed. Bentham's ideas did not prevail in his own time, but they eventually influenced

Peter Singer, author of the 1975 best-seller *Animal Liberation* that kickstarted the modern animal rights movement.

Anthropocentric ideas are still in vogue today. In his 2004 book, *Putting Humans First: Why We Are Nature's Favorite*, libertarian philosopher Tibor R. Machan wrote, "Humans are more important, even better, than other animals, and we deserve the benefits that exploiting animals can provide." Because humans are the most important species, Machan continued, "it is right to exploit nature to promote our own lives and happiness."

The notion of human superiority is even entrenched in landmark international environmental agreements. The first global eco-summit, held in Sweden in 1972, produced the Declaration of the United Nations Conference on the Human Environment (more commonly known as the Stockholm Declaration). It proclaimed, "Of all things in the world, people are the most precious." The 1992 Earth Summit in Brazil resulted in the Rio Declaration on Environment and Development, which stated, "Human beings are at the centre of concerns for sustainable development."

The notion that humans are distinct from, and superior to, other animals permeates Western legal systems, producing outcomes that are at odds with reality. For example, any biologist will tell you that humans are animals. But the law disagrees. *Black's Law Dictionary*, the most widely used law dictionary in Canada and the United States, still defines an animal as "any animate being which is endowed with the power of voluntary motion. In the language of the law the term includes all living creatures *not human*" (emphasis added). Other legal definitions of "animal" are even more absurd. In the U.S., the Animal Welfare Act includes a definition of animal that explicitly excludes rats, mice, reptiles, amphibians, fish, and farm animals. Why? To ensure that even the limited protections offered by that law are not available to animals used in agriculture or research or caught in fisheries.

Property

The idea that nature is merely a collection of things intended for human use is one of the most universal and unquestioned concepts in contemporary society. Hundreds of years ago, influential legal scholar William Blackstone, author of the authoritative *Commentaries on the Law of England*, wrote, "The Earth, and all things herein, are the general property of mankind, exclusive of other beings, from the immediate gift of the creator."

It is remarkable to reflect on the fact that although there are millions of species on Earth, a single species of hyperintelligent primates—*Homo sapiens*—has laid claim, through the assertion of legal ownership, to almost every square metre of the 148 million square kilometres of land on the planet. There is virtually no more *terra nullius*, or "nobody's land," as the famous explorers described land uninhabited by their kind of people. In today's world, land is either private property or state-owned property. Private or public, it's all owned by humans.

Among the planet's few exceptions to the universal assertion of human ownership are a pair of places, linked by their remoteness and utter inhospitality to humans. One is a desolate and uninhabited area of the Antarctic known as Marie Byrd Land. It's protected from future human ownership claims through an international treaty. Another chunk of land where until recently humans did not claim ownership is Bir Tawil, an 2,072-square-kilometre stretch of mountains, sand, and rock in the desert between Egypt and the Sudan. A longstanding boundary dispute between the two African nations resulted in both asserting jurisdiction over a larger parcel of productive land, known as Hala'ib, and renouncing their ownership of Bir Tawil. In 2014, American Jeremiah Heaton journeyed to Bir Tawil and staked an ownership claim. Heaton had promised to make his daughter, Emily, a real princess and was seeking to keep his word. He made up a flag for what he calls the Kingdom of North Sudan and planted it in Bir Tawil on Emily's seventh birthday. As the self-proclaimed king, Heaton was able to fulfill his promise. He even claims to have opened a European embassy in Copenhagen. Unbeknownst to Heaton, British journalist Jack Shenker had made the same journey four years earlier, planting his flag and asserting sovereignty over and ownership of Bir Tawil.

The high seas—the open ocean beyond any country's jurisdiction—are another refuge from humanity's sweeping assertion of ownership. Yet, while not "owned," the high seas are treated as a global commons for human exploitation, a shared resource where massive factory fishing trawler nets vacuum up life from the seas and renegade whaling nations still hunt whales under the guise of scientific harvests. Deep-sea mining, previously unthinkable, is now becoming a reality.

In addition to owning all the land, humans claim ownership of the species that live upon that land: Animals are regarded as property, things, or objects, no different in the eyes of the law than shoes, tables, or trinkets. This includes both domestic and wild animals. From a legal perspective, ownership of an animal includes the rights to possess, use, transfer, dispose of, and exclude others from taking it. Wildlife, even on privately owned land, is owned by state and provincial governments. For example, under New York's Environmental Conservation Law, "The State of New York owns all fish, game, wildlife, shellfish, and protected insects in the state." Legislation in Oregon is more concise: "Wildlife is the property of the state." Courts have reinforced these rules of ownership. In a prosecution of a man for illegally hunting deer, a court held that poachers "have no respect whatsoever for the State of Mississippi's sovereign ownership of such magnificent God-given creatures of the wild, entrusted to mankind for his consumption and/or enjoyment." Animals that are sold are considered "goods" under the U.S. Uniform Commercial Code, just like televisions, trucks, or toys.

In Canada, the law is the same. Wildlife and fish belong to the government until they are lawfully captured or killed, at which point they become private property. Section 2 of the BC Wildlife Act is called Property in Wildlife and states, "Ownership in all wildlife in British Columbia is vested in the government. . . . A person who lawfully kills wildlife and complies with all applicable provisions of this Act and the regulations acquires the right of property in that wildlife." Manitoba's Fisheries Act states, "The property in all wild fish, including wild fish that have been unlawfully caught, is vested in the Crown, and no person may acquire any right or property in such fish other than in accordance with this Act." The Supreme Court of Canada has confirmed that "the fisheries resource includes the animals that inhabit the seas." No matter where wildlife lives, it belongs to humans.

When you stop to think about it, our arrogance is breathtaking. We've divided the diversity of life on Earth into two categories—people and things. Us and them. We're the only species with rights to the land, water, wildlife, and ecosystems of the planet. Old-growth forests, rainforests, cloud forests, rivers, lakes, soil—these natural wonders are all considered natural resources, and thus property owned by humans. To say we share this planet with millions of other species is ecologically incontrovertible, but legally incorrect. If we are the only species with rights, we are the only species that really matters.

While property rights are deeply rooted in Western legal systems, the concept of property responsibilities is largely absent. In one-third of a second, Google produced 31,700,000 hits for the phrase "property rights," but only 19,000 hits for "property responsibilities." Similarly, Google found 154,000,000 results for "human rights," but only 41,000 for "human responsibilities."

Indigenous Worldviews

There are exceptions to the widespread beliefs of human superiority, property rights, and the primacy of economic growth. A contrasting perspective asserting that non-human entities have rights, and that humans have corresponding responsibilities, has deep roots in cultures around the world. More than 1,000 years ago, a Sufi scholar wrote a book called *The Animals' Lawsuit Against Humanity*, in which all members of the animal kingdom—domestic and wild, from bees and mules to frogs and lions—asserted that their rights were being systematically violated by humans. Adherents of Jainism, Hinduism, and Buddhism endorse, to varying degrees, the doctrine of *ahimsa*, which advocates reverence for all life and non-injury to all living things.

Indigenous cultures across the world cultivate complex understandings of human responsibilities toward the natural world.

Despite centuries of Western colonial thought, many still perceive human beings as interdependent—part of, rather than separate from and superior to the rest of the natural world. A key element of the legal systems of many Indigenous cultures is a set of reciprocal rights and responsibilities between humans and other species, as well as between humans and non-living elements of the environment. Luther Standing Bear described the beliefs of his people, the Lakota: "The animals had rights—the right of a man's protection, the right to live, the right to multiply, the right to freedom, and the right of man's indebtedness—and in recognition of these rights the Lakota never enslaved the animal, and spared all life that was not needed for food and clothing." In an essay called "The Right of Animal Nations to Survive," Haudenosaunee scholar John Mohawk wrote, "The Indian cultures accept the legitimacy of the animals, celebrate their presence, propose that they are 'peoples' in the sense that they have an equal share in this planet and, like peoples, have the right to a continued existence. Animals have the right to live as animals. If all of the above are true, humans have no right to destroy animal habitat, or hunt or fish them to extinction." Dr. Gregory Cajete of the University of New Mexico, a Tewa Indian, wrote, "Among Native people animals have always had rights, and were equal to human beings in terms of their right to their lives and to the perpetuation of their species."

Haida lawyer and artist Terri-Lynn Williams-Davidson wrote, "In the Haida worldview, the cedar tree is known as 'every woman's sister,' providing for and sustaining our existence. This ancient sister lies at the root of Haida culture. She permeates every facet of Haida life, beginning in the cradle and continuing to the grave and, finally, ending at the memorial potlatch and raising of memorial totem poles to commemorate and celebrate one's life and contributions to the community." There is no doubt that seeing cedar trees as sisters instead of natural resources dramatically changes human attitudes toward, and use of, forests.

In an Earth Covenant drafted by Williams-Davidson, responsibilities to the Earth come first, before rights. These responsibilities include recognizing and respecting that we're all part of an interconnected world, conserving and restoring the Earth and the species and cultures she nurtures, managing our use of the Earth in ways that maintain her cycles and interrelationships and do not exceed planetary limits, and respecting future generations. Once these responsibilities have been fulfilled, then people have concomitant rights and privileges to live in a healthy environment and to benefit from the Earth and other species.

In 2003, the Navajo Tribal Council amended the Navajo Nation Code to recognize certain "fundamental laws," including the rights of nature. Title 1 of the Code declares and teaches that "all creation, from Mother Earth and Father Sky to the animals, those who live in the water, those who fly and plant life have their own laws, and rights and freedom to exist."

In 2015, the Ho-Chunk Nation, an Indigenous people based in Wisconsin, added a clause acknowledging the rights of nature to the bill of rights portion of its constitution. They are the first tribal nation in the U.S. to do so. The amendment states, "Ecosystems and natural communities within the Ho-Chunk territory possess an inherent, fundamental, and inalienable right to exist and thrive." Fossil-fuel extraction is identified as a violation of the rights of nature. Juliee de la Terre of Viterbo University, who assisted the Ho-Chunk, said to Wisconsin Public Radio that the amendment intends "for nature to be protected by giving a voice through a human intervenor like a lawyer that can talk on behalf of the oak trees and the water systems and everything else." Jon Greendeer, the executive director of Heritage Preservation with the Ho-Chunk Nation, told *Rolling Stone*, "What the rights of nature does is translate our beliefs from an indigenous perspective into modern legislation."

Rights

Rights have a long and convoluted backstory. Moral rights are claims about what constitutes ethical behaviour, but are not necessarily recognized by governments. For example, most people agree that Blacks in South Africa had moral rights, but these were not recognized by law and were systematically violated under the apartheid regime. Legal rights, in contrast, are enshrined in law and are thus enforceable through societal institutions. Human rights expert Alan Dershowitz, a retired Harvard Law School professor, argues that rights emerge from wrongs, transgressions of what we believe to be ethical behaviour. Thus the horrors of World War II were the impetus for the Universal Declaration of Human Rights.

New wrongs can and do emerge as our perceptions of what constitutes ethical behaviour evolve. There was a time when slavery and the ownership of other human beings was not seen as wrong by the majority of people. But beginning with a handful of individuals, a movement emerged denouncing slavery as a brutal and barbaric practice. Defenders of the status quo argued that slaves were less than human, and therefore not worthy of moral consideration. As pressure mounted, defenders of slavery offered to improve standards of treatment. Abolitionists were not impressed. Eventually, the beliefs of the majority shifted from acceptance of slavery to abhorrence. Today, the right not to be enslaved is a basic human right. Rights are symbolically and politically powerful, as the history of the civil rights, women's rights, Indigenous rights, and gay rights movements demonstrates. They are not a magic wand that can be waved to solve problems instantly, but they are a proven means of securing progress in the way society embraces previously mistreated communities.

Changing Values, Changing Cultures, Changing Laws

Evolution—of ideas, law, technology, even life itself—is not a smooth or gradual process. Instead it happens in fits and starts, in what scientists call punctuated equilibrium. Think of a geological fault line, where two of the Earth's tectonic plates overlap. The plates are in constant motion, as they have been since all the continents were united in one large land mass. The plates move slowly, just a few centimetres every year. They would move faster or further but cannot because other plates are in the way. Pressure builds over decades, centuries, or even millennia. Then the pressure reaches a breaking point, the plates slide, and the earth quakes.

That same process happens with science, culture, and laws. Ideas push against the status quo. Activists ramp up the pressure, using every lawful means and sometimes even breaking the law. They are chastised, ridiculed, imprisoned, and killed. But eventually, opinions, values, and paradigms shift.

Science can play a central role in these transformations. For eons, humans believed that Earth was the centre of the solar system, and that the sun revolved around us. Those who challenged this worldview were ostracized, excommunicated, even burned at the stake. But eventually, the heliocentric model was proven, and people came to accept that the Earth, in fact, travelled around the sun.

Over the past fifty years, scientists have produced remarkable discoveries about the intelligence, emotions, and cultures of other species of animals, as well as the interconnectedness of ecosystems and the human impacts on those systems. Scientists who specialize in classifying species recently changed our place in the taxonomy of nature. These specialists now place all the great apes (chimpanzees, gorillas, bonobos, and orangutans) in the family *Hominidae*, previously reserved for humans alone.

Our beliefs and values about other animals, other species, and the Earth are undergoing a sea change. Most people today are horrified by stories of cruelty to individual animals or the extinction of endangered species. We've all seen the images of Earth from outer space, a tiny blue dot in an immense universe of stars, planets, black holes, and dark matter. There is a growing sense that something is amiss in our relationship with the unique planet that we call home. Yet our laws and our actions have not yet changed to keep pace with the evolution of our values.

Protecting the environment is impossible if we continue to assert human superiority and universal ownership of all land and wildlife to pursue endless economic growth. Today's dominant culture and the legal system that supports it are self-destructive. We need a new approach rooted in ecology and ethics. Humans are but one species among millions, as biologically dependent as any other on the ecosystems that produce water, air, food, and a stable climate. We are part of nature: not independent, but interdependent. As conservationist and writer Aldo Leopold wrote, "Conservation is getting nowhere because it is incompatible with our Abrahamic concept of land. We abuse land because we regard it as a commodity belonging to us. When we see land as a community to which we belong, we may begin to use it with love and respect." Similarly, American philosopher Thomas Berry wrote about an "Earth community," referring to all life forms, human and "other than human." From the radical perspective of Leopold and Berry, other species and ecosystems are not merely for our enjoyment and exploitation.

The legal revolution described in this book has the potential to achieve three vital outcomes:

- reducing the harm suffered by sentient animals,
- stopping human-caused species extinction, and
- protecting the planet's life-support systems.

To achieve these objectives, we urgently need to establish and enforce a new set of rights and responsibilities. The rights belong to non-human animals, other species, and ecosystems. The responsibilities rest with humans. Science and values have evolved—now our laws, institutions, cultures, economies, and behaviours need to do the same.

Fortunately, there is evidence from across the world that people, legislatures, and courts are beginning to acknowledge and protect the rights of other members of our planet's community. Laws are protecting the rights of great apes and cetaceans (whales, dolphins, and porpoises). Lawsuits are seeking (and in some cases winning) freedom for chimpanzees, killer whales, and other animals held in captivity. Court decisions are placing the survival of endangered species above human interests in cases involving snail darters, narwhals, northern spotted owls, and Asiatic lions. From New Zealand to Ecuador, constitutions, laws, and judges are recognizing the rights of rivers, forests, and ecosystems. This book chronicles a legal and cultural revolution that appears to be blossoming in the nick of time.

The
RIGHTS *of* ANIMALS

"We are living through an ethical revolution when it comes to animals—shifting from seeing them as objects, commodities and resources, to seeing them as beings in their own right."

Andrew Linzey, theologian, Oxford University

THE HONORARY VERTEBRATE

"Despite being mollusks, like clams and oysters, these animals have very large brains and exhibit a curious, enigmatic intelligence."
PETER GODFREY-SMITH, professor of philosophy and author of *Other Minds: The Octopus, the Sea, and the Deep Origins of Consciousness*

An octopus named Paul gained global fame in 2010 when he correctly predicted the outcome of eight World Cup soccer matches, including the final. He would choose between two containers, each holding one of the competing teams' national flags. Of course, this was just a fluke, but the story gained global attention in part because it fit with emerging scientific evidence about the surprising intelligence of octopuses.

It's easy to imagine that orangutans, chimpanzees, dolphins, whales, and elephants are highly intelligent animals, with rich emotional lives and complex social networks. Even though we may never have seen these creatures in the wild, we have a comfortable familiarity with them, telling our children stories about Babar, Free Willy, and Curious George.

An octopus is more alien to us. On the tree of evolution, humans and octopuses diverged about 600 million years ago. It shows. They have eight arms equipped with hundreds of flexible suckers that can not only grip but also taste. Technically, octopuses are mollusks, like oysters, clams, and snails, yet through evolution they have shed their external shell. They have a beak, like a parrot. Cells that sense light are embedded in their skin. Different species of octopus range in size from the pygmy octopus, full grown at less than an ounce, to the Pacific giant octopus, which can weigh more than 200 pounds. They employ jet propulsion, shooting water through a funnel to move, dig holes in sand, or target pests. They can grow back an arm, if one gets detached. They have three hearts and blue blood. Some octopus species can shoot jets of ink, creating clouds that enable them to disappear. Others have venom that they inject into their prey. Australia's blue-ringed octopus can kill a human. Perhaps most strikingly, they challenge our basic ideas about the mind-body relationship. As well as a centralized brain, the octopus has a decentralized brain, enabling the arms to act independently.

And yet, for all the profound differences, there is something engaging and attractive about octopuses. Maybe it's their eyes, which are nearly identical in structure to human eyes. Canadian zoologist N.J. Berrill called this similarity "the single most startling feature of the whole animal kingdom." The big difference is that while we have round pupils, octopuses have horizontal slits.

The attraction could also be because octopuses are really smart and have individual personalities. Octopuses have hundreds of times more neurons than any other invertebrate. In fact, with an estimated 500 million neurons, they are well ahead of mice and rats and very close to cats (700 million).

The more scientists learn about these eight-armed invertebrates, the more remarkable they seem. Their ability to escape from captivity is legendary. Octopuses held in aquariums are infamous for escaping their tanks at night, climbing into other tanks to eat a few snacks, and then returning to their tanks, leaving aquarium employees baffled the next day. Thanks to the absence of bones, they can squeeze their entire bodies through amazingly small cracks and holes. An octopus can sneak into a fisherman's crab trap, eat all the crabs, and leave.

Inky was a wild octopus found tangled in a crayfish trap by a fisherman and taken to the National Aquarium of New Zealand in the coastal city of Napier. For two years, Inky was one of the aquarium's main attractions, but in 2016 he disappeared. He took advantage of a gap at the top of his enclosure left by a negligent maintenance worker, got out of his tank, moved across the floor, found a fifteen-centimetre-wide drainpipe that led back to the ocean, squeezed his way into it, and escaped. And when flounders in a special research project at the same aquarium began disappearing from their tank, another octopus was identified as the culprit, despite being in a different tank over four metres away.

Octopuses are tool users. They seek out rocks to narrow and camouflage the entries to their dens. The coconut octopus hides in shells, and got its name because it sometimes carries a coconut shell around to serve as an emergency shelter. Octopuses also have the extraordinary ability to change their shape, skin colour, and texture to camouflage themselves against their surroundings. Almost instantly, their skin can transform to mimic sand, coral, algae, or rock. They can dismantle Lego and even open the childproof lids on pill bottles. They like to play with toys and improvise their own games. One octopus used jets of water to push a bottle in circles around her aquarium. They can navigate mazes, solve problems such as unlocking a series of boxes to access food, and remember the solutions. An octopus at the University of Otago in New Zealand figured out that she could turn off a light outside her tank by shooting jets of water at it. Replacing the light became so expensive that the university returned the octopus to the ocean.

Jennifer Mather, a psychologist at the University of Lethbridge and author of *Octopus: The Ocean's Intelligent Invertebrate*, believes that these animals have personalities, and that they can be shy or bold, active or passive, emotional or reserved. In the 1950s, a Harvard scientist named Peter Dews conducted an experiment with three octopuses named Albert, Bertram, and Charles. Albert and Bertram quickly learned that if they pulled a lever, a light would come on and they would receive a piece of sardine. Charles also figured this out, but was more interested in the light and the lever. He wrapped his tentacles around the light and pulled it into his den. He also spent much of his time shooting jets of water at Dews. Finally, Charles pulled on the lever with such force that it bent and eventually broke, prematurely terminating the experiment.

Other experiments have confirmed that octopuses can recognize and distinguish specific humans. Scientists also believe that the changing colours of an octopus reflect its state of mind, like a mood ring. A giant Pacific octopus is white when relaxed and red when agitated or excited.

The octopus is so intelligent that in 1993 it became an "honorary vertebrate," the only invertebrate to be given special protection under the British law governing the licensing of animal experiments. In 2010, the European Union placed strict limits on research experiments involving octopuses because "there is scientific evidence of their ability to experience pain, suffering, distress and lasting harm."

Chapter 1
BREAKTHROUGHS IN
UNDERSTANDING ANIMAL MINDS

"Given that we now know that we live in a world of sentient beings, not one of stimulus-response machines, we need to ask, how should we treat these other emotional, thinking creatures?"

VIRGINIA MORELL, *Animal Wise*

Humans often forget, or deliberately ignore, the fact that we are animals. Consider the sign commonly posted on doors at stores and malls: "No animals allowed." If taken literally, this would be catastrophic for business! Or take the expression "behaving like an animal." Well, how else is a person supposed to behave?

As recently as the 1970s, the prevailing wisdom was that non-human animals were automatons that merely reacted instinctively to external stimuli. Then along came Dr. Donald Griffin, an American zoology professor who originally rose to prominence in 1944 when he figured out that bats use echolocation to navigate. In 1976, after decades of observing different species in labs and in the wild, Griffin suggested that scientists should study animal minds and attempt to learn how they think. Griffin maintained that animals are conscious, even if they might think about different things and in different ways than humans. He opened the door to a whole new field of science called cognitive ethology—the study of the minds, awareness, and, yes, even the consciousness of non-human animals.

Since Griffin issued his challenge, there has been an extraordinary proliferation of scientific research about the minds of animals, overturning many of our previous understandings. There are currently more scientists observing and studying more species than at any time in history. Peer-reviewed scientific articles on animal cognition and capabilities are being published at an unprecedented rate. There have been breakthroughs in our understanding of animal brains through the fields of neuroanatomy, neurochemistry, and evolutionary biology.

The notion of human superiority that runs from Aristotle's hierarchy of existence through Descartes's erroneous belief that animals were automatons should have been obliterated by Darwin and subsequent discoveries about evolution. But myths about who and what we are die hard. Humans have long resisted acknowledging that we are distant cousins to all other animal species, diverging from common ancestors millions of years ago. Yet recognizing that other species are special in no way detracts from the fact that humans are also special. The qualities that humans have relied upon historically in efforts to distinguish ourselves from other species—the "hallmarks of humanity"—include intelligence, emotions, language, tool use, memory, culture, foresight, cooperation, altruism, and self-awareness. Scientists are systematically demonstrating that we share these traits with other animals.

Intelligence

Scientists believe that the large brains of primates, cetaceans, and elephants evolved for dealing with social complexity—recognizing friends and foes, engaging in lifelong social relationships, co-operating for mutual benefit, and developing unique cultures. Humans were supposed to have the biggest brains, and thus the gold medal, in animal intelligence. Not so fast. The brains of *Homo sapiens* are outweighed by those of dolphins, elephants, and whales. In our defence, we cunningly deemed brain weight to be an unfair comparison, so we calculated brain-to-body-weight ratios. Then the tree shrew bests us, so that can't be right. Despite being smaller than whale brains, human brains have more neurons (aha!), but whale brains have more glia, specialized cells used in information processing.

There is no question that dolphins, whales, primates, and elephants are highly intelligent. Dolphins not only have big brains, but possess extraordinary abilities such as sonar or echolocation, with which they send out sound waves that bounce back as echoes, providing extensive information about their surroundings. Echolocation enables dolphins to "see" through solid objects, like a superhero's X-ray vision. For example, dolphins can tell if another dolphin, or a human, is pregnant, using their sonar to detect two separate heartbeats. A few years ago, scientists discovered that dolphin brains contain large numbers of specialized spindle neurons, previously thought to be unique to great apes. These neurons are believed to rapidly transmit important social/emotional information. In fact, dolphins' brains have more spindle neurons than humans'. Dale Peterson writes in *The Moral Lives of Animals* that dolphins "have excellent memories and high levels of social and self-awareness, are excellent at mimicking the behavior of others and can respond to symbolic presentations, form complex and creatively adaptive social systems, and show a broad capacity for the cultural transmission of learned behaviours." In short, dolphins are really smart.

The phrase "bird brain" has long been employed as a put-down, but may now be seen as a compliment. In 2004, scientists completely renamed the parts of avian brains based on new knowledge about their evolution. The brains of birds, contrary to previous understanding, are structurally similar to mammal brains. Despite having relatively small brains, crows, ravens, and jays—members of the corvid family—have proven to be talented problem solvers and tool users. In one experiment, a New Caledonian crow overcame a series of eight obstacles before acquiring a piece of aluminum and bending it with uncanny accuracy into a hook that it used to retrieve a morsel of food. The crow accomplished this feat on its first attempt.

Intelligence is not limited to primates, cetaceans, and birds. Archerfish can instantly calculate complicated mathematics of distance, speed, and time when blasting their prey with jets of water. They can learn to be better hunters by watching skilled individuals of their species. Many species, from monarch butterflies and humpback whales to Pacific salmon and Arctic terns, undertake amazing migrations every year without map, compass, or GPS.

A variety of different species practise deception, behaving in ways intentionally designed to mislead predators or even members of their own group. In his best-seller *The Parrot's Lament*, Eugene Linden chronicles acts of deception by parrots, elephants, orangutans, dolphins, and hawks. Some birds feign injury to lead predators away from their nests. Jays will not cache food when other animals are watching, or will subsequently re-cache the food in a different location. Chimpanzees and gorillas will pretend not to notice desired food items when accompanied by more dominant members of their family. The less dominant primates will return later, unaccompanied, to collect the food. The zone-tailed hawk imitates the flying style of a vulture, a scavenger that poses no threat to other birds, then dives to attack unsuspecting birds. These uses of deception suggest that some species may have the ability to understand what other animals are thinking.

Emotions

In her book *How Animals Grieve*, Barbara J. King defines grief as "when a survivor animal acts in ways that are visibly distressed or altered from the usual routine, in the aftermath of the death of a companion animal who had mattered to him or her." Dolphins, primates, and elephants exhibit behaviour that clearly appears to be grief. According to Jeffrey Kluger, writing in *Time* magazine, "It's well established that elephants appear to mourn their dead. They will linger over a family member's body with what looks like sorrow, and African elephants have a burial ritual, covering dead relatives' bodies with leaves and dirt. Elephants show great interest—some scientists suggest it may even be respect—when they come across the bones of dead elephants, examining them closely, with particular attention to the skull and tusks." Similarly, great apes will remain close to a dead troop mate for days.

There are stories from Africa and Asia of elephant herds and tigers taking revenge on targeted human settlements or hunters for having slaughtered members of their families, stolen their food, or attempted to kill them. Baby elephants sometimes throw what can only be described as temper tantrums if their mothers deny them milk. In addition to observation, scientists can now use physiological data to track changes in the emotional state of animals. Recent studies have demonstrated that dogs feel elation in their owners' presence.

In the 1970s, a captive killer whale named Orky at Marineland in Palos Verdes, California, ran his rostrum up and down the belly of his mate, Corky, four or five times, in much the same way a doctor might run ultrasound equipment over a pregnant woman's abdomen. Immediately afterwards, Orky slammed his head against the wall of the tank over and over. This behaviour had never been seen before. Two hours later, Corky had a miscarriage. Since orcas have the ability to monitor pregnancies, Orky may have been expressing some kind of anguish or grief.

Language

Humans may be the only species with a written language, but many animals have sophisticated means of communication that greatly exceed our understanding, including the use of sound and sonar. Primates have learned symbol and sign languages. Scientists studying wild chimpanzees have identified at least sixty-six distinct gestures, such as beckoning and waving. Kanzi, a bonobo "owned" by the Great Ape Trust and held at a research centre in Iowa, is famous because he knows some 400 words in sign language. When fed kale, he described it as slow lettuce, because it took longer to chew. When fed pizza, he signed *cheese tomato bread*. More significantly, he knows words that express emotions and abstract concepts such as *happy*, *sad*, *be*, and *tomorrow*.

Humpback whales sing songs that travel vast distances across the oceans. Thanks to the release of decades' worth of records amassed by the U.S. Navy as part of its antisubmarine monitoring program in the Atlantic Ocean, scientists have an unprecedented understanding of this communication. In a press release, Dr. Chris Clark of Cornell University said, "We now have evidence that they are communicating with each other over thousands of miles of ocean. Singing is part of their social system and community." New evidence proves that elephants can communicate with each other across huge distances by low frequency rumbling and by stomping on the ground, sending seismic signals that can travel more than thirty kilometres. These sounds are inaudible to humans but are picked up by special cells in elephant feet. Border collies can understand commands and hundreds of words for objects, and dogs generally understand non-verbal human communication such as pointing. Even bees communicate with each other, using a sophisticated code embedded in what entomologists describe as a dance. Bees perform this dance as part of collective deliberations about choosing a new hive site.

Tool Use

For a long time, humans were regarded as the only animals that used tools. Then Jane Goodall made her startling discoveries about chimpanzees that stripped leaves off small branches so they could extract termites from termite mounds. Scientists in the Ivory Coast's Taï Forest observed adult chimpanzees showing young chimpanzees how to use rocks to smash open hard-shelled nuts. The researchers excavated the area and learned that this material culture had been passed down for at least 4,300 years by hundreds of generations of chimpanzees.

Ravens and crows use rocks to break open foods with hard exteriors, from nuts to shellfish. Sea otters balance shellfish on their chests while floating on their back, cracking them open with a rock clutched between their paws. Bottlenose dolphins off the coast of Australia place sea sponges on their rostrums like face-guards when rooting among sharp corals, discarding the sponges when fish dart out from the coral. Alligators and crocodiles have been observed balancing branches or sticks on their snouts and then partially submerging. Herons and other wading birds searching for nest-building materials are lured into the trap.

Orangutans have earned a reputation among zookeepers for their imaginative use of tools to facilitate escapes. The legendary Fu Manchu escaped repeatedly from an exhibit at the Omaha Zoo in Nebraska by using a piece of wire (which he kept hidden in his cheek) to pick locks. In 2016, new scientific studies reported discoveries about tool use by capuchin monkeys, bonobos, and even the California sheephead wrasse (a fish). The sheephead, like otters, uses rocks as anvils to break open and crush sea urchins before eating them. In 2017, bumblebees became the first invertebrate species to demonstrate their ability to use tools to achieve a desired outcome.

Memory

Closely related to intelligence is memory. Despite our prodigious smarts, we've all experienced the frustration of misplacing keys, wallets, and other important items. In that light, consider the memory power of the Clark's nutcracker, a bird with a brain the size of a kidney bean. This small bird gathers seeds from pinyon pine trees in the fall, jams them into a pouch in its throat, flies as far as twenty kilometres to a higher elevation, and hides them in caches of one to fourteen seeds. In total, an individual bird will hide thousands of seeds. During winter and spring, the Clark's nutcracker retrieves them, even when they're buried by snow. Obviously these birds have an incredible spatial memory. Even more impressively, nutcrackers and jays eat cached foods in a particular order, based on anticipation of when the food is likely to spoil.

Then there is the chimpanzee. At Kyoto University's Primate Research Institute, a chimp named Ayumu frequently embarrasses its human competition in short-term memory contests. The numbers one to nine are randomly scattered across a computer monitor with touchscreen technology. As soon as you touch the number one, the other numbers are blacked out but you must tap them in sequence. Ayumu can correctly memorize the location of the nine numbers almost instantly, while humans struggle to recall the correct sequence most of the time, even after prolonged efforts to memorize them. As researcher Tetsuro Matsuzawa told the *Guardian*, "No one imagined that chimpanzees—young chimpanzees at the age of five—would have a better performance in a memory task than humans."

Culture

Like humans, many other animal species live in social groups that have recognizable and particular cultures. Culture can be defined as separate populations developing different ways of doing things through learning, rather than genetic inheritance. An essential element of culture is the transmission of knowledge to subsequent generations, such as chimpanzees training younger ones in tool use. Mounting recent scientific evidence proves that animals—from ants and bees to elephants and whales—live in complex social systems. Years of painstaking research by Professor Nigel Franks at the University of Bristol revealed that individual rock ants serve as teachers to other rock ants. Some species, including but not limited to primates, strategize politically, form alliances, and reconcile after disagreements.

Elephants possess substantial intellectual and cognitive abilities, demonstrate extensive emotional depth, and have complex social networks. Extended families of up to 100 animals live together, and elephants have been observed feeding those who are sick, injured, disabled, or otherwise unable to use their trunks. They use tools and work co-operatively to solve problems. Long-term studies of wild African elephants revealed the critical importance of elder matriarchs to herd survival because of their knowledge, experience, and wisdom. These older females know other elephants' personalities, landscapes, migration routes, water holes, food sources, and strategies for avoiding or combating predators. Sadly, these are the individuals most targeted by poachers because of their long tusks. Who knows what cultural knowledge is being lost as these female elephants are killed?

Killer whales, like elephants, live in matrilineal family units for their entire lives. They travel together, hunt together, play together, and stay together. Dr. Hal Whitehead of Dalhousie University is a pioneer in the study of cetacean culture and has observed that "dolphins and whales live in these massive, multicultural, underwater societies."

Foresight

Humans once believed that we were the only animals with foresight. Yet creatures from blue jays to squirrels cache food for future consumption. If jays or ravens see other animals watching them hide food, they will wait until those animals leave, then move the food. A zoology student at the University of Cambridge—the aptly named Christopher Bird—found that the rook, a member of the crow family, could figure out that dropping stones into a pitcher partly filled with water would raise the level high enough to drink from it. The rooks even selected the largest stones first, recognizing that this would raise the level faster. Aesop wrote a fable called "The Crow and the Pitcher" about a bird that managed precisely the same feat about 2,500 years ago. It took a twenty-first-century scientist to show that the fable was factual.

Co-operation

Some animals co-operate to raise and protect their young, share food, groom each other, or take turns watching out for danger. Hyenas and killer whales both hunt in groups. There's a video on YouTube of a group of orcas near Antarctica that locate a seal adrift on an ice floe. The killer whales circle the ice floe for a period of time, then all but one leave. Moments later they return, swimming side by side at high speed toward the seal before rapidly braking. Their actions propel a powerful wave of water that washes the hapless seal off the ice floe into the mouth of the orca that remained behind.

Scientists in Hawaii have repeatedly witnessed bottlenose dolphins playing a game where they lie on the head of a humpback whale. The whale slowly lifts its head, and the dolphin slips tail-first back into the water, like a child on a waterslide. In Australian waters, male dolphins co-operate to select and capture females for mating. Chimps co-operate in hunting and in conflicts with other groups of chimps. Experiments with elephants and birds have demonstrated that they will work together to secure food rewards. Biologists have observed many remarkable examples of cooperation between coyotes and American badgers in hunting ground squirrels together. Even fruit-fly brothers co-operate, rather than fight, in pursuit of a mate. Tommaso Pizzari, a zoologist at the University of Oxford, concluded that brother flies live longer as a result.

Self-Awareness

Self-awareness refers to the ability to recognize oneself as an individual distinct from the environment and other individuals. In 1838, Charles Darwin watched an orangutan at the London Zoo looking at herself in a mirror. He naturally wondered what she was thinking. More than a century later, scientists inspired by Darwin began placing animals in front of mirrors to explore the question of self-awareness. Animals are marked on their head or body (with paint or a sticker, for example) and then exposed to a mirror. If they touch the mark on themselves rather than on the mirror, scientists conclude that the animal perceives the reflected image as itself, rather than another animal. Experiments indicate that dolphins, orcas, Eurasian magpies, elephants, and some primates recognize themselves in mirrors.

Other scientists bristle at the notion that animals responding to seeing themselves in a mirror should be an indicator that they possess self-awareness. For example, in *Beyond Words*, conservationist Carl Safina argues that the day-to-day behaviour of many different species provides clear evidence of self-awareness. He concludes that "maybe a mirror is mainly a test for which species is the greatest narcissist."

Altruism

Altruism involves behaviour benefitting someone who is not a close relative, despite some personal cost or risk. Field researchers in Africa have observed chimpanzees assisting unrelated chimps without expecting favours in return. Lab tests done decades ago demonstrated that rhesus monkeys will consistently choose to go hungry if their decision to secure food would result in another unrelated rhesus monkey being subjected to an electrical shock. Dolphins have saved humans and seals from sharks and helped rescue whales stranded on rocks or beaches. In *The Moral Lives of Animals*, Dale Peterson recounts stories of a wild elephant in Kenya that defended an injured man from a herd of wild buffalo, a bonobo in an English zoo that saved a starling that had crashed into a window, and a gorilla at Chicago's Brookfield Zoo that rescued a three-year old who fell into her exhibit, landing on a concrete floor.

In 2016, the journal *Marine Mammal Research* published a remarkable article about the seemingly altruistic behaviour of humpback whales. In dozens of recorded observations from around the world, humpbacks responded to the distress calls of other species—including seals, sea lions, and grey whales—that were being attacked by groups of killer whales. In each case, the humpback whales disrupted the hunt by harassing the orcas and driving them away. Scientists cannot find any plausible biological explanation for why the humpbacks would place themselves at risk on behalf of other species, and are left to speculate that this is an example of altruism.

These studies mark huge leaps in our scientific understanding of animal intelligence and consciousness in recent decades. From elephants and cetaceans to ants and fish, animals clearly feel, think, and reason. They are sentient creatures, not machines. As humans, we may never fully understand the intelligence, emotions, or morality of other species. We can study other types of animals, observe their behaviour, analyze their DNA, carry out sophisticated experiments, and attempt to imagine what goes on inside their minds, but knowing is probably an impossible task.

In 2012, a multi-disciplinary group of scientists who study how brains work produced the Cambridge Declaration on Consciousness, stating, "The weight of evidence indicates that humans are not unique in possessing the neurological substrates that generate consciousness. Non-human animals, including all mammals and birds, and many other creatures, including octopuses, also possess these neurological substrates." The declaration noted that many animals experience pain in ways similar to humans—the same chemical reactions in the brain and body (such as the production of adrenalin and other hormones) and the same observable physical reactions (like dilated pupils and elevated heart rates). Scientist Philip Low, one of the authors of the declaration, said that numerous colleagues approached him afterwards and said, "We were all thinking this, but were afraid to say it." Reviewing the evidence, the *New York Times* concluded, "The overwhelming tendency of all this scientific work, of its results, has been toward *more* consciousness. More species having it, and species having more of it than assumed."

From a scientific perspective, the myths of human superiority and exceptionalism have been repeatedly and convincingly debunked. As Charles Darwin observed almost 150 years ago, the difference between humans and other animals is one "of degree, not of kind." After studying chimpanzees for more than forty years, in her foreword to *Building an Ark: 101 Solutions to Animal Suffering*, Jane Goodall concluded, "It is clear that there is no sharp line between us and chimpanzees, between us and the rest of the animal kingdom. The more we learn, the more blurry the line becomes. We are not the only beings on the planet with personalities and minds capable of rational thought and feelings." The knowledge that animals feel, think, and reason has profound consequences for our relationship with them. As journalist Elizabeth Kolbert observed in the *New York Review of Books*, "To acknowledge that we are separated from other species by 'degree, not kind' is to call into question just about every aspect of modern life." We have a powerful moral imperative to change the way we relate to, interact with, and exploit other animals.

LUCY

Lucy was born in 1975 in Sri Lanka. At age two, she emigrated to Canada, moving to Edmonton, where she has lived ever since. Her home is small, with concrete floors. She lived alone for twelve years, then had a roommate, Samantha, for a while. Samantha moved out in 2007, and since then Lucy has been alone again. Because the climate is so much colder in Canada than Sri Lanka, there are many days in winter when Lucy does not go outside. Lucy is quite overweight and suffers from rheumatoid arthritis, a degenerative disease that affects joints. It can be made worse by lack of exercise, being overweight, standing on concrete or hard floors, and cool, damp conditions. Her feet are often swollen, with pus-filled, bleeding abscesses. She takes anti-inflammatory medicine almost every day to reduce her pain. She also suffers from a persistent respiratory illness.

Lucy is a forty-two-year-old Asian elephant. She was captured in Sri Lanka's tropical forest as a baby. Edmonton's Valley Zoo bought Lucy from a wildlife dealer in 1977. Her tiny outside space is 2,000 square metres, and her indoor space, at about 185 square metres, is the size of an average North American house. Elephants in the wild walk many hours daily across vast home ranges and are not known to suffer from arthritis.

Elephants are among the most social mammals in the world, living long lives in tight-knit family units. The Valley Zoo admits that its conditions do not meet generally accepted zoo standards, which explicitly state that female elephants should never be kept without other elephants for companionship. Internationally renowned elephant experts and veterinarians have testified that Lucy suffers from chronic health problems and is being harmed by the lack of elephant companions. Medical records chronicling Lucy's respiratory illness over a period of years describe thick discharge from her trunk as white, green, yellow, and "like cottage cheese." According to Dr. Joyce Poole, one of the world's leading elephant experts, "The Valley Zoo does not come close to meeting Lucy's physical and social needs." In an affidavit she swore in support of a lawsuit against the Valley Zoo, Poole notes that Lucy "has lacked, and continues to lack, the basic necessities and comforts of life, and that her poor health is a condition resulting from this lack. I have no reservations in concluding that she is currently subjected to undue hardship, privation and neglect."

Advocates for Lucy have long campaigned for her to be moved to an elephant sanctuary in California, which would be larger, warmer, and offer an opportunity to interact with other elephants. They filed a lawsuit seeking a declaration that the Valley Zoo was violating zoo standards under Alberta's Animal Protection Act. The case was dismissed by the Alberta Court of Appeal despite a powerful dissent from Chief Justice Catherine Fraser, who wrote that the evidence of neglect "packs a powerful punch. It holds up a mirror for all to see—provided one is prepared to look into the mirror. What it reveals is a disturbing image of the magnitude, gravity, and persistence of Lucy's ongoing health problems and the severity of the suffering she continues to endure from the conditions in which she has been confined. And it also exposes who is responsible for those conditions and that suffering."

Activists have offered to pay for Lucy's transferral to an elephant sanctuary—a move that should significantly improve Lucy's physical and emotional health. However, the zoo warns that she is fragile and may not survive such a journey. Poole responded to this argument in her affidavit, stating, "With all the deprivation and suffering that Lucy has already endured in her life, the last thing I would do is recommend a move if I thought it would be detrimental to her physical or psychological well-being." She added that there are no recorded incidents where elephants died in transit from a zoo to a sanctuary.

Responding to public pressure and belatedly recognizing that Canada's climate is unsuitable for elephants, zoos in Toronto and Calgary transferred their pachyderms to sanctuaries in Florida, California, and Washington, DC. In another recent victory, after more than 130 years, the Ringling Bros. and Barnum & Bailey Circus allowed their elephants to retire, moving them to a sanctuary in Florida. So far, the Valley Zoo refuses to relocate Lucy.

Chapter 2
THE EVOLUTION OF ANIMAL WELFARE

"Until we extend the circle of compassion to all living things, we will not find peace."

ALBERT SCHWEITZER, doctor, author, and
winner of the Nobel Peace Prize

People who love animals and seek to improve their well-being are divided into two main camps—those who focus on improving animal welfare, and those who insist on recognizing animal rights. To the animal welfare community, incremental changes that reduce the suffering of individual animals constitute success. In their view, using animals for human purposes—food, research, or entertainment—is acceptable as long as the benefits (to humans) exceed the harms (to animals), and unnecessary pain and suffering is avoided. The animal welfare movement has identified five fundamental freedoms, which they deliberately avoid describing as rights: freedom from hunger, thirst, and malnutrition; freedom from fear and distress; freedom from physical discomfort; freedom from pain, injury, and disease; and freedom to express normal patterns of behavior. Animal welfare advocates argue that because extending rights to animals faces fierce opposition, the more pragmatic approach is to close existing gaps in the law (such as loopholes excluding protection for farm and research animals), establish stronger rules for specific animals (for example, by eliminating battery cages for egg-laying chickens), strengthen the enforcement of these rules, and make better information available to consumers to inform their purchasing decisions.

To their credit, animal welfare advocates have a long track record of improving the lives of many different species in many different ways. These successes continue and may even be accelerating today.

Improving Animal Welfare

For centuries, people have struggled to improve the living conditions of animals used in human society. The first American law prohibiting cruelty to animals was passed by the Puritans of the Massachusetts Bay Colony in 1641: "No man shall exercise any tirranny or crueltie towards any bruite creatures which are usuallie kept for man's use." Animal welfare organizations were created in the eighteenth and nineteenth centuries, and since that time have secured many victories. An early English case placed limits on vivisection (cutting into or dissecting a living animal) in 1876.

The pace of progress has accelerated. The U.S. Humane Society reports that since 2004, local, state, and federal governments have enacted more than 1,000 animal protection laws. Just thirty years ago, the most serious animal cruelty offences in all but four American states were designated as misdemeanours, minor infractions of the law with minimal penalties. By 2014, all fifty states had made animal cruelty a felony offence, subject to far more serious punishments. In his legal paper "Animals as More Than 'Mere Things,' but Still Property," Professor Richard L.

Cupp of the Pepperdine School of Law said, "In terms of legal change, that reflects an abrupt turnabout in our societal mindset regarding the seriousness of animal cruelty." There have also been substantial improvements in the past decade in Canadian animal welfare laws, with the provinces of Manitoba, Nova Scotia, British Columbia, and Ontario leading the way. However, a federal private members' bill championed by Liberal member of parliament Nathaniel Erskine-Smith that would have closed many loopholes permitting animal abuse was defeated.

According to annual report cards issued by the Animal Legal Defense Fund, recent improvements in laws protecting animals include providing stiffer penalties for offenders, mandatory reporting by veterinarians of animal cruelty cases, requiring mental health evaluations and counselling for offenders, and banning individuals convicted of cruelty from owning animals in the future. Florida strengthened rules governing the confinement and treatment of pigs during pregnancy to prevent the cruel and inhumane treatment of these animals. In at least eighteen American cities, bylaws have been passed to change the legal status of pets from "property" to "companions." Going in the opposite direction, Nebraska passed a law prohibiting cities in that state from defining the legal status of animals in "any manner inconsistent with the status of animals as personal property."

An American law enacted in 2000, the Chimpanzee Health Improvement, Maintenance, and Protection (CHIMP) Act, requires chimpanzees to be retired in sanctuaries instead of being killed when they're no longer needed for research. Thus in 2013, when the U.S. National Institutes of Health decided to retire 90 percent of their chimpanzees, these chimps were not euthanized but sent to sanctuaries. In 2015, the U.S. Fish and Wildlife Service classified all U.S.-based chimpanzees as endangered under the Endangered Species Act, meaning that any ongoing or future invasive research projects would require a special permit, and permits would only be allowed for work that enhances the survival of chimpanzees in the wild.

Governments around the world are changing laws to protect animal welfare. An international assessment published by World Animal Protection evaluated the extent to which laws and policies in more than fifty countries protect animals and improve their welfare. At the top of the rankings, with A grades, were Switzerland, Austria, the UK, and New Zealand. Despite recent progress, Canada and the U.S. were assigned a D grade.

One vital legal step toward protecting animal welfare is recognizing that animals are not merely things but are sentient beings. Sentience is more than the ability to respond to stimuli—it means that animals have emotions and can experience both physical and psychological pleasure and pain.

And the legal system is catching up with the science. New Zealand passed the Animal Welfare Amendment Act, which recognizes that animals are sentient beings, bans cosmetic testing on animals, and establishes strict new rules regarding the use of animals for research. Prior to conducting experiments on animals, researchers must demonstrate that they have assessed "the suitability of using non-sentient or non-living alternatives." The president of the New Zealand Veterinary Association, Dr. Steve Merchant, said, "Expectations on animal welfare have been rapidly changing. The bill brings legislation in line with our nation's changing attitude on the status of animals in society." The European Union's

Treaty of Lisbon, which came into force in 2009, recognizes that animals are sentient beings and requires member states to "pay full regard to the welfare requirements of animals" in agriculture, fisheries, transport, and research. In 2015, France's parliament officially recognized domestic animals as "living beings gifted with sentience" rather than things, updating a legal status that dated from Napoleonic times.

Also in 2015, Quebec unanimously passed a new law called An Act to Improve the Legal Situation of Animals, recognizing that "animals are not things. They are sentient beings and have biological needs." This was a North American first. A Canadian Press news story noted that "until now an animal in Quebec had the same legal rights as a piece of furniture." Agriculture Minister Pierre Paradis said he was inspired by the recent French law. Even flushing a live goldfish down the toilet could run afoul of the new law, leading Minister Paradis to say, "Don't get a goldfish if you don't want to take care of it."

Recognizing that animals are sentient beings spurs other legal changes to improve their well-being. The European Union phased out battery cages for hens, veal crates for calves, and gestation crates for sows as of 2012. (These practices are still allowed in Canada and the U.S.) The EU prohibited experimental research on great apes in 2010 and banned cosmetics testing on all animals in 2013—important steps, as the 2010 directive says, "towards achieving the final goal of full replacement of procedures on live animals for scientific and educational purposes as soon as it is scientifically possible to do so." Following a precedent set by Sweden, the EU also banned the use of antibiotics in agriculture except to treat animals suffering from disease. These drugs are still used to accelerate livestock growth in Canada and the U.S., contributing to the serious problem of antibiotic resistance. In the Netherlands, it is now illegal to keep a goldfish alone in a barren bowl. Countries such as Costa Rica have pledged to phase out zoos, circuses, rodeos, and other activities that exploit animals for human entertainment.

Animal welfare has the potential to improve even further with the co-operation of industry, and hardly a week goes by without some corporate giant making an announcement that they will change practices to treat animals more humanely. Grocery giants Safeway and Costco pledged to stop purchasing pork from suppliers unless they switched from gestation crates, which are too small for sows to even turn around, to group housing that ensures freedom of movement. In the past two years, nearly 200 U.S. companies have pledged to use only cage-free eggs by 2025, including major grocery and fast-food chains that buy billions of eggs monthly. Petco and PetSmart stopped sourcing pets from puppy mills and then ceased selling dogs and cats altogether. These corporations now assist animal rescue organizations in finding homes for pets.

While these commitments represent real progress, they need to be scrutinized closely to ensure that the changes are substantive, and not cosmetic. For example, McDonald's proclaimed that it will only buy eggs from suppliers who give hens 72 square inches of cage space, which is 50 percent more than required under American law. This sounds good, but it is important to realize that 72 square inches is smaller than a standard sheet of paper (which has an area of more than 90 square inches)! Although small steps will improve the well-being of animals in factory farms, the overall quality of life endured in these artificial environments is still miserable.

Stricter Enforcement of Animal Cruelty Laws

Although laws governing animal welfare have become stronger, investigating and prosecuting offences against animals take a back seat to the enforcement of laws where humans are the victims. Criminal sentences for stealing cars and other property crimes are far more severe than those imposed in even the most horrific cases of animal cruelty. In the UK, the maximum sentence for animal cruelty is twelve months in prison, while the maximum sentence for theft is seven years.

Penalties for animal cruelty under Canadian and American laws have become stronger in the last decade. Previously, judges in Canada overseeing the prosecution of appalling acts of cruelty inflicted on animals had complained that the maximum sentences available to them were out of step with societal values. No matter how brutal the actions of the accused, the maximum sentence that judges could impose was six months. The animal cruelty sections of the Criminal Code were amended in 2008, making maximum jail sentences up to five years for serious offences.

In a 2010 case involving gruesome injuries inflicted on two dogs—Abby and Zoey—by their owner's boyfriend, a judge observed that the "amendments to the Criminal Code were no mere housekeeping changes; rather, they represent a fundamental shift in Parliament's approach to these crimes. Such a dramatic change in a penalty provision is virtually unheard of in our criminal law." Despite observing that the pattern of injuries could only have been inflicted through the intentional torture of Abby and Zoey, the judge imposed a jail sentence of just twelve months, which an appeal court reduced to six months. In another case, the judge wrote that Parliament "made it clear that the willful infliction of unnecessary pain and suffering on animals violates one of the basic tenets of our society and is deserving of punishment. It is also conduct which most members of our society find repugnant and morally reprehensible."

Sentences have begun to increase. An Ottawa man was sentenced to two years in jail for beating his dog Breezy with a shovel and callously tossing her into a dumpster. But the courts have applied these new sentencing rules erratically, a progressive decision often followed by a regressive one. In the tourism downturn after the Olympics, a BC man, Robert Fawcett, slaughtered more than fifty sled dogs owned by a Whistler company. He was sentenced to probation, community service, and a $1,500 fine.

In the U.S., sentencing laws vary from state to state but are generally more severe and vigorously applied than in Canada. In 2010, a man who dragged Buddy the dog to death behind his truck at Colorado National Monument was sentenced to three years in prison. In 2013, eight individuals involved with dog fighting were handed sentences ranging up to eight years. A judge in South Carolina recently sentenced a man to thirty years in jail for six felony counts of dog fighting, the longest prison term ever handed down in a dog-fighting case. In 2015, an Alabama man was sentenced to ninety years in prison for starving and neglecting purebred collies on his grandparents' property, although the nine 10-year sentences will run concurrently.

In Oregon, the state Supreme Court has ruled that police do not need to obtain search warrants before seizing animals in jeopardy. The same court ruled that individual animals can be considered victims of crimes rather than merely property. In an earlier case, a man accused of badly mistreating twenty horses and goats was charged with just one count of animal abuse. The Supreme Court's decision that individual animals can be treated as separate victims raises the stakes. It means that a defendant who harms twenty animals could be charged with twenty counts of animal abuse, raising the spectre of a much longer jail sentence. Oregon is also the first state to employ a prosecutor whose sole job is to tackle animal-related crimes. Jake Kamins, Oregon's animal cruelty deputy district attorney, has prosecuted animal abusers in more than fifteen counties since he was hired in 2013. Because animal abuse cases tend to be complicated and time-consuming, Columbia County district attorney Steve Atchison said that "it makes a big difference" to have a specialized prosecutor involved. Following Oregon's example, British Columbia has appointed a prosecutor to act as a province-wide resource-person for animal cruelty cases.

Factory farms have started to be prosecuted for animal cruelty, often after research conducted by animal advocates who capture brutal acts on video. In 2009, an undercover investigation by People for the Ethical Treatment of Animals revealed workers mutilating, torturing, and maliciously killing turkeys at a factory farm owned by Aviagen, one of the world's largest poultry companies. Three men were convicted, one of whom was sentenced to a year in jail—the longest to date in the U.S. for a crime involving factory-farmed animals. In 2015, a New Zealand man who managed a dairy farm was sentenced to four and a half years in jail after pleading guilty to twelve charges of animal cruelty, including breaking the tails of hundreds of cattle and shooting one in the kneecaps before executing her. In 2016, after Mercy for Animals Canada released a disturbing undercover video of cows being savagely abused, twenty charges of animal cruelty were laid against Chilliwack Cattle Sales, one of Canada's largest dairy operations, as well as seven of its employees. The company pled guilty to three charges and was fined almost $260,000, while one of its directors also pled guilty and was fined $86,000. Several employees will go to trial later in 2017.

Animal cruelty laws still exclude common but violent practices used in agriculture, medical and scientific research, fishing, hunting, and trapping. Standard industry practices are regarded as generally acceptable, and much of the harm inflicted on animals is deemed "necessary." Only the most extreme cases of violence, cruelty, and neglect are brought to the law's attention—ordinary violence, cruelty, and neglect are routine. If a human activity is enjoyable (e.g., zoos, circuses, fishing), convenient (e.g., fast food hamburgers or a can of tuna) or profitable (e.g., the livestock industry) then harm to animals is deemed justified and lawful. Despite the scientific advances in our understanding of animal sentience, Canadian law professor Lesli Bisgould concludes in her book, *Animals and the Law*, that "vested interests perpetuate activities that have, by any modest ethical standard, lost all credible defences." Many people are either ignorant of the degree to which animals are harmed, or turn a blind eye to this suffering to avoid having to change their behaviour. Most of us could use our power as consumers to reduce animal abuse through daily actions such as eating less meat and choosing ethically sourced meat.

Despite the modest improvements in conditions for some domestic and captive wild animals in Canada, the U.S., and globally, two irrefutable facts remain. First, most animals are still treated as property. Second, far more animals are being captured, exploited, or killed now than ever before. Every year, humans kill over 100 billion animals, and the number is rising. That is at least fifteen animals per person, per year.

In light of these facts, incremental improvements in animal welfare are unlikely to reduce animal suffering to a degree that would satisfy animal advocates. As Sue Donaldson and Will Kymlicka write in *Zoopolis: A Political Theory of Animal Rights*, "The sheer scale of animal exploitation continues to expand around the globe, and the occasional 'victory' in reforming the cruelest forms of animal abuse simply nibbles at the edges of the systemic human mistreatment of animals." From Argentina to Canada, activists, lawyers, judges, and politicians are striving for breakthroughs in our troubled relationship with other species by forcefully invoking the rights of individual animals.

Chapter 3
CAN A CHIMPANZEE BE A LEGAL PERSON?

"What we're trying to do is change the way people view non-human animals. Right now the line between human beings and non-human animals is at an irrational place. If you're a human, you have rights. If you're not human, you don't. We're saying that's wrong."

STEVEN WISE, animal rights lawyer,

in *Unlocking the Cage*

Steven Wise is obsessed with the idea that the law must evolve to recognize certain animals as legal persons with rights. It's an idea he has taught in law schools, written about in books, and filed lawsuits to achieve. He also wrote a book about an extraordinary eighteenth-century legal case in England, highlighting the vision and courage of a judge who took a stand against slavery despite warnings of economic catastrophe if he endorsed the right of freedom. Wise is the antithesis of a slick corporate lawyer. He has unkempt grey hair, several chins, a pockmarked face, and a generally dishevelled appearance. Much of the time he wears hoodies, T-shirts, and blue jeans. Wise dresses up for court in rumpled suits with ties that are knotted but hang loose several inches below his collar. He comes alive in the presence of the animals whose lives he seeks to transform for the better. His eyes sparkle when he speaks about the remarkable abilities of chimpanzees. When visiting Kanzi, the bonobo famous for language skills, Wise beamed as Kanzi used symbols to ask, "Did the visitor bring a ball?" Seeing these intelligent, complex animals essentially imprisoned breaks his heart and compels him to continue his legal odyssey.

Wise was a regular trial lawyer until he read Peter Singer's classic book *Animal Liberation* in 1980. The book's horrific details about the abuse humans inflict on animals, coupled with the fact that few people seemed to be standing up for them, led Wise to become an animal protection lawyer. For more than thirty years, Wise has represented non-human animals in courtrooms. He has been ridiculed by judges, the media, and the public. "People used to bark at me when I walked into the courtroom," Wise recalled in *Unlocking the Cage*. On his office wall is a poster that says, "We may be the only lawyers on Earth whose clients are all innocent."

In 1991, Wise filed the lawsuit that led him to rethink his legal strategy. The case was filed on behalf of Kama, a six-year-old dolphin, against the New England Aquarium. Wise argued that transferring Kama to the U.S. Navy for training at the Naval Ocean Systems Center in Hawaii violated the Marine Mammal Protection Act. "The lawyer for the aquarium was so outraged," Wise told the *New York Times*. "He kept saying, 'Judge, our own dolphin is suing us!' And I understand that outrage. He felt: 'We own this. This is completely ours, and what is ours is now claiming we can't do something to it?'" The judge ruled that Kama had no standing to bring a lawsuit because she was not a person in the eyes of the law. That defeat sparked Wise's interest in legal personhood.

Wise realized that filing lawsuits on behalf of animals was futile because of the great legal wall that divides humans from other animals. To enable animals to secure legal rights would require overturning centuries of precedents. Wise thought it would probably take thirty years to prepare and file lawsuits challenging this notion. It took twenty-two.

In 1996, Wise founded the Nonhuman Rights Project, an organization dedicated to securing legal rights for certain animals that he regarded as having advanced intelligence. After exhaustively researching the latest science for his book *Rattling the Cage*, Wise concluded that great apes, elephants, African grey parrots, and cetaceans "are not just conscious, they are self-conscious (they are conscious that they are conscious), they demonstrate complex abilities to communicate, and possess some or all the elements of a 'theory of mind.'" Wise has brought lawsuits, and plans to bring more, on behalf of individual members of these species being held in captivity, seeking acknowledgement that they possess some rights that our legal system should recognize and protect.

In December 2013, assisted by dozens of volunteers, Wise filed unprecedented habeas corpus lawsuits on behalf of four chimpanzees who were being held in captivity in the state of New York. Habeas corpus (Latin for "you have the body") is an ancient common law remedy for unlawful imprisonment, dating back to the twelfth century. Wise felt justified in bringing these first habeas corpus cases on behalf of the four chimps because of the knowledge accumulated about their species over the past fifty years. Hercules and Leo, two young males, were being used for research experiments at Stony Brook University. Tommy was a privately owned chimp held alone "in a small, dank, cement cage in a cavernous dark shed," as Wise described in his legal brief. Kiko lived in a cement building at his owner's residence in Niagara

THE RIGHTS OF NATURE

Falls. Wise did not want to focus on the animal welfare issues of whether the chimps were being mistreated or held in inadequate conditions. Instead, he wanted to argue that the chimps were legal persons, and being held in captivity violated their rights. He sought court orders transferring the chimpanzees to a large refuge in Florida called Save the Chimps.

Wise filed more than 100 pages of affidavits from some of the world's leading primatologists, summarizing the cognitive abilities of chimpanzees and the physical and psychological suffering they endure in captivity. The affidavits are clear: chimpanzees display emotions, communicate, have memory, learn, make choices, and suffer physically and psychologically from not being able to move about freely. Wise told reporters, "Sometimes people think we're trying to get human rights for chimpanzees. We're not. We're trying to get chimpanzee rights for chimpanzees." The cases present judges with an uncomfortable choice. Are chimpanzees mere things, or would it make more sense to designate them as legal persons despite the significant consequences that would flow from such a determination?

Tommy's case went first. As Steven C. Tauber reports in *Navigating the Jungle*, Judge Joseph Sise listened to Steven Wise and then said, "You make a very strong argument. However I do not agree . . . I'm sorry I can't sign your order, but I hope you continue. As an animal lover, I appreciate your work." Sise basically invited Wise to appeal. Wise did just that, and successfully petitioned the appeals court to issue an order forbidding Tommy from being moved out of New York. Tommy's appeal was bolstered by Professor Laurence Tribe, a renowned constitutional law scholar from Harvard, who filed an amicus curiae (friend of the

Court) brief. Tribe wrote, "The lower court fundamentally misunderstood the purpose of the common law writ of habeas corpus" and "reached its conclusion on the basis of a fundamentally flawed definition of legal personhood." The Center for Constitutional Rights—a leading legal advocacy organization on issues of civil liberties and human rights—also filed an amicus curiae brief supporting the chimps.

It was a bumpy hearing. In front of five stern-looking appeal judges, Wise began with the traditional opening "may it please the Court" and doggedly made the case that Tommy was effectively imprisoned, and the Court should grant his release. He argued passionately, waving his hands in the air and gesturing at judges. Karen K. Peters, the first female presiding judge of the New York Supreme Court, Appellate Division, Third Department, interrupted and rebuked him: "You assert he's a person. We haven't decided that."

In rejecting Tommy's appeal, the Court observed that "animals have never been considered persons for the purposes of habeas corpus relief, nor have they been explicitly considered as persons or entities capable of asserting rights for the purpose of state or federal law." In the Court's eyes, the absence of any precedents was strike one. The inability of chimpanzees to carry out the responsibilities that accompany rights was strike two. Strike three was the existence of other laws that offered some degree of protection for animals, including chimps. The Court was unwilling to break new ground. Instead, they suggested that Wise ask the legislature to increase legal protection for chimpanzees.

In Kiko's case, Justice Ralph A. Boniello III of the State Supreme Court for the County of Niagara called Wise's legal arguments "excellent" but concluded, "I am not prepared to make this leap of faith." The judge held that a chimp is not a person and suggested a change in the law should be made by the legislature, not the judiciary. The appeals court dodged the legal personhood issue altogether. Instead, they decided that habeas corpus was not appropriate in the circumstances because Wise was not seeking the release of Kiko, but merely a transfer to another facility.

The case brought on behalf of Hercules and Leo received a friendlier judicial reception. Justice Barbara Jaffe of the New York Supreme Court is known as a compassionate and open-minded judge, having served on a committee on LGBT issues for the New York County Lawyers' Association. She is also a careful judge, telling an interviewer, "I have decided thousands of motions in serious civil matters, in hotly contested civil cases involving a lot of money, and I've been reversed only once."

In response to Wise's written legal arguments, just before Earth Day 2015, Justice Jaffe ordered Stony Brook University and its president Samuel Stanley to "show cause," meaning they needed to justify their detention of the two chimpanzees, and explain why Hercules and Leo should not be immediately transferred to the Save the Chimps sanctuary. Wise broke down in tears—he and his colleagues misinterpreted the news as acknowledging that chimps are legal persons and granting their writ of habeas corpus. The Nonhuman Rights Project issued a news release claiming this legal breakthrough was a first in world history. But they had jumped the gun. Justice Jaffe wanted Stony Brook and the Nonhuman Rights Project to appear in her courtroom and make their arguments.

Wise made his case well. Justice Jaffe was clearly interested and well informed, asking several pointed questions of both Wise and his opponent, Assistant Attorney General Christopher Coulston. Dressed in a sharp black suit, Coulston warned that the case "could set a precedent for the release of other animals . . . housed at a zoo, in an educational institution, on a farm, or owned as a domesticated pet." Coulston emphasized that no court anywhere in the world had ever determined that an animal is a legal person.

In the end, Justice Jaffe wrote a sympathetic decision, concluding that "efforts to extend legal rights to chimpanzees are understandable. Someday they may even succeed." She found herself bound by the higher court's decision in Tommy's case, although she suggested the court of appeals would be the right court to break new ground regarding chimps as legal persons. Justice Jaffe wrote, "Not very long ago, only Caucasian male, property-owning citizens were entitled to the full panoply of legal rights under the United States Constitution. Tragically, until passage of the Thirteenth Amendment of the Constitution, African-American slaves were bought, sold, and otherwise treated as property with few, if any, rights. Married women were considered the property of their husbands, and before marriage were often considered family property, denied the full array of rights accorded to their fathers, brothers, uncles and male cousins."

She also quoted U.S. Supreme Court justice Anthony Kennedy, who wrote in a 2003 Supreme Court decision overturning a Texas law that made homosexual intercourse a crime, that "times can blind us to certain truths and later generations can see that laws once thought necessary and proper in fact serve only to oppress."

Steven Wise didn't expect to make an historic legal break-through in his first round of lawsuits. He admitted to the *New York Times Magazine*, "For me this has been a twenty-five-year plan. . . . If we lose, we keep doing it again and again, until we find a judge who doesn't feel that the way is closed off. Then our job is to produce the facts that will allow that judge to make that leap of faith. And when it happens, it will be huge." The Nonhuman Rights Project is preparing to file further lawsuits on behalf of other great apes, elephants, dolphins, and whales. Wise will never stop fighting for the rights of the animals who he believes should be recognized as non-human persons.

In 2016, Louisiana University's New Iberia Research Center, which was renting Hercules and Leo to Stony Brook University, covertly took the chimps back to Louisiana. This end run around the lawsuit was lawful since they "owned" the chimps. However, under growing public pressure from the lawsuit and a critically acclaimed documentary about the Nonhuman Rights Project called *Unlocking the Cage*, New Iberia made a startling announce-ment. The company would not only transfer Hercules and Leo to a chimp sanctuary being created in Georgia, but would do the same for all 220 of their chimpanzees.

Chapter 4

THE EXPANSION OF ANIMAL RIGHTS

Although the notion that animals should have rights is not a new idea, it began attracting widespread interest in North America in 1975 when Peter Singer published his book *Animal Liberation*. Singer argued that "to discriminate against beings solely on account of their species is a form of prejudice, immoral and indefensible in the same way that discrimination on the basis of race is immoral and indefensible." Since the mid-1970s, organizations such as Mercy for Animals and People for the Ethical Treatment of Animals have arisen to defend animal rights.

Animal rights advocates take a variety of positions grounded in emerging science about animal intelligence, consciousness, communication, and culture. Some argue that animals already have certain rights, and that these rights simply need to be better enforced. For example, almost everyone would agree that it's unacceptable to torture or starve a dog, cat, bird, horse, or other animal. This could mean that animals have a right not to be subjected to torture or other forms of intentionally cruel behaviour. In rights language, this is a classic negative right—the right to be free from harm imposed by others. It is also argued that domestic animals have a right to be provided with adequate food, water, and shelter. These positive rights impose a responsibility on animal guardians to fulfill them.

Other animal rights advocates take a more radical view, asserting that all human uses of animals constitute exploitation, are morally wrong, and should be abolished. In his book *The Case for Animal Rights*, Tom Regan said, "It is not larger, cleaner cages that justice demands in the case of animals used in science, but empty cages; not traditional animal agriculture, but a complete end to all commerce in the flesh of dead animals." Professor Gary Francione of Rutgers Law said on his website AnimalAbolition.com, "It's really not rocket science. If animals are not mere things, if they have moral value, we cannot justify eating, wearing, or using them." He added that "all sentient beings should have at least one right—the right not to be treated as property."

Prodigious amounts of scientific evidence show us that animals are thinking, feeling creatures capable of suffering. As a result, laws increasingly recognize animals as sentient beings, meaning they can think, feel, and suffer. The ensuing moral, legal, and cultural implications are fascinating. If animals are sentient beings, then how are we going to continue to treat them as nothing more than a slightly special class of property?

Various governments are beginning to recognize that some sentient animals have at least some rights that ought to be protected by our legal system. Because their extraordinary capacities are widely recognized, great apes and cetaceans have been the primary focus of these pioneering initiatives. New Zealand passed a trailblazing law in 2000 that recognized that great apes have the right not to be deprived of life, not to be subject to cruel treatment, and not to be subjects of medical or scientific experiments. Laws banning invasive research on great apes have also been enacted in Australia, Japan, the United Kingdom, and the entire European Union.

In 2013, India's Ministry of Environment and Forests banned the practice of keeping dolphins in captivity, stating that dolphins are "non-human persons, and as such should have their own specific rights" and it is "morally unacceptable to keep them captive for entertainment purposes." In 2014, the San Francisco Board of Supervisors passed a measure stating that cetaceans have the right "to be free from life in captivity and to remain unrestricted in their natural environment." The board cited their complex emotional and intellectual capacities, as well as the psychological stress and high mortality rates caused by captivity. Conservationists praised the move as a milestone for marine mammal rights. Laura Bridgeman of the International Marine Mammal Project said, "This resolution reflects an understanding that what we once believed about dolphins and whales—that they are unthinking automatons—is in fact false, and that they deserve to be free." Another California city, Malibu, passed a resolution proclaiming that all cetaceans swimming past its coast have the right to life.

More recently, laws to prevent cetaceans from being held in captivity have been passed by the state of California and the province of Ontario. These laws implicitly recognize cetaceans' right to freedom. California's Orca Protection Act bans captivity and breeding programs, as well as wild or captive orca exports. Animal activist Mike Garrett applauded Ontario's law, saying, "Three years ago here in Ontario a law banning orca captivity would be unimaginable, yet here we are." The Canadian Senate is studying a bill called the Ending the Captivity of Whales and Dolphins Act (S-203). This bill would prohibit importing, exporting, and capturing cetaceans, except for injured animals in need of assistance. Liberal senator Wilfred P. Moore said that he "was shocked to learn that a captive orca's range is only 1/10,000th of 1 percent the size of its natural home range." The bill has a good chance to pass because it enjoys bipartisan support. Conservative senator Janis G. Johnson endorsed the proposed law, noting that "we are behind Costa Rica, India, UK, Italy, New Zealand, Hungary, Mexico and Cyprus. We need to catch up to science." Independent senator Daniel Christmas testified that from his Aboriginal perspective, "We really have to see cetaceans as our equals, as living beings." In the U.S., Congressman Adam Schiff introduced the Orca Responsibility and Care Advancement Act, which would phase out the display of captive killer whales. While these laws do not explicitly mention the rights of cetaceans, they implicitly recognize the right to live free in natural habitat.

In 1977, UNESCO published a Universal Declaration of Animal Rights stating that wild animals have the rights to life, liberty, and procreation in their natural environment. Although not a legally binding document, this declaration played an important role in a precedent-setting Argentine court decision discussed later in this chapter. In 1993, a group of scientists and activists formed the Great Ape Project and have been working since to have the United Nations issue a world declaration on great primates. In their petition, they identify three basic rights for the world's great apes: to life, liberty, and freedom from torture. Similarly, the UK-based Whale and Dolphin Conservation Society is advocating for a declaration of rights for cetaceans that acknowledges their complex minds, societies, and cultures and asserts their rights to life, liberty, and well-being.

Some animal rights activists are upset by the focus on great apes and cetaceans. Professor Gary Francione advocates for the recognition that all sentient animals have rights and warns that "focusing on the humanlike cognitive characteristics of some non-humans who are declared to be 'special' is like having a human rights campaign that focuses on giving rights to the 'smarter' humans first in the hope that we will extend rights to less intelligent ones later on." Given our growing understanding of the sentience and remarkable qualities of many other species beyond primates, whales, and dolphins, Francione's warning is astute.

On the frontiers of legal change, there is a growing global movement to recognize non-human animals as legal persons, a radical change that would endow them with a variety of legal rights. Animal rights advocates are not saying primates, cetaceans, or elephants are people. They are saying that the law should recognize them as legal persons. A 'legal person' is not necessarily a human being, but rather an entity to which the law grants specific rights. A corporation is considered a legal person, as are ships, churches, and municipalities. The rights and responsibilities of a legal person vary according to the nature of the entity. Corporations and human beings have different sets of legal rights and duties. For example, corporations may assert freedom of expression, but are not protected by the right to life.

Over time, the boundaries of what is considered a legal person have evolved in concert with our values. For centuries, slaves were not considered to be legal persons, and thus had no rights. In Canada, women were not regarded as persons in the eyes of the law until shockingly recently. Until 1882, pursuant to a legal doctrine called coverture, Canadian women lost their status as legal persons when they married. In 1929, the Supreme Court of Canada, in a famous case inspired by Nellie McClung and other women's rights activists, ruled that women were not persons in the eyes of the law and were therefore ineligible to be appointed to the Senate. That decision was overturned in 1931 by the UK's Judicial Committee of the Privy Council, marking an important milestone in the advancement of women's rights in Canada. Aboriginal people in Canada did not enjoy the full array of legal rights until 1960, when they became eligible to vote in federal elections.

Lawyers around the world, like Steven Wise in the U.S., are striving to expand the boundaries of the phrase "legal persons" to include individual animals. Lawsuits on behalf of individual animals have been filed in countries as far-flung as Argentina, Austria, Brazil, and Switzerland. One of the leading approaches involves asserting their rights through habeas corpus, a remedy which is available to a legal person. At the request of the Brazilian Great Ape Project, public prosecutors filed a habeas corpus application on behalf of Suica, a chimp living in a tiny enclosure in a municipal zoo in the city of San Salvador, though she died before the court could hear her case.

Like the lawsuits filed by Steven Wise on behalf of chimpanzees Tommy, Kiko, Hercules, and Leo, the cases brought in Austria and Switzerland ran into judges without the vision to expand the definition of a legal person. A case was filed in Austria on behalf of Hiasl, a twenty-six-year-old chimpanzee, after a wildlife sanctuary where he lived went bankrupt. A donor had given almost $10,000 to the sanctuary to care for Hiasl just before it went bankrupt. Lawyers sought to have the chimp recognized as a legal person, so that they could appoint a legal guardian to secure the donated funds for the chimp's benefit. Judge Barbara Bart ruled that Hiasl was neither mentally handicapped nor in imminent danger, thus failing to meet Austrian law's criteria for appointment of a legal guardian. Austria's Supreme Court rejected Hiasl's appeal. Neither Austrian court directly tackled the question of whether a chimp can be a legal person. In 2010, the European Court of Human Rights refused to hear Hiasl's case.

In Argentina, however, the legal wall separating humans and other animals has been breached. In 2013, the Argentine Association of Professional Lawyers for Animal Rights (AFADA) filed a habeas corpus writ on behalf of Sandra, a Sumatran orangutan held for twenty years in a Buenos Aires zoo, alleging the "unjustified confinement of an animal with proven cognitive ability." The word "orangutan" is Malay for "person of the forest." Orangutans, like all great apes, possess advanced cognitive abilities. AFADA lawyers argued that Sandra should be considered a legal person instead of a thing, and that as a non-human person, she had been illegally deprived of her liberty.

In 2014, judges unanimously agreed that Sandra was a "non-human person [who] has some basic rights, including freedom and avoiding suffering from being in captivity." The court ruled that she should be transferred to a sanctuary. AFADA lawyer Pablo Buompadre said the court decision "opens the way not only for other great apes, but also for other sentient beings who are unfairly and arbitrarily deprived of their liberty in zoos, circuses, water parks, and scientific laboratories." The court's decision and associated publicity triggered the announcement in 2016 that the Buenos Aires Zoo would close completely. In making the announcement, the city's mayor, Horacio Rodríguez Larreta, said, "This situation of captivity is degrading for the animals." As this book goes to press, the courts are reviewing plans developed by an expert committee for relocating Sandra and the zoo's 2,500 other animals to appropriate sanctuaries within Argentina.

A second Argentine case decided in late 2016, on behalf of a chimpanzee named Cecilia, resulted in a globally important precedent for animal rights. Lawyers for AFADA filed a habeas corpus case, seeking to have Cecilia transferred from a small concrete enclosure in the century-old Mendoza Zoo to the Sorocaba chimpanzee sanctuary in Brazil. Cecilia is twenty years old, and she had been alone for years following the death of her two companions.

Dr. Fernando Simón, state attorney of Mendoza, argued that Cecilia was still a thing under Argentine law. He agreed that animals deserve protection but not legal personhood or rights. Simón argued that only humans have rights of liberty and freedom of movement and even posited that neither AFADA nor Cecilia had standing to bring the lawsuit.

Judge María Alejandra Mauricio wrote a powerful and at times poetic decision ordering that Cecilia be released from the Mendoza Zoo and transferred to the Sorocaba sanctuary within six months. The judge cited the Universal Declaration of Animal Rights and Argentina's constitution. She concluded that rights evolve over time and "to classify animals as things is not a correct standard." Judge Mauricio described the remarkable capabilities of chimpanzees and clarified, "This is not about granting them the same rights humans have, it is about accepting and understanding once and for all that they are living sentient beings, with legal personhood and that, among other rights, they possess the fundamental right to be born, to live, grow, and die in the proper environment for their species."

Acknowledging the potential controversy ignited by her decision, Judge Mauricio said that once people understand "the circumstances that resulted in my decision, they will feel the satisfaction of knowing that acting collectively as a society we have been able to give Cecilia the life she deserves." Judge Mauricio closed her decision by quoting the words of philosopher Immanuel Kant: "We may judge the heart of a man by his treatment of animals."

Cecilia underwent thirty days of special medical care and observation, and has now been transferred to the chimpanzee sanctuary in Brazil. Her victory has energized legal efforts for other chimpanzees in zoos throughout Argentina and around the world. "Considering that they are very close to humans, it is an absurdity that they are still in captivity," said primatologist Aldo Giúdice of the University of Buenos Aires.

An even more radical approach to using courts to advance the rights of animals has been used by People for the Ethical Treatment of Animals (PETA). In 2011, PETA lawyers filed a lawsuit on behalf of five orcas—Tilikum and Katina at SeaWorld Orlando, and Kasatka, Corky, and Ulises at SeaWorld San Diego. These killer whales were among dozens captured in the wild and then confined in tiny aquariums by companies like SeaWorld. Tilikum was captured near Iceland at the age of two and used by a variety of aquariums. He killed trainers in 1991 and 2010, and is suspected of killing a man who broke into SeaWorld in 1999 and was found dead in his tank.

PETA's lawsuit accused SeaWorld of violating the U.S. Constitution's thirteenth amendment, which abolished slavery and involuntary servitude in 1865, by forcing the whales to live in small tanks and perform shows daily to entertain SeaWorld's customers. PETA's lawyers argued the whales deserved the same protection from slavery as humans—marking the first time an American court heard arguments about whether the Constitution could protect animals. Jeff Kerr, general counsel to PETA, said, "It's a new frontier in civil rights. Coercion, degradation, and subjugation characterize slavery, and these orcas have endured all three."

Kerr became an animal rights lawyer by accident. He was planning to attend a social justice lecture, but the original speaker got stuck in traffic. The substitute presenter's subject was the abuse of animals in the U.S. The presentation hit him "right between the eyes." Kerr recalled, "I went straight home and threw out every food item in my house that had any animal product in it and went vegan." He responded to an ad in the *Washington Post* for a staff attorney at PETA and has been with the organization ever since.

Not surprisingly, SeaWorld rejected PETA's assertions in the 2011 case. Their lawyer argued, "Neither orcas nor any other animal were included in 'We the people' . . . when the Constitution was adopted." SeaWorld argued that if PETA's lawsuit was successful, the precedent would have devastating consequences for everything from agriculture and medical research to dogs used by police to detect bombs and drugs. Even among lawyers advocating for animal rights, the case was deemed a stretch given the lack of precedents. Steven Wise pulled no punches, arguing, "It was idiotic to invoke the Constitution the first time around. You know maybe in fifty years, after you've already laid a foundation of courts recognizing that non-human animals could be considered legal persons under the common law." Other critics argued that it was preposterous, reprehensible, and an affront to human dignity to compare the problems facing captive killer whales to the evils endured by African American slaves.

Laurence Tribe, a constitutional expert and professor at Harvard Law School, acknowledged that some people might find the comparison with slavery offensive, but said, "The Constitution is an essentially aspirational document. Its bold language and broadly expressed principles offer themselves to each generation as we struggle to define our national values in an ever-changing world. . . . So it seems to me no abuse of the Constitution to invoke it on behalf of non-human animals cruelly confined for purposes of involuntary servitude."

The PETA lawsuit was dismissed by Judge Jeffrey Miller of the U.S. District Court for Southern California, who wrote in his ruling that "the only reasonable interpretation of the Thirteenth Amendment's plain language is that it applies to persons, and not to nonpersons such as orcas." Judge Miller relied on an 1872 decision of the U.S. Supreme Court in the Slaughterhouse Cases, which held that the use of the word "involuntary" in combination with the word servitude meant that the Thirteenth Amendment only protected humans. His conclusion did not take into account the advances in scientific evidence about animal intelligence and con-sciousness. Despite dismissing the case, Judge Miller noted, "Even though Plaintiffs lack standing to bring a Thirteenth Amendment claim, that is not to say that animals have no legal rights; as there are many state and federal statutes affording redress to Plaintiffs, including, in some instances, criminal statutes that 'punish those who violate statutory duties that protect animals.'"

While PETA's attempt to secure the constitutional rights of

killer whales failed in the U.S., a decision of the Supreme Court of India proves that the approach is neither misguided nor doomed to fail. The Animal Welfare Board of India and the Indian branch of PETA filed a lawsuit challenging the legality of *jallikattu*, a traditional event that involves taming bulls by mistreating them. The Supreme Court took the unprecedented step of extending the protection of Article 21 of India's Constitution, which protects the rights to life and liberty, to all animals. According to the Court, bulls have a constitutional right "to live in a healthy and clean atmosphere, not to be beaten, kicked, bitten, tortured, plied with alcohol by humans or made to stand in narrow enclosures amidst bellows and jeers from crowds."

All social change is fraught with challenges, however, and the *jallikattu* case is no exception. The Supreme Court decision has been hotly contested by the event's proponents, who claim it is an important traditional event in the state of Tamil Nadu. Some people have ignored the Court's order and been arrested. The state legislature tried to legalize the practice once again and was rebuffed by the Court, but the controversy is ongoing.

Since the Indian Supreme Court decision, and despite the protests sparked by the *jallikattu* case, many other animal rights cases have been filed involving elephants, dogs, roosters, horses, and exotic birds. India's constitution makes it a fundamental duty of all citizens "to have compassion for all living creatures." In a case involving the mistreatment of circus animals, the Kerala High Court wrote, "It is not only our fundamental duty to show compassion to our animal friends, but also to recognize and protect their rights . . . If humans are entitled to fundamental rights, why not animals?"

Recognizing that animals have rights does not mean that they have human rights, as critics love to suggest. Obviously, the right to vote is nonsensical in the context of chimps, chickens, or killer whales. However, in recognition of their sentience, intelligence, and consciousness, it seems reasonable to insist that animals enjoy animal rights appropriate to their species. Bats, birds, and primates will have bat rights, bird rights, and primate rights, which will differ according to their needs. There will be a common core, however, which includes rights to life, freedom, and suitable habitat. Sue Donaldson and Will Kymlicka, the authors of *Zoopolis: A Political Theory of Animal Rights*, make a compelling case that animal rights need to be distinguished for different species in three broad categories—domestic, wild, and liminal (wild species that have adapted to life among humans, such as crows and raccoons). Domestic animals are dependent on humans, but the authors propose that they be treated as co-citizens of our community, leading to a more extensive set of positive rights for the creatures and corresponding responsibilities for people. These animals have rights to food, water, shelter, medical care, normal behaviour (requiring living space of adequate quality and quantity, and in some cases company of the animal's own kind), compassion, and respect. Wild animals flourish when undisturbed by humans, so their rights are akin to sovereignty rights and self-determination. These rights go beyond the right to be left alone: they include positive human interventions that further their rights but protect their autonomy, such as habitat restoration projects or environmental cleanups. There is no expectation that humans will be obligated to intervene in nature to protect one animal from killing another. The territory of wild animals, under this theory, includes all habitat not already settled or developed by humans (effectively ending the expansion of human settlements and agriculture). Donaldson and Kymlicka identify a hybrid set of animal rights and human obligations for the liminal species based on our mutual coexistence in shared habitat.

While the animal welfare movement has secured improvements in the way animals are treated in contemporary society, this progress is outweighed by the growth in the sheer number of animals being used and abused by humans. Steven Wise is correct when he calls the current legal system's rigid distinction between humans and animals "arbitrary, unfair, and irrational." The notion that animals should be granted rights is controversial, yet the progress in scientific understanding and the concomitant evolution of societal values seem to compel movement in this direction. Science is opening our eyes and our minds to the real nature of animals. They are complex individuals, living in elaborate social networks, relationships, and communities. We should treat them with greater respect, a simple dictum that will require huge societal changes.

The law, which in recent centuries has treated non-human animals as property intended for human use and exploitation, is beginning to catch up with the science. An assessment of the laws governing the treatment of animals and their rights leads to an encouraging conclusion—more and more people, and more and more countries, are recognizing that animals deserve significantly stronger rights than they have been granted in the past. It must be acknowledged that factory farming is an outlier, as only the most modest strides have been made in reducing the prodigious suffering inflicted upon animals by this industry. Elsewhere, the momentum is almost all in the same direction—toward stronger animal cruelty laws, greater punishments for those convicted of animal cruelty, and legal acknowledgement that animals are sentient beings. At the leading edge are legal changes recognizing that animals have rights that, while different from human rights, still must be respected, protected, and fulfilled. For primates, cetaceans, and elephants, some remarkable legal victories have been secured. But protecting the fundamental interests of all individual animals can only be assured through the systemic recognition of animal rights, just as protecting fundamental human interests requires recognizing the rights of all humans.

For wild species, however, an even more pressing question than the quality of the lives of captive individuals is the survival of the species as a whole. The global biodiversity crisis, with many species going extinct and thousands more becoming endangered, has raised a vitally important legal question: Do endangered species have the right to survive?

The
RIGHTS *of* SPECIES

*"[The] balancing of interests between the commercial fishing
fleet and the porpoise is irrelevant; the porpoise must prevail."*

U.S. Court of Appeals for the District of Columbia, 1976

A FISH, A DAM, AND A
LAWSUIT THAT CHANGED THE WORLD

Professor Zygmunt Plater is a balding, bespectacled legal scholar with a penchant for wearing bow ties. Although best known as one of America's top academics in the field of environmental law, Plater's crowning achievement was leading a team of students at the University of Tennessee in a six-year legal battle that sent shock waves across the U.S. and around the world.

Plater was a university student at Princeton and Yale in the 1960s when the Tennessee Valley Authority (TVA) sought permission to build the Tellico Dam on the Little Tennessee River. The project would improve flood control, store water for irrigation, and create a large waterfront real estate development. Plater had no idea that he would end up leading a lawsuit about the dam that reached the U.S. Supreme Court, led to skirmishes and dirty tricks in Congress, and was ultimately decided by President Jimmy Carter. The saga would mark a critical turning point in the relationship between human beings and other species on this planet.

The Tellico Dam was just the latest in a long line of thousands of dams that blocked the flow of America's once-wild rivers. Environmental damage and destruction were seen as the price paid for progress. The TVA assumed that it would easily clear the regulatory hurdles for the dam, as it had so many times in the past.

But thanks to Congress and President Richard Nixon, environmentalists had new shields they could use to try to defend nature from industrialization's onslaught. A law called the National Environmental Policy Act was passed in 1969, requiring major projects to undergo a type of review called environmental assessment. TVA skipped this process, leading local farmers and residents to file a successful lawsuit that delayed work on the dam for several years. But then TVA completed the environmental assessment and resumed construction.

By 1973, Zygmunt Plater had graduated from Yale Law School and secured a job as an assistant professor at the University of Tennessee law school, teaching property law and environmental law. One day in 1974, a shaggy-haired student named Hiram (Hank) Hill approached Plater with a proposed term paper topic. According to Hill, fisheries students with whom he'd been drinking beer told him that their biology prof had found a tiny, tan-coloured, bottom-dwelling fish he'd never seen before in the Little Tennessee River, downstream from the proposed dam. Hill said, "The Endangered Species Act had some teeth added to it last year, so an endangered fish might be able to block the Tellico Dam. Do you think that's enough for a ten-page paper?"

The hitherto-unknown fish discovered by University of Tennessee ichthyologist David Etnier would be named the snail darter (based on its quick movements and the freshwater snails that are its favourite food). Its only known habitat would be eradicated if the Tellico Dam was completed. The snail darter is not a fish that stirs the blood of sports fishermen or tantalizes the palates of American chefs. No, it's a plain-looking creature, less than four inches long. Plater and Hill petitioned the government to list the snail darter as an endangered species, and in 1975 the government complied, inadvertently opening the door to a legal challenge.

As Plater tells the story of the case, his voice grows and his passion flows. "This is a David and Goliath story, and Goliath is a bastard." At a meeting of local residents whose land was going to be expropriated for the project, farmers passed around a hat soliciting donations for a second legal challenge. They managed to raise twenty-nine dollars. The fee to file the case was fifteen dollars, so they had fourteen dollars left over for the remaining expenses. Plater and his colleagues were acting pro bono (not charging for their services). He begged national environmental groups for help and was turned down. A spokesperson for TVA reportedly said, go ahead and sue us, "we have 100 lawyers and our own federal judge." Plater and Hill accepted the challenge, filing a lawsuit arguing that completing the dam and wiping out the snail darter would violate the Endangered Species Act.

When the case went to trial, the lead attorney for Plater's team was Boone Dougherty, a descendant of Daniel Boone. Dougherty had a reputation as a hard-nosed litigator and the added attraction of being the trial judge's neighbour. Judge Robert Taylor, appointed by President Harry Truman in 1949, was the sole federal judge in the Eastern District of Tennessee. A small man wearing round glasses and a long black robe, Taylor called the lawyers into his office for a pre-trial conference. Knowing the judge had attended Yale Law School, Zygmunt Plater wore his Yale tie. Judge Taylor asked, "You went to Yale?"

Plater replied "Yes, your honour."

"Well, I hear they don't teach much law there these days."

Not a great start to the case, but a sign of things to come. At one point in the trial, Judge Taylor asked Dougherty, "Do you really think that Congress would want me to stop an important project for just any endangered creature, for some red-eyed cricket?"

The TVA hired a former Cornell University professor, Ed Raney, to serve as their fisheries expert. Raney was a hired gun, providing industry-friendly opinions to whoever paid his fees. He testified that the snail darter might not be a separate species, that it might be found elsewhere, that it could be transplanted to other rivers, and that it might flourish even if the dam was built. Boone Dougherty ripped Raney apart during cross-examination, forcing him to admit that he'd done most of his "research" on snail darters from a helicopter. Members of the public seated in the audience laughed out loud.

Not surprisingly, Judge Taylor dismissed the case. In his decision, Taylor acknowledged that the dam would harm the snail darter and its habitat. However, he ruled that the economic importance of the project trumped the adverse impacts on an insignificant fish. He concluded, "It would be foolish to issue an injunction."

Plater and his team appealed to the U.S. Court of Appeals for the Sixth Circuit, seeking to overturn Taylor's decision. This time, Plater handled the legal arguments. As he spoke, he was encouraged to see Judge Wade McCree furiously scribbling notes—he assumed the judge was jotting down his compelling points to shape a decision favourable to the fish. In fact, the appeal was successful, with all three judges agreeing that the law was clear: by completing the dam and harming the darter, TVA would violate the Endangered Species Act. A law clerk with the Court of

Appeals later told Plater that Judge McCree wasn't taking notes but was composing a limerick:

> Who can surpass the snail darter?
> The fish that would not be a martyr.
> It stymied the dam,
> Near the place where it swam.
> Can you think of a fish any smarter?

It was TVA's turn to appeal, and the next stop for the case was the U.S. Supreme Court. Appearing before your country's highest court is usually the pinnacle of a lawyer's career. For the occasion, Zygmunt Plater wore a snail darter T-shirt (inside out so that it was invisible) beneath his white dress shirt. On the other side of the courtroom was a squadron of elite government and industry lawyers, led by the U.S. attorney general himself, Griffin Bell. Bell was a former judge and had recently been named to a list of best-dressed Americans. The pressure was excruciating, and Plater admits having to clench his bowels as he approached the podium, facing nine dour-faced Supreme Court judges. Less than a minute into his argument he was interrupted by Justice Blackmun. Hostile questions flew fast and furious. Plater was flailing, struggling to make a coherent argument. Justice Stewart came to his rescue with an easy query. Then Chief Justice Burger asked whether the discovery of an endangered fish would require the government to tear down a $300- or $400-million-dollar dam. Justice Powell asked, "What purpose, if any, is served by these little darters? Are they used for food? Are they suitable for bait? I'm a bass fisherman." Plater eventually gained his footing, informing the Court that the darter relies on "clean, clear, cool flowing river water." After building more than sixty-five dams in the Tennessee River watershed, Plater continued, the TVA had destroyed the habitats of the snail darter "one by one, until this last thirty-three river miles is the last place on earth where this species, and human beings as well, have the quality of that habitat."

Despite his strong concluding statement, Plater thought they'd lost. Two months passed. On June 15, 1978, the Supreme Court issued its decision. With a six-to-three vote, the Court determined that completing the dam would violate the Endangered Species Act. Justices Burger and Marshall, whose questions during the hearing suggested they were squarely on TVA's side, turned out to be part of the majority.

In a powerful and enduring judgment, the Supreme Court stated that "the plain intent of Congress in enacting [the Endangered Species Act] was to halt and reverse the trend toward species extinction, whatever the cost." As the Court acknowledged, their decision, and their interpretation of the law, "will produce results requiring the sacrifice of the anticipated benefits of the project and of many millions of dollars in public funds. But examination of the language, history, and structure of the legislation under review here indicates beyond doubt that Congress intended endangered species to be afforded the highest of priorities."

Consider three key words in the Supreme Court's judgment: "whatever the cost." No other environmental law in the U.S. or any other nation has ever contained such a phrase or been interpreted to have such a meaning. For a law to set out to achieve its goal "whatever the cost" must mean that the objective being pursued is of incalculable value. And the objective, in the case of the Endangered Species Act, is preventing extinction. It is little wonder that many legal experts regard this piece of legislation as the strongest environmental law in the world.

Environmentalists' initial celebrations were short-lived. By the time the case was decided by the Supreme Court, the dam was almost complete. TVA had barged ahead, either willfully blind to the risk of a legal setback or arrogantly confident that nothing could stand in its way. The court's decision ignited a firestorm of debate. Conservative pundits depicted the Endangered Species Act as a radical environmental bogeyman that epitomized government's growing disregard for private property rights. TVA lobbied furiously for an exemption from the law's requirements.

Congress bent but didn't break, amending the Endangered Species Act to establish a formal exemption process carried out by an Endangered Species Committee. This committee is chaired by the secretary of the interior, while other members include five senior administration officials and one individual from each affected state (who collectively share one vote). Congress inserted several roadblocks in the exemption process: there can be no reasonable alternatives to the proposed action; the benefits of the proposed action must outweigh the benefits of protecting the endangered species and their habitat; and five of the seven committee members must vote for the exemption in order to authorize an activity that threatens the future of an endangered species.

Media nicknamed this committee "The God Squad." The TVA immediately applied for an exemption. Amazingly, the committee voted unanimously not to grant an exemption for the Tellico Dam. Undaunted, the TVA and the Tennessee congressional delegation responded by pushing Congress to pass a bill specifically giving the Tellico Dam the green light, overriding the Endangered Species Act. Reinforced by environmental allies who now understood the snail darter's symbolic value, Plater and his team worked the corridors of power in Washington, DC, and won two narrow votes. Then TVA's relentless supporters slipped a rider into a multi-billion-dollar appropriations bill, granting Tellico Dam an exemption. A rider is an undemocratic tactic by which a completely unrelated but controversial provision is appended to a proposed law that enjoys wide popularity. The appropriations bill and the rider passed. Years and years of fighting for the snail darter were tossed in the trash by unscrupulous southern lawmakers.

Only President Jimmy Carter could stop the completion of the dam now, by vetoing the appropriations bill. Carter initially told the media that he planned to use his veto power on behalf of the snail darter. Days later, Plater's phone rang. It was the president calling from Air Force One. Carter said he was going to sign the bill, not veto it. Plater argued desperately that the president should change his mind and demonstrate environmental leadership, but to no avail. When he hung up, Plater berated himself for failing to appeal to President Carter's strong Christian beliefs by saying something like "Mr. President, you do realize that if you don't deliver a veto when you get off that plane you'll be the first person in human history to hold a species created by God in his hand and consciously condemn it to extinction." Plater then sat in his office and cried.

The TVA completed the dam, but in the story's final twist, snail darters were discovered in Chickamauga Creek near Chattanooga, and transplanted darters prospered in the Hiwassee and Holston

Rivers. To reflect its wider range and higher numbers, the species was downlisted from endangered to threatened.

When recounting the snail darter story, Plater jokes that he wished the case had involved a beautiful whooping crane instead of a cold, slimy little fish. But in some ways, the case is all the more striking because it involved a seemingly insignificant species. Even the snail darters of this world have the right to live, and the right to have their habitat protected from destruction.

Chapter 5

SAVING ENDANGERED SPECIES:
"WHATEVER THE COST"

"[The Endangered Species Act] made us the only nation on Earth to declare a basic right of existence for species other than our own."

JOEL SARTORE, *National Geographic* photographer

In the late nineteenth and early twentieth centuries, the first stirrings of a new ethic began to emerge—that it's wrong for humans to drive another species to extinction. International treaties were signed and national laws enacted to protect polar bears, migratory birds, whales, and other species whose populations were in free-fall because of human activities. National parks and wildlife refuges were created. In Canada, a law was passed in 1877 to protect the dwindling buffalo herds that once caused the Prairies to shake. That law, however, and others like it, were never implemented or enforced.

Fast-forward a century, and the year 1973 seemed unlikely to mark a turning point in human attitudes toward other species. It was an *annus horribilis*, marred by nuclear tests, plane crashes, terrorist attacks, the Arab–Israeli War, and the start of the first OPEC oil crisis. In other news, President Nixon finally ended the war in Vietnam, *The Godfather* swept the Academy Awards, Billboard's number-one song was "Tie a Yellow Ribbon Round the Ole Oak Tree" by Tony Orlando and Dawn, Hank Aaron hit his 700th home run, and a dozen eggs cost twenty-five cents.

And yet 1973 was also the year that two landmark legal developments signalled the emergence of a revolutionary idea—that species other than humans have the right to live and to flourish in their natural habitat, or at the very least, the right not to be eliminated from the face of the Earth. The first was the enactment of the U.S. Endangered Species Act, still regarded as one of the world's most powerful environmental laws. The second was the negotiation of a new international treaty called the Convention on International Trade in Endangered Species of Wild Fauna and Flora (CITES), which some scholars described as a Magna Carta for animals. Both laws reflected kangaroo-sized bounds forward in humankind's attitudes toward other species.

It's important to view these legal breakthroughs in their historical context. By 1970, environmental concerns were reaching unprecedented heights around the world. Rivers were catching on fire, lakes were dying, and oil tankers were rupturing and coating beaches in black muck. The media was electrified, and coverage grew. Concerns about air pollution, water pollution, toxic chemicals, and the disappearance of wildlife galvanized the public. Rachel Carson's book *Silent Spring* had been a major spark, its influence growing in the years since its publication in 1962, and it ignited the environmental movement. The crashing bald eagle population verified Carson's warnings. The pesticide DDT accumulated in food chains, and it was causing eagle eggs to thin to the point that the shells broke before the chicks could hatch. By 1970, there were only 400 nesting pairs of bald eagles left in the lower forty-eight states. Over a million people marched on

Earth Day 1970. Greenpeace was founded in 1971. The first major global eco-summit was held in Sweden in 1972. The times were a-changin'.

A few years earlier, with little fanfare, the United States had passed a modest piece of legislation called the Endangered Species Preservation Act of 1966. This law was inspired by the alarming downward trajectory of treasured species such as the whooping crane. It authorized the secretary of the interior to place native American species of fish and wildlife on an endangered species list and take modest steps to protect them. Even fifty years ago, biologists understood that loss of habitat was the main threat to most species, while a minority of creatures, such as alligators and crocodiles, were threatened by hunting, fishing, or poaching. The new law ordered federal land agencies such as the U.S. Forest Service to protect endangered species' habitat on lands and waters under their control. The U.S. Fish and Wildlife Service was allocated the princely sum of fifteen million dollars annually to buy lands providing habitat for the listed species.

In March 1967, seventy-eight species were listed as endangered, including thirty-six fish, twenty-two birds, fourteen mammals, and six reptile and amphibian species. This initial group, including the American alligator and the California condor, became known as "The Class of '67.'" In 1968, the U.S. Fish and Wildlife Service bought its first endangered species habitat: 2,300 acres in Florida for the key deer.

These small steps did not arrest the decline in species' populations, so in 1969, Congress revamped the law and renamed it the Endangered Species Conservation Act. This new law added restrictions on international and interstate commerce in endangered species. Any species threatened with extinction glob-ally could no longer be imported into the U.S. The revised law expanded the scope of protection to less sexy species including invertebrates such as mollusks and crustaceans. Perhaps most importantly, the amended law also instructed the U.S. government to host an international meeting, with the intent of developing a treaty to conserve endangered species. That meeting was held in Washington, DC, in February 1973 and produced the Convention on International Trade in Endangered Species of Wild Fauna and Flora, discussed in the next chapter.

As public pressure on politicians to protect the environment spiked in the early 1970s, Congress responded by passing laws to protect the country's air and water through the pioneering Clean Air Act and Clean Water Act. People were not only concerned about human health; they were also genuinely concerned about the prospect of losing magnificent species forever. Greenpeace, founded in 1971, ran a prominent Save the Whales campaign, and used a tiny Zodiac boat to place themselves within the harpoon range of massive Russian whaling ships. A report from the House of Representatives' Merchant Marine and Fisheries Committee (now the House Committee on Natural Resources) summarized the problem in blunt terms: "Recent history indicates that man's impact upon marine mammals has ranged from what might be termed malign neglect to virtual genocide. These animals, includ-ing whales, porpoises, seals, sea otters, polar bears, manatees and others . . . have been shot, blown up, clubbed to death, run down by boats, poisoned, and exposed to a multitude of other indigni-ties." In 1972, the U.S. enacted the Marine Mammal Protection Act to prohibit human activity from jeopardizing whales, dolphins, and seals, setting a precedent that the U.S. would build upon the very next year.

In 1973, Congress turned to the third iteration of American legislation to protect imperiled species in just seven years. In keeping with the heightened environmental concerns of the time, the Endangered Species Act was designed to protect "critically imperiled species from extinction as a consequence of economic growth untempered by adequate concern and conservation." The House of Representatives passed the Endangered Species Act 355 to 4, while the bill passed, without dissent, on a voice vote in the Senate. Laws rarely receive such uniform bipartisan support.

Republican president Richard Nixon, who was embroiled in the Watergate scandal, signed the act into law three days after Christmas in 1973. It is unlikely that Nixon had any inkling of the powerful legal defences the law created for non-human species. In a cliché-ridden statement to the media, Nixon said, "Nothing is more priceless and more worthy of preservation than the rich array of animal life with which our nation has been blessed. It is a many-faceted treasure, of value to scholars, scientists, and nature-lovers alike, and it forms a vital part of the heritage we all share as Americans. I congratulate the ninety-third Congress for taking this important step toward protecting a heritage that we hold in trust for countless future generations of our fellow citizens. Their lives will be richer, and America will be more beautiful in the years ahead."

The 1973 version of the U.S. Endangered Species Act was drafted using clear, straightforward language: if a proposed human activity jeopardized the existence of a listed endangered species, then that activity could not proceed. If a proposed activity would destroy or damage critical habitat for an endangered species—whether on federal, state, or private land—that activity could not proceed. The act's protection extended not only to charismatic megafauna such as bald eagles and grizzly bears, but to all species, including microfauna such as the blunt-nosed leopard lizard, Pacific pocket mouse, and El Segundo blue butterfly. Decades later, in the 1992 law review article "Do Species and Nature Have Rights?" American law professor James L. Huffman asserted, "The Endangered Species Act is the most ambitious law ever adopted for the purpose of preserving animal and plant species." Huffman added, "Congress enacted the Endangered Species Act, like much of its legislation, without really understanding what it was doing."

The snail darter case brought by Zygmunt Plater revealed that Congress had gone further than even the most impassioned environmental activists anticipated. In the 1990s, the Endangered Species Act was again at the heart of a bitter controversy, this time over a bird instead of a fish. The northern spotted owl lives in the old-growth forests of the Pacific Northwest. Despite compelling scientific evidence that logging was pushing this owl toward extinction, the U.S. Fish and Wildlife Service rejected calls to list the species under the Endangered Species Act.

Environmentalists sued to enforce the law. In a case called *Northern Spotted Owl v. Hodel*, a federal court judge concluded that the government had "disregarded all the expert opinion on population viability, including that of its own expert, that the owl is facing extinction." Justice Zilly ordered the government to obey the law and list the owl as endangered. The U.S. Fish and Wildlife Service complied but, acutely aware of the looming impact on the logging industry, put off designating critical habitat for the owl.

Again, the government was sued. Again, Judge Zilly ordered them to follow the clear legal requirements of the Endangered Species Act.

Loggers, timber companies, and conservatives were outraged. Environmentalists in Oregon and Washington were assaulted. Recipes for spotted owl soup were published in rural newspapers. The Bureau of Land Management applied to the God Squad, seeking exemptions for forty-four timber sales in critical habitat for the owl. The committee convened and reached a five-to-two decision, approving the exemption for thirteen of the forty-four proposed sales. Before any trees were cut, another lawsuit launched by environmentalists led to a court decision that three members of the God Squad had been in illegal contact with then president George H.W. Bush. The timber sales were cancelled, and the government developed a sweeping plan to ensure the northern spotted owl's survival by protecting ten million acres of old-growth forest.

The God Squad has been asked to issue an exemption to the Endangered Species Act's powerful protection just six times in forty years. It is a testament to the emerging ethic that causing extinction is wrong that only once—in the Grayrocks Dam case—did the God Squad agree to issue a potential death warrant for a species. The Grayrocks Dam in Wyoming was expected to have a negative impact on whooping cranes downstream on the Platte River in Nebraska, potentially jeopardizing their survival as a species. The exemption was granted subject to significant actions to reduce the downstream impacts of the dam, including not only maintaining but also enhancing habitat for the cranes.

Environmental groups—led by Earthjustice and the Center for Biological Diversity—routinely use the Endangered Species Act as a basis for lawsuits and rely on the Supreme Court decision in the snail darter case. As recently as 2008, a court reaffirmed that Congress made it "abundantly clear that the balance has been struck in favour of affording endangered species the highest of priorities." In 2011, the Center for Biological Diversity settled a landmark lawsuit under the Endangered Species Act, forcing the U.S. Fish and Wildlife Service to accelerate the listing process for more than 750 species that had been languishing on a waiting list. By the end of 2016, more than 175 of these species had gained legal protection, including several critically endangered Hawaiian birds and an orchid that spent forty-one years on the waiting list. In 2016 alone, the Center for Biological Diversity used the law to secure protection for 2.5 million acres of critical habitat, including 1.8 million for Sierra Nevada amphibians.

In some cases, lawsuits have been brought in the name of the endangered species itself. In addition to the northern spotted owl lawsuits, there was a case called *Palila et al. v. Hawaii Department of Land and Natural Resources*. The palila, a pretty yellow-headed bird belonging to the Hawaiian honeycreeper family, was facing a variety of threats, including feral goats and sheep wreaking havoc on its habitat. The goats and sheep were eating the shoots and saplings of māmane and naio trees in the forests around Mauna Kea on the Big Island. Instead of protecting the palila, the government was protecting the sheep and goats on behalf of hunters. The Federal Court, Ninth Circuit, stated, "As an endangered species under the Endangered Species Act . . . the bird . . . has legal status and wings its way into federal court as a plaintiff in its own right . . . represented by attorneys for the Sierra Club, the Audubon Society, and other environmental parties." In *Marbled Murrelet v. Babbitt*, the Court ruled that because marbled murrelets (small coastal birds dependent on old-growth forests) are protected under the Endangered Species Act, the species "has standing to sue in its own right." Other cases featuring species as named plaintiffs included *Hawksbill Sea Turtle v. FEMA*, *American Bald Eagle v. Bhatti*, *Mt. Graham Red Squirrel v. Yeutter*, *Florida Key Deer v. Stickney*, and *Loggerhead Turtle v. County Council of Volusia County*.

On the other hand, some American courts have rejected the idea that endangered species can be plaintiffs in litigation. In a case involving a different endangered Hawaiian bird, a court ruled that the 'alalā did not have standing to maintain a suit challenging the implementation of a program under the Endangered Species Act. The court denied the 'alalā standing because the bird was not a person, and court rules allowing lawsuits on behalf of infants or incompetent persons did not apply to animals. It ruled that the case could be brought forward in the name of environmental groups working to protect the species.

Similarly, in a 2004 case called *Cetacean Community v. Bush*, challenging the U.S. Navy's use of sonar, the Court of Appeals, Ninth Circuit, concluded that cetaceans do not have standing to sue, even under the Endangered Species Act and the Marine Mammal Protection Act.

Is the Endangered Species Act making a difference? In the 1960s, populations of California condors, black-footed ferrets, and whooping cranes had each fallen below twenty-five. Today there are more than 200 condors in the wild and more than 200 in captivity, producing chicks for release into the wild. There are more than 600 whooping cranes and more than 1,000 black-footed ferrets. More than thirty species have recovered so fully, they no longer need the act's protection. Species removed from the list include the bald eagle, peregrine falcon, gray whale, grizzly bear, gray wolf, brown pelican, Steller sea lion, and Virginia northern flying squirrel. The Center for Biological Diversity identified more than twenty endangered American wildlife species whose populations have increased over 1,000 percent in recent decades, including a 2,206 percent increase in Atlantic green sea turtle females nesting on Florida beaches. The bottom line: an astonishing 90 percent of species listed under the Endangered Species Act are on track to meet their recovery targets. The United States recognizes that species have the right to live, the right to habitat, and the right to exist at healthy population levels.

This radical rethinking of our relationship with non-human species has been emulated across the planet. More than 100 other countries have enacted laws or regulations that embody the spirit, if not the letter, of the American Endangered Species Act. None of these laws are quite as powerful or as effectively implemented, yet they do reflect a genuine effort to prevent the irreversible loss of other life forms, a challenge to conventional wisdom about property, and a tacit acknowledgement that species jeopardized by humans have a right to exist and recover.

A DIRTY COP AND THE UNICORN OF THE SEA

Gregory Logan was an RCMP officer for twenty-five years, from 1978 to 2003. He grew up in New Brunswick but spent most of his career in Grande Prairie, a small city in northern Alberta. For a brief time, from 1982 to 1985, he was posted to the eastern Northwest Territories, a vast icy expanse now known as Nunavut. That experience opened the door to a lucrative criminal enterprise that made Logan rich but also led to his downfall.

The narwhal is one of the world's quirkiest animals. A member of the whale family, it has a long, spiraling tusk protruding from the centre of its face. That tusk is actually a tooth that grows through the face. In the classic novel *Moby Dick*, author Herman Melville speculated that the tusk was used as "a rake in turning over the bottom of the sea for food" or "for an ice-piercer," enabling it to break through the Arctic ice to breathe. To this day, there is scientific debate about the tusk's purpose. Some scientists believe that it's like the male peacock's tail, a symbol of virility intended to attract females. Others believe it's used in aggressive behaviour, like a sword. A more recent and controversial theory is that the tusk is actually a sensory organ that provides the narwhal with information about the dark, cold Arctic waters it lives in. A flaw in this theory is that female narwhals rarely have tusks. In any event, the tusk is made of ivory, like an elephant or walrus tusk, although narwhal tusks are the only ones that grow straight. Up to three metres in length, the tusks command a huge price on black markets in countries where they cannot be legally imported or sold. On rare occasions, a narwhal will grow a double tusk, which can sell for close to 100,000 dollars.

In the Middle Ages, when Vikings began selling narwhal tusks in Europe, they were rumoured to prove the existence of the mythical unicorn and became one of the world's most highly coveted artifacts. Tusks sold for far higher prices, pound for pound, than gold or silver. Legends suggest that Queen Elizabeth I traded an entire castle for a jewel-encrusted narwhal tusk. Pope Clement VII reportedly gifted a narwhal tusk to the French royal family in the sixteenth century as a wedding present. The Holy Roman Emperor wielded a narwhal tusk as a sceptre. Not to be outdone, a Danish king in the seventeenth century had a throne made of narwhal tusks. The tusks were also believed to have aphrodisiac qualities and to serve as a potent antidote to poisons.

Nowadays the only people legally allowed to kill narwhals are the Inuit in Canada and Greenland. Canada's Department of Fisheries and Oceans allocates an annual quota of roughly 500 narwhals, divided among the Inuit communities. For more than 1,000 years, the Inuit have hunted narwhals, not so much for their tusks as for the thick outer layer of blubber, called muktuk. The blubber is rich in vitamin C and enables the Inuit to avoid scurvy despite a traditional diet virtually devoid of fruit or vegetables.

In 2009, law enforcement officials with Environment Canada received a tip from their American counterparts. For five years, the U.S. Fish and Wildlife Service had been investigating a wildlife smuggling ring. The operation began when customs officials at JFK Airport in Washington intercepted a package containing over 500 sperm whale teeth. A Ukrainian man, Andrei Mikhalyov, had sent the teeth to David Place, a Nantucket antique store owner who ran a side racket in illegal wildlife artifacts. The wildlife cops discovered an email trail revealing that Place was also buying narwhal tusks from two Canadians, Gregory Logan and his wife, Nina.

It took eight Environment Canada wildlife officers from across the country to handle the complex investigation, code-named Operation Longtooth. They used stakeouts, vehicle tails, search warrants, and production orders requiring banks and phone companies to hand over the Logans' records. Investigators had to exercise extreme caution, as their prime suspect was a former cop who knew all the tricks and would be on high alert. They kept tabs on Logan at his New Brunswick residence, and one day followed him from the suburbs of Saint John across the U.S. border and into Maine. He stopped on the way and drove down a little road to nowhere. Using binoculars, Environment Canada officials watched him take a package of tusks from beneath his vehicle and place them in the bed of his truck. Then Logan got back on the highway, drove to a FedEx outlet in Bangor, and sent his package disguised in a custom-made shipping sleeve. American officials intercepted it and found a pair of two-metre-long narwhal tusks. Logan was officially busted.

On December 14, 2011, Gregory and Nina Logan were charged in Canada for violating an environmental law with a very long name, the Wild Animal and Plant Protection and Regulation of International and Interprovincial Trade Act (WAPPRIITA). This law implements Canada's obligations under the Convention on

International Trade in Endangered Species. Between 2003 and 2009, the Logans had smuggled over 250 narwhal tusks into the U.S. using a Chevy pickup truck and a utility trailer with a false bottom (a crude secret compartment installed underneath it by simply screwing on a sheet of plywood).

Logan went to trial in New Brunswick Provincial Court in 2013, while charges against his wife were dropped. His lawyer—high-priced, Toronto-based criminal lawyer Brian Greenspan, whose clients include Justin Bieber and supermodel Naomi Campbell—emphasized Logan's strong record as an RCMP officer who'd received positive evaluations throughout his career. Logan told the Court about enduring brutal experiences, such as coming upon decapitated bodies and amputated limbs at crime and accident scenes. He had retired in 2003 with a full pension after twenty-five years of service, but a year later was diagnosed with post-traumatic stress disorder.

Video footage taken outside the New Brunswick courtroom shows Logan as a stocky man with a shaved head, wearing an expensive-looking suit, blue shirt, and striped silk tie and carrying a fancy leather attaché case. He looks a little bit like actor Michael Chiklis, who played a corrupt cop in *The Shield*. Refusing to face the camera, Logan behaves more like a criminal than a police officer. Now sixty years old, he has refused to grant any interview requests since his initial arrest. There was no question that Logan was guilty. The question was how steep a price he would pay for his crimes. Logan pled guilty to seven charges of violating WAPPRIITA.

At the sentencing hearing, lawyer Brian Greenspan said that it had been a terrible experience for his client to go from law enforcer to law breaker. In classic defence lawyer understatement, Greenspan claimed that "a modest side hobby became a bit of a supplement to his medical and RCMP pensions." The judge was not impressed. In the stiffest sentence ever doled out under WAPPRIITA, Logan was fined $385,000, ordered to serve an eight-month conditional sentence (tantamount to house arrest), and prohibited from possessing or purchasing marine mammals for ten years. In addition, he was ordered to forfeit his truck, trailer, and shipping supplies. As an ex-cop, Logan probably breathed a deep sigh of relief that he had avoided a stint in prison.

His co-conspirators in the U.S. didn't fare as well. David Place was sentenced to thirty-three months in jail for his role in smuggling teeth and tusks. Andrei Mikhalyov was lured to the U.S., arrested, put in jail for nine months, and then deported back to the Ukraine. Jay Conrad, a roofing contractor with a penchant for collecting weird curios like shrunken heads, was also in cahoots with Logan. Conrad and his partner Eddie Dunn bought hundreds of tusks from Logan and re-sold them for millions of dollars. Conrad died while awaiting sentencing. Another co-conspirator was Andrew Zarauskas, a New Jersey construction worker who served as an informant in the whale tooth case but turned out to be involved with Logan's narwhal business. Like Place, he ended up with a thirty-three-month prison sentence. In imposing the sentence, district court judge John Woodcock said, "You should know, Mr. Zarauskas, that the narwhals are worth more to the rest of us alive than they are to you dead."

Gregory Logan wasn't off the hook yet. American authorities notified Canada that they wanted to extradite Logan to the U.S. to face additional charges. There's a basic principle of criminal law called the rule against double jeopardy, which means you can't be tried twice for the same crime. Logan fought the extradition process all the way to the Supreme Court of Canada, but the Americans prevailed. Logan had been tried and convicted in Canada for wildlife smuggling, whereas the U.S. wanted to charge him with a variety of money-laundering offences. The double jeopardy defence didn't apply; these were very different charges. In 2016, Logan was extradited to the U.S., where he agreed to plead guilty to one count of conspiracy to launder money and nine counts of money laundering. As this book went to print, Logan was being held in an American prison without bail. He faces a sentence of up to thirteen years.

Chapter 6
ENDANGERED SPECIES LAWS GO GLOBAL

"We are always only a single generation away from a new sense of what is normal."

J.B. MACKINNON, *The Once and Future World*

In 1973, eighty countries signed the Convention on International Trade in Endangered Species of Wild Flora and Fauna (CITES). By early 2017, 183 nations had ratified CITES, committing themselves to protecting endangered species through a combination of domestic and international action.

It shocks many people to learn that the illicit trade in animals and plants is the third largest international crime, after drugs and weapons. Global estimates of the value of this illegal activity amount to billions of dollars annually. Wildlife and plant smugglers sell everything from teak, rosewood, and ivory to aquarium fish, reptiles, and traditional medicine products, such as bear gall-bladders, rhino horns, and tiger penises.

In the preamble of CITES, the parties to the agreement recognize that "wild fauna and flora in their many beautiful and varied forms are an irreplaceable part of the natural systems of the earth which must be protected for this and the generations to come." Species whose survival is in serious jeopardy are listed in

Appendix 1 of CITES. The agreement states that "trade in specimens of these species must be subject to particularly strict regulation in order not to endanger further their survival and must only be authorized in exceptional circumstances." Examples of the more than 900 species appearing in Appendix 1 today include gorillas, rhinos, tigers, walruses, grey parrots, and green turtles.

CITES also requires action on threatened species, for whom the possibility of extinction is serious but not as urgent. These species, including narwhals, are listed in Appendix 2 and are subject to more modest trade limitations, including a scientific assessment to ensure that trade will not seriously affect the population of a species. In total, more than 35,000 species receive some degree of protection under CITES.

CITES was followed by a series of international agreements that reinforced the right of species to live and flourish in the wild. But these subsequent agreements went even further: while CITES protects species for present and future generations of humans, the later agreements refer to the protection of species for their own sakes. In 1982, the UN agreed upon the World Charter for Nature. This charter states, "Every form of life is unique, warranting respect regardless of its worth to humans, and to accord other organisms such recognition, humans must be guided by a moral code of action." In 1980, the International Union for the Conservation of Nature (IUCN) published a World Conservation Strategy. The revised version from 1991 stated, "Every form of life warrants respect independently of its worth to people. Human development should not threaten the integrity of nature or the survival of other species." Also, throughout the 1990s, people from across the planet, led by the unlikely combination of Canadian industrialist/activist Maurice Strong and former Russian president Mikhail Gorbachev, united to craft the Earth Charter. Formally released in March 2000 after much re-drafting, the charter places humans within a broader community of life that includes other species as well as future generations of life on Earth. While none of these documents creates legally binding obligations, they artic-ulate an emerging ethic that nature has intrinsic value—a stepping stone toward recognizing both the rights of other species and the rights of nature.

From CITES in the 1970s and the World Charter for Nature in the 1980s to the opening of discussion in 1991 that led to the Earth Charter, the world was moving inexorably toward 1992's Earth Summit in Rio. There, the world's leaders agreed upon the UN Convention on Biodiversity, a legally binding treaty that imposes extensive obligations upon governments to protect the diversity of life. The text of the convention acknowledges "the intrinsic value of biological diversity and the ecological, genetic, social, economic, scientific, educational, cultural, recreational and aesthetic values of biological diversity and its components." In 2010, parties to the convention met in Aichi, Japan, and agreed to achieve the ambitious targets of protecting at least 17 percent of their land and 10 percent of marine areas by 2020, especially regions rich in biodiversity.

Laws to protect endangered wildlife have now been passed in almost every country. The Convention on Biodiversity prompted Canada to pass the Species at Risk Act in 2002, filling a longstand-ing gap in the federal government's framework of environmen-tal laws. And a growing number of laws and regulations around the world acknowledge the intrinsic value of other species. Since being articulated in the World Charter for Nature, World Conservation Strategy, Earth Charter, and the Convention on Biodiversity, intrinsic value has been incorporated into laws in Costa Rica, Canada, Bangladesh, Japan, Tanzania, New Zealand, and the European Union. As an example, in 1998, Costa Rica, widely recognized as a world leader in protecting nature, enacted its Biodiversity Law, whose first principle is "respect for all forms of life. All living things have the right to live, independently of actual or potential economic value."

In Canada, the Northwest Territories' Wildlife Act 2013 is a recent law whose development was heavily influenced by Indigenous peoples. Section 2 states, "Wildlife is to be conserved for its intrinsic value and for the benefit of present and future generations." Israel's National Biodiversity Plan (2010) states that "it is incumbent upon humankind to respect and protect biodiversity, also (or even mostly) due to its intrinsic and existence value." New Zealand's Resource Management Act requires all decision-makers to pay attention to the intrinsic value of ecosystems.

This idea that other species have intrinsic value regardless of their utility to human beings is a radical departure for modern legal systems. For thousands of years, the prevailing wisdom in Western thought has been that other species are here on Earth to serve us. Just as laws recognizing the sentience of animals represent a breakthrough with respect to the rights of individual animals, recognizing the intrinsic value of biodiversity is a breakthrough for the rights of species. If other species have intrinsic value, then they ought not to be considered property. Intrinsic value also demands recognition of their rights to live, flourish, and

evolve. Humans have a responsibility not to violate these fundamental rights through activities that inflict suffering, could lead to
extinction, or undermine ecosystem health.

Another extraordinary trend involves the inclusion of provisions in national constitutions to safeguard these rights.
Switzerland's constitution states that the federal government
"shall protect endangered species from extinction." The Brazilian
constitution specifically requires the government to prohibit all
practices that cause the extinction of species. New constitutions
in the Sudan, South Sudan, the Maldives, Egypt, Bolivia, and
Ecuador also obligate governments to restrict activities that could
adversely affect endangered species or cause extinction. Given that
constitutions are the highest and most supreme law of a nation,
intended to reflect a society's most deeply cherished values, these
are profound commitments, even if fulfilling these commitments
is sometimes delayed by poverty and war.

Once laws are on the books, they must be implemented and
enforced. When laws are violated, courts and judges are sometimes called upon, as was the case in the snail darter and northern
spotted owl controversies. From Canada to Costa Rica and India,
judges have created a body of law clarifying that now, in the early
years of the twenty-first century, it is fundamentally wrong for
humans to push other species over the edge of the abyss into eter-
nal oblivion.

As indicated by Gregory Logan's prosecution for smuggling
narwhal tusks, Canada's Wild Animal and Plant Protection
and Regulation of International and Interprovincial Trade Act
(WAPPRIITA) is being vigorously implemented. Although

enforcement of many Canadian environmental laws is notoriously lax (public libraries collect more dollars in fines for overdue books than governments collect for violations of pollution laws), policing illegal wildlife trade is a priority. Annually, Canada conducts 3,000 to 5,000 inspections and carries out 300 to 500 investigations. In addition to Gregory Logan's $385,000 fine for exporting narwhal tusks, a company that imports traditional Chinese medicines was fined $100,000 for smuggling endangered orchids into Canada. In recent unrelated incidents, two Canadians have been arrested for smuggling turtles by taping them to their legs beneath baggy trousers. Engineering student Kai Xu had apparently shipped thousands of turtles to China before being nabbed travelling from Michigan to Ontario with fifty-one live baby turtles taped to his legs. He thanked wildlife cops "for stopping the darkness of my greed and ignorance," but despite his remorse was sentenced to five years in an American jail. Dong Yan was arrested while attempting to enter Canada with thirty-eight baby turtles taped to his legs. He was sentenced in Canada, where judges are more lenient. Yan was fined $3,500, placed on probation for two years, and banned from owning turtles for ten years.

Since Canada enacted the Species at Risk Act, successful lawsuits have been brought on behalf of killer whales, humpback whales, greater sage-grouse, Nooksack dace (a small fish that resembles the snail darter), woodland caribou, marbled murrelets, and Nechako white sturgeon. Normally conservative Canadian judges have criticized the federal government for "egregious delays" and "enormous systemic problems." A federal court judge wrote, "To state the obvious, the Species at Risk Act was enacted because some wildlife species in Canada *are at risk*. As the applicants note, many are in a race against the clock as increased pressure is put on their critical habitat, and their ultimate survival may be at stake." Canadian governments and industry still have much work to do to alleviate pressure on endangered species, especially in protecting habitat, but recent laws and court decisions point the way forward.

In Costa Rica, courts have ordered the government to take immediate action to protect endangered species such as sea turtles, scarlet macaws, and sharks. Court orders made it illegal to hunt endangered green turtles or collect their eggs; courts struck down permits for logging in endangered scarlet macaw habitat; and they ordered the government to stop the wasteful practice of shark finning. The Constitutional Court of Costa Rica even ordered the government to expropriate privately owned lands slated for a tourist development because they were located too close to a beach used for nesting by endangered sea turtles. As the Court concluded in a 2008 case, "Human life is only possible in solidarity with nature."

India is perhaps the most fascinating example of the growing recognition of the rights of other species to survive and flourish. The Indian constitution imposes a "fundamental duty" on all citizens to "protect and improve the natural environment including forests, rivers, and wildlife, and to have compassion for all living creatures." It also mandates that governments "protect and improve the environment and safeguard the forests and wildlife of the country." Gandhi, who once said that "the greatness of a nation and its moral progress can be judged by the way its animals are treated," would likely be pleasantly surprised.

The Supreme Court of India is famous for its progressive environmental judgments in cases protecting the iconic Taj Mahal from air pollution, stopping toxic discharges from tanneries into the sacred Ganga River, ordering New Delhi to replace diesel buses with cleaner natural gas vehicles, and safeguarding eco-systems from destructive industrialization. In 1983, the Supreme Court took into consideration the "broad interests of the entire valley" in a decision to halt all mining operations in the Doon Valley. In a similar case, the internationally acclaimed Sariska Tiger Reserve in the Aravalli Hills of Rajasthan was being jeopardized by marble mining. In 1992, the Court ordered the closure of 400 mines to protect the endangered cats. In another case, involving iron ore mining in Kudremukh National Park, the Supreme Court endorsed the World Charter for Nature's statement that "mankind is part of nature and life depends on uninterrupted functioning of natural systems" and warned that by "destroying nature man is committing matricide."

More recently, the Supreme Court of India issued two ground-breaking biodiversity decisions. The decisions about the Asiatic wild buffalo and the Asiatic lion criticized the anthropocentric bias of sustainable development and endorsed an eco-centric approach to human decision-making and action. The opening line of the Court's 2012 judgment telegraphed its perspective: "Asiatic wild buffalo is reported to be the most impressive and magnificent animal in the world." However, these buffalo are endangered in India, and petitioners were in court to compel the government of India to rescue this species from its colli-sion course with extinction. The defendant state of Chhattisgarh argued that it was already taking steps to protect the buffalo, including the designation of a sanctuary and the relocation of villagers who had been living there.

The Supreme Court made the remarkable observation that "laws are man-made, hence there is likelihood of anthropocentric bias towards man. Rights of wild animals often tend to be of secondary importance, but in the universe man and animal are equally placed." The court determined that existing government efforts were inadequate and directed the state to implement, within three months, a comprehensive program to save the Asiatic wild buffalo from extinction. Actions included prevention of interbreeding between wild and domestic buffalo, research and monitoring programs for buffalo in the Udanti Wildlife Sanctuary, training programs for forestry officials, and the development of a comprehensive recovery plan.

In its revolutionary 2013 decision about the fate of the Asiatic lion, India's Supreme Court went even further than in the Asiatic Buffalo decision in articulating the rights of non-human species. The Asiatic subspecies is a bit smaller than the African lion, but a non-biologist would be hard pressed to tell them apart. The main prey species hunted by these lions in India are herbivores including chital, nilgai, sambar deer, four-horned antelope, chinkara, and wild boar. The Asiatic lion's range originally stretched from the coastal forests of North Africa and Greece all the way through the Middle East and across Southwest Asia to Eastern India.

Today the Asiatic lion's population and range have been dramatically reduced. The only wild survivors live in India's Gir Forest, in the state of Gujarat. That there are any lions at all is thanks to the pioneering conservation efforts of the Nawab of Junagadh, Muhammad Rasul Khanji Babi, and his son Muhammad Mahabat Khan III, who created a protected zone and limited hunting over

100 years ago. The ensuing British administration also regulated hunting and safeguarded the lion's last bastion. After independence, India's forest department took over the task of managing the Gir Forest National Park and Wildlife Sanctuary.

The national park is only about 1,400 square kilometres, or roughly twice the size of the city of Calgary, while the sanctuary adds another 1,150 square kilometres. The reserve is surrounded by a buffer zone, where some human activities are restricted. The lions are not fenced in. Their survival requires the co-operation of local farmers and villagers, who must live with lions in their midst. In a documentary called *India's Wandering Lions*, filmmaker Praveen Singh of the Discovery Channel chronicled the incredible tolerance of local people to the big cats, and vice versa. As the lions venture beyond the boundaries of the park and sanctuary, they travel through agricultural fields, grasslands, and villages. Singh said to the *Daily Mail*, "People are proud to have lions in their state and most know that they are not going to injure or attack humans unless provoked. Many farmers said that they didn't mind the lions in their fields or mango orchards as they kept deer and other wild herbivores away from their crops." It's an encouraging story of coexistence between humans and wild predators.

There were roughly 400 Asiatic lions left in the wild in 2010, a number that has grown steadily since the mid-1960s, when the population dipped below 200. The 2015 census counted over 500 lions. (Another 200 or so Asiatic lions live in zoos worldwide.) The single wild population in the Gir Forest is acutely vulnerable to unpredictable events such as a disease outbreak, a drought, or a large forest fire. A major flood in 2015 killed thirteen of the big cats.

The plight of the Asiatic lions reached the Indian court system because the Biodiversity Conservation Trust of India and other organizations filed a lawsuit seeking to have a small group of lions relocated to a second sanctuary, in the state of Madhya Pradesh, where land suitable for lions had been purchased over time. Wildlife biologist Ravi Chellam is an expert on the Gir lions and an outspoken advocate for the relocation project. He also served as an advisor to the Supreme Court on the case. Chellam has survived many close encounters with lions and warns children to be wary when a lion wags its tail or growls. Regarding the lions' future, Chellam told the *Times of India*, "A second home away from Gir is like an insurance policy for the lions' survival." The State of Gujarat, a defendant in the case, argued that the lions have the best chance of surviving in their current location, highlighting the state's success in increasing the size of the protected area and the number of lions. Gujarat also pointed to a failed relocation experiment in 1979, when a group of lions were relocated to Uttar Pradesh but did not survive.

Lawyer Ritwick Dutta worked on the lion relocation case for seven years. Dutta is a powerful speaker and one of the country's leading environmental lawyers, having worked on more than 350 cases. He frequently works for free or is paid in fruits, vegetables, or hand-woven clothes. Dutta made legal arguments based on India's constitution, international commitments, and domestic environmental laws and policies. He highlighted India's National Wildlife Action Plan, which states that every species has the right to live, and every endangered species must be protected to prevent its extinction. The court concluded, in response to Dutta's arguments, "We are committed to safeguard this endangered species because this species has a right to live on this earth, just like human beings." This is an extraordinary statement.

At the heart of the Supreme Court's judgment is a remarkable passage in which the Court critiques the idea of sustainable development as anthropocentric. In contrast, the Court endorses eco-centrism, which "is nature-centered, where humans are part of nature and non-humans have intrinsic value. In other words, human interest does not take automatic precedence and humans have obligations to non-humans independently of human interest." The court addressed the specific question of whether Asiatic lions need a second home from the lions' perspective. What would be in the best interests of the lions? In the words of the Court, given that other species have the right to life, "We, as human beings, have a duty to prevent the species from going extinct and have to advocate for effective species protection regimes."

Pursuant to the Supreme Court's order, a committee has been established to oversee the relocation of a group of lions from the Gir Forest to the Kuno-Palpur sanctuary in Madhya Pradesh. Experts, including Ravi Chellam, recommended moving eight to ten lions, including five to seven females, and their cubs. The Supreme Court also asked the Ministry of Environment and Forests to "take urgent steps" and implement recovery plans for some of India's other endangered species—the great Indian bustard, Bengal florican, Manipur brow-antlered deer, dugong, and wild buffalo. Lawyer Ritwick Dutta says that adopting an eco-centric approach and respecting the rights of other species is "the need of the hour—the only way we can successfully meet our environmental and social challenges."

The Supreme Court of India continues to set extraordinary

precedents related to the rights of nature (and the closely related rights of Indigenous people). In 2013, the Court defended the sacred Niyamgiri Mountain and the rights of the Dongria Kondh peoples from bauxite mining by the company Vedanta. The court ruled that the project could not proceed without the consent of the tribal peoples whose land and culture would be affected. The Dongria Kondh community overwhelmingly rejected the mine. In 2014, following the decisions of the tribal people and the Supreme Court, the Indian Ministry of Environment and Forests revoked Vedanta's permits, effectively ending the project.

Today, most people agree that it is morally wrong for humans to knowingly or negligently cause other species to become endangered or to go extinct. In 2015, in his *Laudato Si*, Pope Francis clearly articulated this global consensus: *"It is not enough, however, to think of different species merely as potential 'resources' to be exploited, while overlooking the fact that they have value in themselves.* Each year sees the disappearance of thousands of plant and animal species, which we will never know, which our children will never see, because they have been lost forever. The great majority become extinct for reasons related to human activity. Because of us, thousands of species will no longer give glory to God by their very existence, nor convey their message to us. *We have no such right"* (emphasis added).

That a major religious leader would decry the human-caused extinction crisis and frame this as a moral issue is significant. The basic rights of all species include the rights to exist, reproduce, and evolve, all of which require protection of substantial habitat and natural ecological systems and processes.

The types of laws and lawsuits described here have achieved some remarkable, even improbable, successes. New Zealand's black robin was down to a single pair in 1980. Today, there are more than 250 black robins. In Canada, creatures that have recovered and no longer need the protection of the Species at Risk Act include the white pelican, Baird's sparrow, and Caspian tern. Dozens more have been downlisted to less dire categories to reflect their improving circumstances, including sea otters, wood bison, and the Rocky Mountain tailed frog. Globally, many whale populations, including humpback, gray, and fin whales, have enjoyed tremendous recoveries since international law placed strict limits on commercial whaling.

The first national park in the world, setting aside land for nature, was Bogd Khan Uul in Mongolia, established in 1778. A century later, Yellowstone National Park in the U.S. and Banff National Park in Canada were created a little over a decade apart. Over the course of the past century and a half, nations around the world have designated over 25 million square kilometres of land as parks and wildlife sanctuaries, an area the size of North America. Many of these protected areas prohibit certain types of harmful activities, from hunting and fishing to logging, mining, and oil and gas extraction. While this represents significant progress, it's still only 15 percent of the Earth's land surface, and in some countries, the protections written on paper are not implemented in practice. Even in parks, human desires for recreation and commercial development are sometimes placed ahead of the needs of wildlife. It seems blindingly unfair that one species can allocate 85 percent of the planet's land to itself, while leaving only 15 percent to the millions of other species.

A growing number of ecologists, including pre-eminent Harvard biologist E.O. Wilson, have reached the conclusion that "nature needs half," meaning that to pre-empt the looming cataclysm of biodiversity loss, humans will have to relinquish their claim of priority to at least 50 percent of every ecosystem in the world. Some countries are already surprisingly close to this ambitious goal, including Bhutan, Seychelles, Slovenia, and Turks and Caicos. Others, such as Austria, Belize, Benin, Brazil, Costa Rica, Croatia, France, Germany, Morocco, Namibia, New Zealand, Norway, Slovak Republic, Spain, Tanzania, and Zambia are all over 25 percent.

Considering that the U.S. and Canada are hovering between 10 and 15 percent of their land in protected areas, and that these gains have often come after protracted and divisive debates, it may be difficult to envision the calls of conservation biologists being heeded in the short term. Yet both countries have made international commitments to boost the percentage of land protected to 17 percent by 2020.

The idea that nature has intrinsic value, regardless of its utility for humans, is spreading rapidly across the globe and is reflected in international treaties and laws in more than 100 countries. By emphasizing that causing extinction is morally wrong, recognition of biodiversity's intrinsic value could serve as a precursor to the expanding recognition of nature's rights. While most of the world's legal systems continue to treat nature, from individual animals to entire ecosystems, as property, cracks in the law's outdated approach are appearing. The rights of nature have gained revolutionary legal protection in Ecuador, Bolivia, Colombia, and India during the past decade.

The
RIGHTS *of* NATURE

From Trees to Rivers and Ecosystems

"The extension of legal rights to nature represents the
logical evolution of rights."

Professor Roderick Nash,
University of California (Santa Barbara)

WALT DISNEY, THE SIERRA CLUB, AND THE MINERAL KING VALLEY

In the late 1960s, Walt Disney proposed building a massive ski resort in a wild part of the Sierra Nevada Mountains in California. The development was to be located in the Mineral King Valley, at the headwaters of the Kaweah River, an area much loved by hikers and backpackers. The resort was to include a new highway, power lines, hotels, restaurants, swimming pools, parking lots, and downhill skiing infrastructure that would sprawl across eighty acres. It would have attracted over five million visitors annually, transforming the valley from remote wilderness into a heavily used outpost of modern civilization. The U.S. Forest Service approved the project in 1969.

The Sierra Club responded by filing a lawsuit that came oh so close to revolutionizing the American legal system. Their lawyers argued that the project should be halted, and its permits cancelled, but the government challenged the Sierra Club's standing to bring the lawsuit. Historically, standing to commence a lawsuit required an aspiring litigant to demonstrate some direct personal, property, or economic injury. Initially, at trial, the Sierra Club was granted standing on the basis of their long history of advocating for the protection of wild landscapes. Then the Court granted the Sierra Club's application for an injunction to block construction of the ski resort. On appeal, however, the lower court's decision was overturned. The Sierra Club was denied standing because there was no evidence before the Court that its members would be directly harmed by the proposed development. The injunction preventing construction of the ski resort was dissolved, giving Walt Disney the green light to proceed. In 1971, the Sierra Club appealed to the U.S. Supreme Court.

At roughly the same time, a young law professor at the University of Southern California, Christopher Stone, was teaching a property law course when he stumbled across the notion that perhaps nature itself should have legal rights. The idea apparently electrified his law students. Stone immediately began developing legal arguments about the rights of nature for publication in an academic journal. In his article, Stone argued that technically there is no legal barrier to granting rights to nature, given that other non-human entities such as ships and corporations have legal rights conferred upon them. Stone wrote that society should "give legal rights to forests, oceans, rivers, and other so-called 'natural objects' in the environment—indeed, to the natural environment as a whole." Anticipating the criticism that natural entities have no voice, Stone wrote, "It is no answer to say that streams and forests cannot have standing because streams and forests cannot speak. Corporations cannot speak, either; nor can states, estates, infants, incompetents, municipalities, or universities. Lawyers speak for them, as they commonly do for the ordinary citizen with legal problems."

Professor Stone was aware that the Sierra Club's lawsuit against the Mineral King ski resort was headed to the U.S. Supreme Court, but lawyers had already made their arguments in the case. It appeared as though his article "Should Trees Have Standing?" would be published too late to have any influence on the outcome. Then Lady Luck intervened.

One of the nine judges of the U.S. Supreme Court, Justice William O. Douglas, was a passionate outdoorsman. As a child he had suffered from a rare form of paralysis, and it was through hiking in the Cascade Mountains of his native Washington state that he rehabilitated and strengthened his legs. In 1950, Douglas wrote a critically acclaimed book called *Of Men and Mountains*, in which he argued passionately that man was part of, not separate from, nature. In his words, "When one stands on Darling Mountain, he is not remote and apart from the wilderness; he is an intimate part of it." Then, in 1965, Douglas wrote *A Wilderness Bill of Rights*, in which he called for a "Bill of Rights to protect those whose spiritual values extend to the rivers and lakes, the valleys and the ridges, and who find life in a mechanized society worth living only because those splendid resources are not despoiled." Fortuitously, Justice Douglas had agreed to edit a special edition of the Southern California Law Review. Professor Stone worked feverishly to finish his article on the rights of nature and then sent it, as part of a package of articles, to the judge.

In his judgment in the Sierra Club's lawsuit against the proposed Mineral King ski resort, Justice Douglas argued that there should be a rule "that allowed environmental issues to be litigated before federal agencies or federal courts in the name of the inanimate object about to be despoiled, defaced, or invaded by roads and bulldozers and where injury is the subject of public outrage. Contemporary public concern for protecting nature's ecological equilibrium should lead to the conferral of standing upon environmental objects to sue for their own preservation. . . . This suit would therefore be more properly labeled as *Mineral King v. Morton*" (instead of *Sierra Club v. Morton*).

Douglas went on to observe that inanimate parties such as ships and corporations are considered capable of launching litigation, and "so it should be as respects valleys, alpine meadows, rivers, lakes, estuaries, beaches, ridges, groves of trees, swampland, or even air that feels the destructive pressures of modern technology and modern life." It was essential, Douglas concluded, that rules of standing be amended to extend to "all of the forms of life . . . the pileated woodpecker as well as the coyote and bear, the lemmings as well as the trout in the streams." Justice Douglas concluded his judgment by quoting Aldo Leopold: "The land ethic simply enlarges the boundaries of the community to include soils, waters, plants, and animals, or collectively, the land."

Justice Douglas attempted to persuade his colleagues on the Supreme Court to join him in embracing the idea that the Mineral King Valley and other elements of nature ought to have certain legal rights, including standing. This would have enabled American lawyers to bring lawsuits on behalf of trees, rivers, valleys, or endangered species, acting as guardians of their best interests in the same way that lawyers sometimes represent children or severely disabled people. Douglas failed to sway a majority of the nine judges, although his colleague Justice Harry Blackmun called Douglas's opinion "eloquent" and insisted that he read it aloud in the courtroom. Justices Blackmun and Brennan did concur with Douglas that it made sense to grant standing to organizations that could speak knowledgably on behalf of the environment.

The majority of the court ruled that there was no evidence on the record to prove that either the Sierra Club or its members would be directly affected by the ski resort. Therefore, the Sierra Club lacked standing. The court left the door open to the Sierra Club to put forward evidence in the future that its members used the area and thus would be directly affected by the proposed development. If Justice Douglas had been able to bring his colleagues on board, their judgment would have sent shock waves through the foundations of the American legal system and changed the world in a profound way. Instead, the case became a brief public sensation, a lasting source of largely academic and philosophical interest, and an inspiration for future efforts to gain recognition of the rights of nature.

At the time, of course, not everyone was impressed. Some members of the legal profession thought that Justice Douglas's proposal for recognizing nature's rights was nonsense. Lawyer John Naff wrote the following poem, which was published in the *American Bar Association Journal* in 1973:

> If Justice Douglas has his way—
> O come not that dreadful day—
> We'll be sued by lakes and hills
> Seeking a redress of ills
> Great mountain peaks of name prestigious
> Will suddenly become litigious
> Our brooks will babble in the courts,
> Seeking damages for torts
> How can I rest beneath a tree
> If it may soon be suing me?

Or enjoy the playful porpoise
While it's seeking habeas corpus?
Every beast within his paws
Will clutch an order to show cause
The courts besieged on every hand,
Will crowd with suits by chunks of land.
Ah! But vengeance will be sweet
Since this must be a two-way street.
I'll promptly sue my neighbor's tree
For shedding all its leaves on me.

A decade later, in 1983, a Michigan appeals court poked fun at the idea of nature's rights. The owner of a tree damaged in a car crash sued the driver, seeking damages for negligence. In affirming the lower court's dismissal of the lawsuit, the judges issued a poem in lieu of writing a normal judgment:

We thought that we would never see
A suit to compensate a tree.
A suit whose claim in tort is prest
Upon a mangled tree's behest;
A tree whose battered trunk was prest
Against a Chevy's crumpled crest,
A tree that faces each new day
With bark and limb in disarray;
A tree that may forever bear
A lasting need for tender care.
Flora lovers though we three
We must uphold the court's decree.

Despite losing their case at the Supreme Court, eventually the Sierra Club prevailed in the court of public opinion. Walt Disney's ski resort was never built. The Mineral King Valley remains wild today, bristling with lakes and waterfalls, providing habitat for black bears, mule deer, and yellow-bellied marmots beneath striking Sawtooth Peak. Cell phones still don't work there, because the valley is so remote and so steep. Mineral King Valley was added to Sequoia National Park in 1978 by the U.S. Congress, protecting it from ill-conceived development forever.

Professor Stone's visionary article continues to be widely discussed in law schools nearly fifty years later. Lawsuits have been filed on behalf of various elements of nature, including a beach, rare species of birds, dolphins, salmon, a marsh, a national monument, a river, and, as Stone anticipated, a tree. The U.S. Federal Court allowed a lawsuit filed in the name of the Byram River (along the border between New York and Connecticut) to proceed against the Village of Chester, based on alleged pollution damage caused by the village. A recent case in the Philippines saw lawyers for a group of whales and dolphins challenge offshore exploration for oil and gas that could harm their habitat. In deciding the case in 2015, the Supreme Court of the Philippines discussed the Mineral King precedent. However, the Court determined that it was unnecessary to give marine mammals legal standing because Filipino rules allow any citizen, as a steward of nature, to bring a lawsuit to enforce that country's environmental laws. In general, courts still prefer to grant standing to humans rather than nature, but that may be on the brink of changing.

Chapter 7
WATERSHED MOMENTS: ASSERTING THE RIGHTS
OF AMERICAN ECOSYSTEMS

"I detest the word 'resource.' How could a wild river, part of nature's
bloodstream, ever come to be regarded primarily as a damned
resource? As if it were no more than a vein of coal, a field of cabbages,
a truckload of cow manure?"

> EDWARD ABBEY, American nature writer,
>
> in *Down the River*

In the U.S., the seeds of the idea that nature should have rights
were planted long ago by two giants of the American environmental movement. In 1867, near the end of a thousand-mile walk from
Kentucky to Florida, John Muir, who later founded the Sierra
Club, reflected on society's loathing of alligators. Muir believed
that gators were "honorable representatives of the great saurians
of an older creation" and wrote, "how narrow we selfish, conceited
creatures are in our sympathies! How blind to the rights of all the
rest of creation!"

Another towering figure in the history of environmentalism is
Aldo Leopold, who was trained as a forester and became one of
the leading wildlife experts in the U.S. He wrote a book called *A*
Sand County Almanac, a series of reflections on humanity's troubled relationship with nature. Published posthumously in 1949,

the book has sold over two million copies. In that book, Leopold's essay "The Land Ethic" laid the intellectual groundwork for later discussions of the rights of nature. He articulated the negative consequences of the concept of property by referring to the Greek myth of Odysseus. After returning from Troy, Odysseus hanged a dozen slave-girls whom he suspected had misbehaved during his absence. There was no ethical issue, no question of right or wrong, because the slave-girls were his property. Leopold wrote, "There is as-yet no ethic dealing with man's relationship to the land and to the animals and plants which grow upon it. Land, like Odysseus's slave-girls, is still property." He described the extension of ethics to land as an ecological necessity, noting that leading thinkers since the days of Isaiah and Ezekiel understood that destroying land was not only inexpedient but morally wrong. In Leopold's words, "We abuse land because we see it as a commodity belonging to us. When we see land as a community to which we belong, we may begin to use it with love and respect."

Muir and Leopold would likely be surprised and pleased to witness the extent to which their radical ideas about the rights of nature have gained traction in the United States in recent years. Nature's rights have evolved from philosophical musings into the decision of the Supreme Court in the Mineral King case, and more recently into revolutionary laws passed by communities right across the country, from California to New York.

For years, Thomas Linzey was regarded as a successful environmental lawyer. He founded the Community Environmental Legal Defense Fund (CELDF) in Pennsylvania to assist communities in their legal battles against industrial pollution and resource exploitation. A powerful, funny, and engaging orator, Linzey won many cases for his clients, but eventually concluded that they were pyrrhic victories. His corporate opponents in mining, oil and gas, factory farming, and other industries had the resources to keep reapplying for permits that courts had initially quashed or revoked. Linzey's clients, in contrast, ran out of the money and energy needed to continue fighting these David and Goliath battles. For a time, Linzey considered closing CELDF. Instead, he chose to reboot the organization with a radical new approach centred on rights. CELDF began to focus on the rights of individuals to live in a healthy environment, the rights of communities to make their own decisions about the kinds of economic activities they support, and the rights of nature. Although he looks like a conventional lawyer, Linzey champions the subversive belief that it's necessary to challenge the entrenched constitutional rights of corporations, which he saw routinely used to trample the rights of people, communities, and ecosystems.

Linzey's right-hand woman at CELDF, Mari Margil, isn't an attorney but possesses an impressive knowledge about law, the environment, history, and democracy. Linzey and Margil make quite an extraordinary claim: environmental laws and regulations don't actually protect the environment. Both of them can sound like talk radio hosts or fiery preachers, describing, in talks laced with profanity, the corporate takeover of America and the associated eco-crisis. According to Linzey and Margil, environmental laws merely slow the rate of environmental damage by requiring corporations to take modest precautions when mining or fracking or polluting, even though these activities are inherently harmful. The environmental agencies of governments approve and legitimize these activities. Environmental laws are constructed this way,

Linzey and Margil argue, because they are based on the bedrock belief that nature is property, an idea at the heart of Western legal systems. In other words, environmental laws treat the environment as a natural resource, a bundle of commodities to be used in our economy, rather than as an ecosystem with intrinsic value and rights.

In response to these systemic problems, Linzey, Margil, and CELDF work with communities to pass local ordinances (known in Canada as municipal bylaws) that prohibit unwanted industrial practices, including factory farms, fracking for oil and gas, large-scale water withdrawals, hazardous waste dumping, and open-pit mining. The first community rights ordinance was enacted in 2000 in Belfast, Pennsylvania—a conservative rural area that votes Republican—to ban factory farming. The ordinance was challenged in court and upheld in 2005. Since that time, other Pennsylvania communities have enacted citizens' rights ordinances that ban mining, spreading sewage sludge on agricultural land, and oil and gas activities that pose a threat to water. There are now hundreds of American communities that have passed ordinances prohibiting specific types of unwanted industrial activities. Some of these local laws spell out the rights of citizens, communities, and nature, while revoking some of the constitutional rights corporations enjoy. With the election of President Trump, local opposition to environmental destruction will gain even greater importance.

The first community ordinance to recognize the rights of nature was passed in 2006 by Tamaqua Borough in Schuylkill County, Pennsylvania. People in that town of 7,000 were deeply concerned about a proposal to dump sewage sludge into old mining pits, fearing that the toxic substances in the sludge could contaminate their drinking water. CELDF assisted the town in drafting the Tamaqua Borough Sewage Sludge Ordinance, "an Ordinance to protect the health, safety, and general welfare of the citizens and environment of Tamaqua Borough by banning corporations from engaging in the land application of sewage sludge; . . . by removing constitutional powers from corporations within the Borough; [and] by recognizing and enforcing the rights of residents to defend natural communities and ecosystems.

The groundbreaking ordinance acknowledges the legal rights of natural communities and ecosystems. It also denies corporations status as persons under the law, and allows the borough or any of its citizens to file a lawsuit on behalf of nature for any harm done by the land application of sewage sludge. The borough is obligated to use any money recovered from environmental violations to restore ecosystems.

The town's solicitor warned that the ordinance was a bad idea and could trigger lawsuits by industry. When half of the council voted against the proposed ordinance, Mayor Chris Morrison stepped in and cast the deciding vote. In *We the People: Stories from the Community Rights Movement in the United States*, Morrison said, "Tamaqua is where I am going to stay and create my future. Our biggest issue is taking care of the environment and I have brought it to the forefront in my tenure as mayor. We shouldn't have to wait until a farmer's sheep or a child die for people to get involved. We need to educate now . . . If I am going to be sued, so be it." As Elizabeth Eaves accurately observed in *Forbes*, "The law flies in the face of thousands of years of Western legal precedent that treats nature strictly as property."

These rights of nature ordinances are now found in communities across the U.S., including Pittsburgh, Pennsylvania; Santa Monica, California; Mora County, New Mexico; Athens, Ohio; Mountain Lake Park, Maryland; and Broadview Heights, Ohio. When national and state environmental laws failed to protect local people and the places they loved, these communities exercised their own law-making powers. Santa Monica's ordinance states, "Natural communities and ecosystems possess fundamental and inalienable rights to exist and flourish in the City of Santa Monica. To effectuate those rights on behalf of the environment, residents of the City may bring actions to protect these natural communities and ecosystems." In 2010, Pittsburgh became the first large city to ban fracking, a practice that injects high-pressure water and chemicals underground to release oil and gas from subterranean shale deposits. Fracking can contaminate drinking water and trigger earthquakes.

Let's take a closer look at how three distinct American communities have employed the rights of nature in their efforts to secure a healthier future for both people and ecosystems.

Grant Versus Goliath

In Grant Township, a small rural community of about 700 people located 130 kilometres west of Pittsburgh, a community bill of rights ordinance was triggered by concerns about the consequences of fracking and, in particular, the disposal of the toxic wastewater produced by that activity. Pennsylvania is in the midst of a fracking gold rush, with the enthusiastic approval of federal and state governments. Over one billion gallons of fracking wastewater is produced annually in the state. This wastewater can contain cancer-causing chemicals, including benzene, toluene, and xylene.

Pennsylvania responded to communities such as Grant Township by ignoring their concerns and listening instead to the lobbying of the oil, gas, and coal industries. The state passed laws that handcuffed the ability of local governments to protect their lands, water, and people. For example, a law passed in 2012—purportedly to update the state's regime for managing the oil and gas industry—included provisions removing the authority of local governments to use mechanisms such as zoning to regulate where fracking would be permitted. Parts of this law were later struck down. It was found that they violated a provision in Pennsylvania's state constitution that protects the human right to live in a healthy environment.

The people of Grant Township rely on private wells for their drinking water, and they fear contamination of that drinking water if deep injection wells for the disposal of toxic fracking wastewater are allowed in the area. (Earthquakes are also a concern, as the U.S. Geological Survey has published studies linking this type of injection well to thousands of small quakes.) In 2014, a company called Pennsylvania General Energy (PGE) applied for and received federal and state permits to convert an existing oil and gas well in Grant Township into a wastewater injection well.

The mother-daughter team of Judy Wanchisn and Stacy Long, residents in the township, appealed the permits issued by the federal Environmental Protection Agency and the Pennsylvania Department of Environmental Protection. At the same time, lacking confidence in these appeal processes, the women also spearheaded the push for a community bill of rights, to establish the rights of both human and natural communities to live in a healthy environment. It helped that Stacy Long was a local elected official. In June 2014, the township enacted a community bill of rights, guaranteeing the people of Grant Township clean air, clean water, and a sustainable energy future. The ordinance recognizes the rights of natural communities and ecosystems—including, but not limited to, rivers, streams, and aquifers—to exist, flourish, and naturally evolve. The Grant Township community is everything: the people and the soils, waters, plants, and animals, or, as Aldo Leopold simply called it, "the land."

The law specifically bans wastewater injection wells and any other means of depositing waste from oil and gas extraction within the township, noting that this prohibition is needed to safeguard the rights of residents and nature. As well, the law removes certain rights from oil and gas corporations operating within the municipality. "We're tired of being told by corporations and our so-called environmental regulatory agencies that we can't stop this injection well," said Stacy Long in a CELDF press release. "This isn't a game. We're being threatened by a corporation with a history of permit violations, and that corporation wants to dump toxic frack wastewater into our township." Long continued, "I live here, and I was also elected to protect the health and safety of this township. I will do whatever it takes to provide our residents with the tools and protections they need to nonviolently resist aggressions like those being proposed by PGE."

In a CELDF blog, Judy Wanchisn said, "Pure water is guaranteed to us by the Pennsylvania Constitution under Article I, Section 27. That right is unalienable, and our governments have no authority to negotiate our rights away. With the passing of this Ordinance, we are securing and protecting our community's rights. Water is our most precious resource, and if we don't take action to protect it for our community and for future generations, who will?"

Confronted by this local opposition, PGE sued Grant Township, seeking to overturn the community's ordinance by asserting the constitutional rights of corporations to undertake activities including underground injection of fracking wastewater. According to PGE, communities do not have the right or the legal authority to say no. PGE asserted that the community bill of rights violated its corporate rights under the U.S. Constitution, and that the ordinance was pre-empted by state law that explicitly authorized wastewater injection wells.

The Grant Township supervisors, as the local councillors are known, retained CELDF to defend their community bill of rights. Thomas Linzey asserted that "this lawsuit, brought by the gas industry to overturn a democratically enacted law threatens the rights of both human and natural communities." CELDF argued that community self-government is at the heart of American society, and dates back to the Mayflower Compact of 1620, the American Revolution, and the Declaration of Independence.

Then things got really interesting. There is a provision in Grant Township's community bill of rights that states "any action brought by either a resident of Grant Township or by the Township to enforce or defend the rights of ecosystems or natural communities secured by this Ordinance shall bring that action in the name of the ecosystem or natural community in a court possessing jurisdiction over activities occurring in the Township. Damages shall be measured by the cost of restoring the ecosystem or natural community to its state before the injury, and shall be paid to the Township to be used exclusively for the full and complete restoration of the ecosystem or natural community."

An application to intervene in the lawsuit was filed on behalf of the Little Mahoning Watershed, igniting a firestorm of controversy. A newspaper headline read "Pennsylvania Ecosystem Fights Corporation for Rights in Landmark Fracking Lawsuit." Through its lawyers, the watershed asserted that PGE's plan to inject wastewater underground threatened to violate its ecological integrity and its legal rights. CELDF lawyer Lindsey Schromen-Wawrin wrote in a brief, "The Little Mahoning Watershed's interests would necessarily be impaired if it is not allowed to intervene, because its rights could not be defended." This was one of the first cases in the world where an ecosystem filed a motion to intervene in a lawsuit to defend its own rights. You can see Professor Stone's fingerprints on the watershed's legal arguments.

While environmental lawyers praised the approach as groundbreaking, critics worked themselves into a lather, describing the idea of nature's rights as absurd, demented, or even dangerous. Oil and gas lawyer Bruce Kramer told *Energywire*, "People who propose this and say that these are valid ordinances are coming close to engaging in legal malpractice. It's crazy." Jim Willis, editor of a pro-fracking website, Marcellus Drilling News, wrote, "The latest nonsense to come from the extreme left is that artificial constructs like watersheds now have rights. . . . This would all be rolling-on-the-floor funny if extremists weren't so hellbent on bastardizing our laws and the U.S. Constitution." A post on the *Natural Gas Now* blog accused CELDF of being "a Marxist group of con artists and revolutionaries seeking to use democracy to destroy democracy."

In a court document responding to the Little Mahoning's application, PGE's lawyers argued that "the Watershed offers no legal support for its absurd attempt to intervene as a party to this lawsuit." In unusually derogatory language, they called the watershed's motion to intervene a "circus act," adding that "a watershed lacks consciousness, intelligence, cognition, communicability, or agency. The Watershed cannot decide to intervene, cannot accept representation or engage with counsel as a client, and cannot appear in court or testify." PGE added that if an animal is not considered a person with standing to sue under federal law, then neither is a "natural condition" such as a watershed.

PGE's lawyers failed to recognize that many of the same arguments they used to attack the watershed's standing are equally applicable to their own client. A corporation is a legal fiction, lacking consciousness, intelligence, and cognition. It is incapable of doing the things the corporate lawyers suggest an ecosystem ought to be able to do, such as testify in court. It is remarkable that PGE's lawyers could describe watersheds as "artificial constructs" while simultaneously believing that corporations are real persons to whom rights naturally belong.

In an unexpected twist in 2015, Pennsylvania's Department of Environmental Protection revoked PGE's permit for the proposed wastewater injection well before the Court could address the watershed's application to intervene in the lawsuit. DEP spokesperson John Poister told the *Indiana Gazette* that "we are supposed to protect the waters of the commonwealth" and explained that the state had determined that "we should review our procedures for granting permits for injection wells." Undeterred by the loss of its permit, PGE went full steam ahead with its lawsuit against Grant

Township. In October 2015, a federal judge in the Western District of Pennsylvania overturned six sections of the Grant Township community bill of rights. Judge Susan Baxter noted that the U.S. Supreme Court has clearly and repeatedly ruled that corporations are legal persons and as such enjoy constitutional rights. Only the Supreme Court can overrule itself, Judge Baxter decided. She agreed with PGE that Grant Township lacked the legal authority to enact key elements in its community bill of rights.

The people of Grant Township responded by voting to become what is known in the U.S. as a "home rule" municipality. Home rule means that a community has greater powers of local control, subject to complying with the federal and state constitutions. This transformation in municipal government structure enabled the township to adopt a new municipal charter similar to its original community bill of rights, again banning wastewater injection wells, recognizing the rights of nature, and removing corporate rights. In other words, Grant Township took Judge Baxter's ruling and figured out a way to circumvent it to reinstate its fracking wastewater ban.

Not surprisingly, oil and gas lawyers remain skeptical about the township's chances of success. Kevin Moody, general counsel with Pennsylvania Independent Oil and Gas Association, which intervened in the lawsuit on the side of PGE, said, "Contrary to what a lot of people believe, just because a municipality declares itself home rule, that doesn't mean it's its own little country. It still can't violate the U.S. Constitution or the Pennsylvania Constitution."

A similar story is playing out in Pennsylvania's Highland Township, where concerns about a wastewater well led to a community rights ordinance that recognized the rights of nature. In response to a lawsuit filed by Seneca Resources Corporation, the local board of supervisors repealed the ordinance. Upset citizens then adopted a home rule charter through a ballot initiative, reasserting the rights of people, communities, and ecosystems over corporations. Seneca sued again. An application by the Crystal Spring Ecosystem to intervene in the lawsuit is currently before the courts.

Cases about the right of American communities to regulate fracking have been decided in other states, with mixed results. Home rule communities in New York, such as Dryden and Middlefield, passed zoning ordinances banning fracking to protect their small-town character, citizens' health, and the environment. A 2014 decision from the New York Court of Appeals upheld the right of these communities to regulate fracking. The state of New York subsequently imposed a statewide ban on fracking. On the other hand, the Colorado Supreme Court struck down anti-fracking rules in Longmont, Fort Collins, and other communities. Writing for a unanimous court, Justice Richard Gabriel wrote, "In matters of statewide or mixed concern . . . state laws supersede any conflicting government regulations." The Ohio Supreme Court also struck down five ordinances that attempted to ban fracking.

In 2016, Grant Township passed a related law that protects its residents from arrest if they engage in civil disobedience to protest PGE's wastewater injection well. Township supervisor Stacy Long said, "It's going to have to be bodies in the road to stop those trucks if the courts fail us." PGE reapplied for its state permit and is challenging Grant Township's charter in court. The corporation is seeking judicial sanctions against the township and CELDF, accusing them of frivolous and unreasonable actions and arguments. PGE is seeking more than one million dollars in damages, no small amount for a township with an annual budget roughly one quarter that amount. While the people of Grant Township have deployed the rights of nature to win a few battles, the jury is still out regarding who will win the war.

Corporate Water Extraction

In New Hampshire, four communities—Barnstead, Barrington, Nottingham, and Atkinson—have enacted community bills of rights, including the rights of nature, in efforts to protect their water. These are quintessential American small towns, with main streets featuring post offices, churches, fire stations, country stores, and community notice boards (advertising everything from upcoming concerts to guns for sale). The land is predominantly rural. In summertime, you can watch kids jumping off Barnstead's town bridge into the Merrimack River. These communities have an idyllic, 1950s atmosphere, with whitewashed Victorian homes surrounded by forests, lakes, and farmland.

Situated in the middle of the state, Nottingham and Barnstead are about thirty kilometres apart, with roughly 4,000 residents each. Both communities felt threatened by corporate proposals to extract massive volumes of water from underground aquifers for bottling and export. Residents depend primarily on well water in both towns.

Passing a community bill of rights that recognizes the rights of nature and challenges the status quo is no easy feat in small, largely rural communities that tend to be conservative. Local business owners wondered if the denial of corporate rights to multinational corporations would spill over and adversely affect their rights. Hunters worried that recognizing the rights of nature might mean they could no longer shoot a deer for fear of being sued in the name of the deer's family members. Loggers expressed concern that the ordinance might make it illegal to cut down trees. Some wags even speculated that the rights of nature might enable hippies and tree huggers to wander around naked in public with impunity.

But in Barnstead, when the fire department votes with you, you win. In March 2006, at the end of a very long discussion, the fire department accepted the logic behind a rights-based ordinance to protect water. The town voted 135 to 1 in favour of the proposed community bill of rights. Jack O'Neill, a grizzled Vietnam vet, said in *We the People*, "We the people of Barnstead threw aside our fears for the generations to come, knowing we were in a battle with the corporations and their legal teams. To the nation, this might be a small battle, but something has to be done, and we the people of the town of Barnstead will walk point." The lone dissenter clung to the supremacy of property rights—the notion that property owners should be able to do whatever they want on their own property.

Neighbouring Nottingham faced a proposal by USA Springs to take over one million litres per day from the local aquifer for bottled water destined to be shipped overseas. Peppered with lakes and ponds, Nottingham is drained by the Pawtuckaway and North Rivers. In 2003, New Hampshire's Department of Environmental Services outlined twenty-seven reasons why they were rejecting USA Springs's application for a water-taking permit. At that time, a test revealed that water levels in neighbourhood wells dropped twelve metres in just ten days, even while less water was being pumped than the company proposed. USA Springs appealed and the state granted a ten-year water extraction permit in 2004.

The citizens of Nottingham were not impressed. Several groups, including Save Our Groundwater and Neighborhood Guardians, filed a lawsuit. Their lawyers argued that because groundwater is held in the public trust, the water extraction permit was invalid because it privatized so much of the community's water supplies. In 2008, New Hampshire's Supreme Court denied that the two community groups had standing in the case and unanimously upheld the permit.

Running out of options, the town passed the Nottingham Water Rights and Local Self-Government Ordinance, similar to Barnstead's law. Section 2 outlines the purpose: "We the People of the Town of Nottingham declare that water is essential for life, liberty, and the pursuit of happiness—both for people and for the ecological systems, which give life to all species. We the People of the Town of Nottingham declare that we have the duty to safe-guard the water both on and beneath the Earth's surface, and in the process, safeguard the rights of people within the community of Nottingham, and the rights of the ecosystems of which Nottingham is a part."

The ordinance prohibits corporate water withdrawals. It also recognizes that natural communities and ecosystems—including wetlands, streams, rivers, and aquifers—have the right to exist and flourish.

The ongoing public opposition made a difference. USA Springs was unable to secure financing to complete its bottling plant and declared bankruptcy. In 2011, a Swiss firm called Malom Group AG attempted to rescue the project. Malom is an acronym for "make a lot of money," and its executives turned out to be con artists who bilked investors out of millions. Four were sentenced to jail terms in the U.S., including one man who is in Canada waiting to be extradited. Two others remain fugitives.

The 189-acre property where water was to be extracted and bottled, which USA Springs claimed was worth 125 million dollars, has been listed for sale for years at an asking price of $1.95 million. As for selling the company, USA Springs president Francesco Rotondo told the *New Hampshire Business Review* in 2013, "Nobody wants it. It's a f------ mess." The ten-year permit from New Hampshire's Department of Environmental Services expired in 2014 and has not been renewed. Jim Hadley, chairman of Neighborhood Guardians, called this a "historic victory" for water and the threatened communities.

Oil and Gas Drilling in New Mexico

New Mexico's Mora County is over a million arid acres of prairies and foothills located to the east of the Sangre de Cristo Mountains. The county is so sparsely populated that it doesn't have a single set of traffic lights. It does, however, face unwanted environmental threats from the oil and gas industry. Like Grant Township, Mora County enlisted the help of CELDF to draft a community water rights and self-government ordinance in 2013. This law recognized the rights of nature and was the first local ordinance in the United States to ban all oil and gas drilling. John Olivas, chair of the Mora County board of commissioners, said in a letter to the *Decorah Journal*, "We decided not only to recognize that Mora residents possess certain civil and environmental rights—to local self-government where they live, to a sustainable energy future, to clean air and water, and to water for agriculture—but that those rights cannot be overriden by corporate 'rights' or nullified by state legislatures." The Mora County ban clashes with both state and federal laws, which regulate but do not prohibit drilling for oil and gas.

The oil and gas industry responded with several lawsuits, arguing that Mora County was violating the constitutional rights of corporations to drill for fossil fuels. The first lawsuit was filed by the Independent Petroleum Association of New Mexico. In the second, a subsidiary of Shell, the sixth-largest oil company in the world, asserted that they have a constitutional right to drill. A decision in the Shell case was handed down in 2015, as district court judge James O. Browning ruled that the Mora County ordinance contradicted federal law. According to Judge Browning, "Historically, a county cannot enact or supersede federal law. The ordinance goes beyond Mora County's historical lawmaking just to deprive a corporation of their rights." Under the U.S. Constitution's Supremacy Clause, any local or state law that conflicts with federal law is invalid. Judge Browning made it clear during oral argument that corporate rights take precedence over community laws and have done so in the U.S. for over 100 years. He struck down the entire ordinance—including citizens' rights, community rights, and nature's rights—on the basis that it violated the corporation's right to extract oil and gas from its leases.

Mora County rescinded the ordinance in 2015. However, neighbouring San Miguel County and Santa Fe County enacted fracking bans. The Independent Petroleum Association of New Mexico warned that CELDF's advocacy for nature's rights is "the beginning of a social movement that is greater than just the oil and gas industry, it is a potential game changer for all of corporate America." Thomas Linzey agrees. In a 2016 film called *We the People 2.0*, he calls for a second American revolution that dismantles the corporate state and replaces it with local self-government.

Since 2006, over three dozen communities in ten U.S. states— including California, Ohio, New York, Maryland, and Maine— have followed in Tamaqua Borough's footsteps, passing local laws that recognize nature's rights. In 2014, 70 percent of voters in Mendocino County, California, approved a community bill of rights that recognized the rights of local ecosystems and banned fracking. Dozens more are in progress, from Spokane and Tacoma in Washington to Greenfield, Massachusetts. In 2017, Lafayette, Colorado passed the first municipal ordinance declaring that both people and nature have the right to live in a healthy climate, and banning oil and gas extraction because that activity would violate these rights. Two Vermont municipalities have adopted resolutions urging the state legislature to amend the Vermont constitution to include the rights of nature. The Vermont amendment would state "that the natural environment of Vermont, including its forests, natural areas, surface and ground waters, and fish and wildlife populations, has certain natural, inherent, and unalienable rights to clean water and air." Campaigns to amend state constitutions are also underway in Colorado, Ohio, New Hampshire, and Oregon. In Colorado, the proposed amendment would authorize local governments to pass laws recognizing the rights of nature. These laws could not be preempted or overturned by state or federal laws, although they would still have to be consistent with state and federal constitutions.

J. Stephen Cleghorn, an organic farmer in Jefferson County, Pennsylvania, became the first landowner in the U.S. to use a conservation easement to recognize and protect the rights of water, forests, and wild ecosystems on his own land. A conservation easement is a voluntary agreement that permanently limits uses of land to protect its environmental values. Concerned by the threat of fracking, Cleghorn said to GlobalExchange.org, "We wanted to preserve organic agriculture on these fifty acres to be sure, but also wanted to employ this recognition of rights of nature to deter any activity that would threaten those rights."

These visionaries are turning American law upside down, suggesting that the rights of people, communities, and, most radically, nature are more important than corporate rights and property rights. It is a historic struggle, and one that will not be easy to win. Corporations have used the legal system to accrue power for centuries. In an otherwise obscure 1886 railway taxation case, the U.S. Supreme Court held that corporations, as legal persons, were protected by the Fourteenth Amendment's Equal Protection Clause. That provision had been added to the U.S. Constitution in 1868 for the sole purpose of safeguarding the rights of recently freed slaves. In 2010, in a notorious case known as *Citizens United*, the U.S. Supreme Court held that limits on election spending by corporations violated their constitutional right to free speech.

As communities across the U.S. assert that the rights of people, communities, and nature ought to take priority over corporate and property rights, they are provoking a massive legal response from big business. In addition to the cases already highlighted, there are similar lawsuits underway in California, Ohio, Colorado, and New York. When the California city of Compton enacted an ordinance banning fracking within city limits, the Western States Petroleum Association sued. Faced with the might of the oil and gas industry, Compton withdrew its ban. An attempt to put forward a ballot initiative in the state of Washington that would have recognized the rights of the Spokane River was struck down by the Washington Supreme Court on the grounds that water rights are governed by existing state law and can't be overridden by local governments.

Industry lawsuits against community bills of rights in Broadview Heights, Ohio, and Blaine Township, Pennsylvania, have been successful. Judge Michael K. Astrab said state law gives the Ohio Department of Natural Resources "sole and exclusive authority" to regulate oil and gas wells, overturning Broadview Heights' voter-approved ban on future wells. Judge Donetta W. Ambrose wiped out large parts of Blaine Township's ordinances, finding that Blaine "does not have the legal authority to annul constitutional rights conferred upon corporations by the United States Supreme Court." She also ruled that the township's drilling restrictions ran afoul of the Pennsylvania Oil and Gas Act.

Courts are striking down community rights of nature ordinances because they are inconsistent with state and/or federal law. To Thomas Linzey, this reinforces his most fundamental point: today's laws and institutions are antithetical to the rights of natural ecosystems and local communities. Linzey concluded in a CELDF press release, "Communities are recognizing the rights of nature in law as part of a growing understanding that a fundamental change in the relationship between humankind and nature is necessary." Gus Speth, co-founder of the Natural Resources Defense Council and the former dean of the Yale School of Forestry, agrees, and said to *Earth Island Journal*, "I am very excited about the move to a rights-based environmentalism. Lord knows we need some new and stronger approaches. And endowing the natural world with rights is a big part of that."

There will be many more legal battles fought in the U.S. before nature's rights enjoy the same protection as corporate rights. While lawsuits capture most of the headlines, CELDF believes it is more important to educate people about the clash between their rights, nature's rights, and corporate rights, as well as how these conflicts can be reconciled in a democracy. Mari Margil concluded an essay in *Exploring Wild Law* about CELDF's efforts to defend the rights of nature with the following exhortation: "The Lorax asked 'who speaks for the trees?' The people of Ecuador, Blaine, Barnstead, Nottingham, and a dozen other communities have answered 'We do.' And now I ask all of you. Will you speak for the trees? For if not you, then who? And if not now, then when?"

Chapter 8
A RIVER BECOMES A LEGAL PERSON

Ko au te awa, ko te awa ko au.

I am the river, and the river is me.
Māori expression

Until recently, every square foot of land on Earth outside Antarctica and Bir Tawil was owned by humans. A single species among tens of millions of species, *Homo sapiens*, purports to hold title to it all. The first small, pioneering cracks in this ubiquitous assertion of human ownership occurred in New Zealand, thanks to recent changes that begin to incorporate Māori worldviews into the legal system. Aotearoa is the Māori name for the country, meaning "land of the long white cloud."

Aotearoa/New Zealand is a small country that has occasionally demonstrated global leadership on fundamental issues of rights. Back in 1893, it became the first country in the world to recognize that women had the right to vote. In the twentieth century, it was the first country to have a female prime minister, chief justice, and governor general at the same time. More recently, Aotearoa/New Zealand has become a pioneer in recognizing the legal rights of ecosystems—first a river, and then a national park.

These internationally important precedents emerged from negotiations between the national government and the Māori people. The agreements, and the laws that implement them, reflect and incorporate Māori cosmology. Although the Māori worldview is unique, it shares many elements with other Indigenous cultures, particularly in terms of the human relationship with nature. Their perspective is starkly different from the Western system of human exceptionalism, anthropocentrism, and separation from nature.

Aotearoa/New Zealand's revolutionary recognition of the rights of nature has roots in the nineteenth century. After arriving from Polynesia in canoes, Māori had lived on Aotearoa for a thousand years prior to the arrival of European explorers and settlers. In 1840, the Treaty of Waitangi led to the British assertion of sovereignty over New Zealand. The negotiation of the treaty was fraught with the challenges one might expect in an exchange between profoundly different cultures, exacerbated by linguistic barriers. There was also clear evidence of fraud, with intentionally different versions of the text prepared in English and in Māori. For example, in the English version the Māori cede sovereignty to the Crown, while the Māori version guarantees *tino rangatiratanga* (absolute authority) to the Māori. These deceptions and misunderstandings are still being sorted out today, nearly two centuries later.

The Waitangi Tribunal is a permanent government commission established in 1975 to investigate Māori claims about wrongful acts of the Crown. The tribunal conducts hearings, reports its findings, and offers recommendations to guide future negotiations. While the government is not legally bound by the tribunal's suggestions, most settlements have been consistent with tribunal direction.

To Māori, nature is not simply property or a source of natural resources. There are two important and interrelated concepts at the heart of the Māori relationship with nature that are profoundly different from Western philosophy—*whanaungatanga* and *kaitiakitanga*, loosely translated as kinship and stewardship. *Whanaungatanga* is actually broader than kinship in the sense that it relates not only to relations between living humans, but also to an expansive web of relationships between people (living and dead), land, water, flora and fauna, and the spiritual world of *atua* (gods)—all bound together through *whakapapa* (genealogy). In other words, the Māori believe that all things in the universe, living and dead, animate and inanimate, are related, going back to Papatūānuku (the Earth), and Ranginui (the sky). Thus all the elements of nature are kin. All are infused with *mauri* (living essence or spirit), and merit the same respect accorded to fellow humans. The people of a particular place are intimately connected to its geographic features—rivers, forests, lakes, and other species—and have responsibilities toward them all. *Kaitiakitanga* is an intergenerational obligation of respect that flows directly from *whanaungatanga* because of the web of kin relationships.

In the Western legal system, fulfilling rights and responsibilities is essential to healthy relationships between people. For Māori, fulfilling rights and responsibilities is viewed as a prerequisite to healthy relationships among humans, and also between humans and nature. This notion of binding responsibilities toward the natural world has the potential to turn centuries of human exploitation of "natural resources" on its head, requiring us to place nature, rather than only humans, at the heart of sustainability.

The Māori's relationship with the natural environment has gradually gained recognition in legislation, court judgments, day-to-day government decision-making, and among the Pākehā (non-Māori) population of New Zealand. Proposals to deposit raw sewage in rivers or the ocean, erect towers for television signals, and build roads through natural areas have been rejected by courts not only because of adverse impacts on the environment, but also due to potential harm inflicted upon the metaphysical relationship between the Māori and certain locations. For example, in 2004, following a lengthy dispute about discharging sewage wastewater into the Whanganui River, New Zealand's Environment Court ruled that "one needs to understand the culture of the Whanganui River *iwi* [tribe] to realize how deeply engrained the saying *ko au te awa, ko te awa ko au* [I am the river, and the river is me] is to those who have connections to the river. Their spirituality is their 'connectedness' to the river. To take away part of the river is to take away part of the *iwi*. To desecrate the water is to desecrate the *iwi*. To pollute the water is to pollute the people."

New Zealand's acceptance of the Māori worldview reached new heights in a 2011 treaty settlement recognizing that the Whanganui River has the rights of a legal person. This trailblazing agreement regarding the legal rights of nature was formalized in legislation in early 2017.

In 2014, a law was enacted that transformed Te Urewera National Park from a region of government-owned property into a legal entity that has the rights of a person, owns itself, and must be managed in a way that respects its rights.

The groundwork for the Whanganui and Te Urewera breakthroughs was laid by earlier treaty negotiations involving the

Te Arawa Lakes and the Waikato River. The Te Arawa Lakes Settlement Act 2006 shifted ownership of a series of lakebeds from the Crown to a newly created body called the Te Arawa Lakes Trust. Under this law, no level of government can authorize any new commercial activities or new structures on the lakes without the consent of the trustees, whose mandate is to put the lakes' interests first. The law also makes it clear that the lakebeds may never be privatized or sold.

The Waikato-Tainui Raupatu Claims (Waikato River) Settlement Act 2010, passed four years later, articulates a very un-Western concept of a river, based on Māori cosmology. To the Waikato-Tainui people, the Waikato River is a *tupuna* (ancestor) that possesses *mana* (prestige) and in turn represents the *mana* and *mauri* (life force) of the tribe. Respect for *te mana o te awa* (the spiritual authority, protective power, and prestige of the Waikato River) is at the heart of the relationship between the *iwi* and their ancestral river. The opening section of the law states, "The overarching purpose of the settlement is to restore and protect the health and well-being of the Waikato River for future generations."

The law acknowledges the personhood of the river in the eyes of the *iwi* and honours the *iwi*'s close spiritual relationship with the river:

> The Waikato River is a single indivisible being that flows from *Te Taheke Hukahuka o Te Puuaha o Waikato* and includes its waters, banks and beds (and all minerals under them) and its streams, waterways, tributaries, lakes, aquatic fisheries, vegetation, flood plains, wetlands, islands, springs, water column,

airspace, and substratum as well as its metaphysical being. Our relationship with the Waikato River, and our respect for it, gives rise to our responsibilities to protect *te mana o te Awa* and to exercise our *mana whakahaere* in accordance with long established *tikanga* to ensure the wellbeing of the river. Our relationship with the river and our respect for it lies at the heart of our spiritual and physical wellbeing, and our tribal identity and culture.

However, that law, enacted in 2010, did not take the additional step of recognizing the legal rights of the river.

The Whanganui River is the third longest river flowing through Aotearoa/New Zealand, stretching from its headwaters on the slopes of Mount Tongariro to its mouth emptying into the Tasman Sea, in the ancestral territory of the Whanganui Māori. To the Whanganui *iwi*, the river is Te Awa Tupua, a living being that is *taonga* (treasure), central to, and indeed inseparable from, their identity, culture, health, and well-being. The Whanganui *hapū* (subtribes) are entrusted with *kaitiakitanga* (guardianship) of this *taonga* so as to protect the *mana* (prestige) and *mauri* (life force) of the river for generations to come. Protecting the river means protecting the people, and vice versa.

The Whanganui Māori have had ongoing disputes with the British colonial government about their customary rights and their relationship with the Whanganui River from the time the Treaty of Waitangi was signed in 1840. At that time, the Māori charged a toll for using the river for transport or shipping, as a means of asserting their authority. In the 1870s and 1880s, as prospectors for gold, coal, and other resources moved into the region, the Māori filed petitions with the New Zealand parliament registering their opposition to industrial activities on the river. They fought against the destruction of their eel weirs by colonists seeking to ease the passage of ships. They brought lawsuits to the Supreme Court of New Zealand in 1895 and 1898 asserting customary fishing rights and seeking compensation for gravel removed from the river. In 1903, the Whanganui *iwi* demanded that the Court stop the Crown from asserting ownership of riparian or riverside lands. Another petition to the parliament in 1927 sought damages for violations of the *iwi*'s native rights. None of these legal actions were successful.

In 1938, the Whanganui *iwi* filed another lawsuit against the Crown, destined to become one of the country's longest-running court cases, alleging multiple breaches of the Treaty of Waitangi. They sought to resolve the question of guardianship over the Whanganui River. In various decisions over the decades, judges from the Native Land Court, Court of Appeal, and Supreme Court concluded that as of 1840, the Māori had owned the river-bed. However, a law passed in 1903—without consultation or compensation—assigned title in all navigable rivers to the Crown.

In 1977, the Whanganui *iwi* petitioned Queen Elizabeth II regarding their treaty rights over the river. The petition was ignored. In the 1980s, concerns about excessive withdrawals from the river for hydroelectricity led the Whanganui *iwi* to file a lawsuit seeking the assurance of minimum flows at all times of the year. Finally in the early 1990s, the Whanganui River Māori Trust Board brought a case to the Waitangi Tribunal concerning their customary and treaty rights, seeking to settle once and for all the issue of Māori *mana* and *rangatiratanga* (authority or sovereignty) in the Whanganui River.

In 1999, the Waitangi Tribunal published a comprehensive report recognizing Māori interests and authority over the whole of the river. The tribunal concluded that "unless the Māori right in the river is settled, properly acknowledged, and provided for, the people will be always on the back foot, responding, without sufficient resources, to complex planning proposals by which others assume control." As Christopher Finlayson, attorney general and minister for Treaty of Waitangi negotiations, acknowledged to the NZ parliament, "The constant position of Whanganui *iwi* for well over 150 years was that they never willingly relinquished possession or control of the Whanganui River and all things that give the river its essential life. For generations they have pursued justice in respect of the river."

Following the tribunal's report, negotiations about reconciling the Māori grievances related to the Whanganui River gained momentum. In 2011, media reports emerged about a radical agreement recognizing that the Whanganui River enjoyed the same legal rights as a person. Finalized in 2014, this agreement recognizes the holistic Māori concept of Te Awa Tupua, referring to the indivisible whole of the Whanganui River, including all its physical and metaphysical elements and extending from the mountains to the sea.

Legislation to implement the agreement was introduced in 2016 and passed in early 2017. Christopher Finlayson seems an unlikely champion for the rights of nature. He is tall and slim, with a prominent forehead. He wears elegant suits and wire-rimmed glasses, looking very much the part of an urban intellectual. Finlayson loves the opera and Shakespeare. Prior to entering politics, he worked at a law firm that often represented Māori communities in their ongoing efforts to settle historical grievances with the government. Finlayson said in a 2009 speech, "I used to love going to the office in the morning when we were suing the Crown."

Now he represents the Crown and says that being treaty negotiations minister "is the best job a person can have." Margaret Mutu, a professor at Auckland University and chief treaty negotiator for a group of Māori, describes Finlayson as "a lawyer with a conscience" and the best-qualified minister she has ever met. When he introduced the revolutionary legislation recognizing that the Whanganui River had legal rights, Finlayson was visibly elated.

The new law goes far beyond the stepping stones of the Te Arawa Lakes and Waikato River laws. The Whanganui Agreement and the legislation include remarkable provisions intended to protect and implement the Māori perspective of the river as a holistic system in which they are physically and spiritually embedded. The most important transformation is that the Whanganui River is recognized as a legal entity with "the rights, powers, duties, and liabilities of a legal person." The bed of the river is no longer property of the Crown. Ownership will be vested in the new legal entity representing the river itself. In the words of Elaine Hsiao, a fellow at Pace Law School's Center for Environmental Legal Studies, "like women and slaves, the Whanganui River has undergone a transformation from property interests to a legal being in its own right."

The new law also recognizes the deep-rooted values that lie at the heart of Te Awa Tupua, including:

(a) *Ko te Awa te mātāpuna o te ora*: the river is the source of spiritual and physical sustenance for the *iwi*, *hapū*, and other communities of the River.

(b) *E rere kau mai i te Awa nui mai i te Kahui Maunga ki Tangaroa*: Te Awa Tupua is an indivisible and living whole from the mountains to the sea, incorporating the Whanganui River and all of its physical and metaphysical elements.

(c) *Ko au te Awa, ko te Awa ko au*: I am the River, and the River is me: The *iwi* and *hapū* of the Whanganui River have an inalienable connection with, and responsibility to, Te Awa Tupua and its health and well-being.

(d) *Ngā manga iti, ngā manga nui e honohono kau ana, ka tupu hei Awa Tupua*: Te Awa Tupua is a singular entity comprised of many elements and communities, working collaboratively for the common purpose of the health and well-being of Te Awa Tupua.

In short, the Whanganui River is no longer owned by humans but by itself, Te Awa Tupua. The river and surrounding ecosystem, plus associated metaphysical elements, have legal rights, standing, and an independent voice. The innate values, interests, and status of the river are to be explicitly considered, respected, and upheld. This is consistent with the Māori vision that rivers and other elements of nature have intrinsic value and are inherently incapable of being owned in the western sense. According to legal scholar Catherine Iorns Magallanes in *Nature as Ancestor*, "this combination of formally legislating for a natural feature as a legal person and upholding its interests for its own sake suggests to all—not just to its Māori descendants—that it is more than just a resource to be exploited."

Many people wonder exactly how the Whanganui River's interests will be protected in practice. The law establishes a new entity called Te Pou Tupua. Two individuals will be appointed to serve as official guardians, one chosen by the Whanganui *iwi* and one by the government. They will be the human face of Te Awa Tupua, symbolizing the new partnership between the Māori and the Crown. The guardians are "to act and speak for and on behalf of Te Awa Tupua," ensuring that the values identified above are consistently applied to safeguard the health and well-being of the river and the people of present and future generations. It is conceivable that, in its own name and via its guardians, Te Awa Tupua could lodge an objection to any proposed activity that might have an adverse impact on the river. For example, Te Awa Tupua could appeal the issuance of permits for developments that are not in the river's long-term interests. Through its guardians, Te Awa Tupua could also file lawsuits seeking injunctions to stop harmful actions or seeking compensation for damage caused by negligent acts by corporations or individuals.

The Whanganui River law clearly contains ideas that challenge some of society's most deeply entrenched beliefs. Amazingly, there has been no opposition. As the bill was "debated" in New Zealand's Parliament, Marama Fox of the Māori Party heaped praise on it and thanked everyone who contributed to it. Metiria Turei, co-leader of New Zealand's Green Party, referred to the importance of the legal status that is afforded the *awa* [river] in this legislation. . . . it is absolutely about time the law caught up with our *tikanga* [customary legal system]. It has been our *tikanga* forever that our environment is entitled to its own integrity, is entitled to be protected and restored from damage and injury *for its own sake* [emphasis added], that our environment, however we want to describe it, is our ancestor and from where we come, and, therefore, we owe our environment everything—our life, our existence, our future. The law slowly is starting to find ways—clumsy and not perfect by any means, but it is slowly trying to find ways to understand that core concept.

Turei concluded her speech by pleading with New Zealanders struggling with the notion of recognizing that a river has rights to reflect on the fact that our legal system has long granted corporations many of the same rights as people. In comparison, she observed, "It is so much more important—so much more important—that we give status for its own sake to the very thing that gives us life, and in Whanganui that is our river."

Maybe it's not surprising that that the Māori Party and the Green Party are on board. But the governing National Party, who describes itself as centre-right, proposed the law. The opposition Labour Party also endorsed it. Labour representative Kelvin Davis said, "It is about time that this House started recognising and legitimising the Māori worldview. . . . I can imagine how outside of these walls the country will be going off: 'Oh, my gosh! These Māoris—what are they on about now?' Well, if in our Pākehā [non-Māori] culture and in our Christian culture we believe someone can walk on water, then we can believe that Te Awa o Whanganui is a person. So it is a beautiful thing." Even the right-wing New Zealand First Party has spoken positively about it. Pita Paraone of the NZ First Party said, "I think it is a real privilege to be part of this process today and see [Māori] intrinsic values come into legislation. It also sets up a framework for future legislation [recognizing nature's rights]." Paraone concluded by simply stating, "I commend this bill to the house."

Because the legal system is recognizing the Māori's special relationship with the natural world, and because of the Māori's traditional approach to guardianship, the Whanganui River is much more likely to be treated in a sustainable manner.

THE LAND WAS HERE FIRST

When you first see Tamati Kruger, you can't help thinking that he must have played professional rugby. His broad shoulders, barrel chest, and bull neck are the hallmarks of a man more comfortable in a rugby scrum than a media scrum. In almost every photo and video, whether meeting with government ministers or celebrating the deal that ended a bitter dispute spanning three centuries, Kruger is wearing a T-shirt or a golf shirt, and a pair of track pants. Yet when Kruger speaks, with quiet authority, it's obvious that he is blessed with singular wisdom, patience, and insight.

As chief negotiator for the Ngāi Tūhoe, a Māori *iwi* from the North Island, Kruger has repeatedly snatched victory from the jaws of defeat. Despite a series of stunning setbacks, he has always pressed on. His challenges were formidable. First, he had to convince his people to place their faith in a government that had dispossessed them, killed them, and betrayed their hopes and dreams for more than 150 years. Then he had to convince the government to relinquish ownership of a vast and much-loved national park in order to settle the Tūhoe claim.

Kruger was eminently qualified to tackle these obstacles. He had served a fifteen-year apprenticeship working for the Tūhoe *iwi* on every kind of committee, including employment, education, health, and welfare. He sought to "learn as much as I could about the dynamics of people and politics." Kruger developed the ability to make seemingly explosive accusations sound like an even-handed explanation of Māori history: "In the 1850s the Crown openly said that they had to exterminate Tūhoe. That's in government records. The view was that Tūhoe could never be rehabilitated from wanting to be masters of their own destiny. So the Crown enacted its scorched earth policy—poison the wells, shoot the cow, burn the house, and destroy the crops to starve Tūhoe to death. Inheriting that history shapes your mind in a certain way. You can become embittered but other things are possible."

In May 2010, after years of intense negotiations, it appeared as though the government and the Tūhoe had reached an agreement in principle to return Te Urewera, their traditional homeland that ranges across hundreds of thousands of hectares, to the Tūhoe. According to Kruger, travel arrangements were made and motels booked for the Tūhoe negotiation team to attend a signing ceremony. Special commemorative pens were even made. Then Kruger received a phone call from Prime Minister John Key. "I'm sorry, Tamati, but this is a bridge too far for me," Key said, referring to the proposed transfer of Te Urewera National Park from the Crown to the Tūhoe. The signing ceremony was cancelled.

The government's abrupt U-turn was a painful reminder of more than a century of broken promises. Most negotiators would have resigned at that point, unable to trust the government and unable to justify the breakdown in negotiations to their people. But not Tamati Kruger. He didn't burn any bridges with the government. Nor did he sugarcoat the depth of betrayal he felt on behalf of his people. On the contrary, he used the prime minister's about-face to increase the pressure on government to settle quickly. Kruger resuscitated the agreement by proposing that the government not return ownership—in the traditional western sense—of Te Urewera to the Tūhoe. Instead, the government would pass a law giving the land—mountains, lakes, rivers, trees, and animals—the rights of a legal person and ownership of itself.

"Land is not property," Kruger said. "The challenge was convincing the New Zealand Government of that." In his own words, "My feeling is that the land was here first, so nobody owns it. If anything, it owns you. The water owns the water, the land owns the land. So our proposition to the government has been 'Let us agree that Te Urewera owns itself.'"

Remarkably, the government agreed.

Chapter 9
TE UREWERA: THE ECOSYSTEM
FORMERLY KNOWN AS A NATIONAL PARK

"True wisdom consists in not departing from nature, and in moulding our conduct according to her laws and model."

SENECA, ancient Roman philosopher

The emergence of the rights of nature in Te Urewera has its roots in a dark chapter of history. As European settlers flooded into Aotearoa/New Zealand and took up land in the nineteenth century, there were occasional armed uprisings by Māori. The government responded with brutal, indiscriminate, and excessive force. A particularly violent episode occurred during the 1860s when the military was in pursuit of Te Kooti, a Māori leader in the armed resistance. The colonial forces employed a scorched earth approach to the Tūhoe people in the Urewera region who were believed to be sheltering the rebel. Innocent men, women, and children were killed, their villages destroyed, crops and food stores razed, livestock and horses slaughtered, and survivors left to starve. The Waitangi Tribunal found that the military had committed grave human rights abuses and concluded, "We find that the Crown was wholly at fault, attacking people who were simply retreating or defending themselves. We cannot overemphasize the reprehensible nature of the wholesale destruction and killing by

Crown forces. Grave breaches of Treaty principle were involved in these events." Also during this period, the New Zealand government confiscated 400,000 acres of Māori land in the Te Urewera region. Only 142 acres were eventually returned to the Māori, and no compensation was paid.

A fundamentally important aspect of this history is that the Tūhoe refused to sign the Treaty of Waitangi. They consistently asserted their desire and intention to retain sovereignty and control over their lands. In the 1890s, negotiations between the Tūhoe and the Crown appeared to reach a historic breakthrough. The New Zealand government enacted a unique law called the Urewera District Native Reserve Act 1896. Rights of self-government, including authority over lands and waters, would be returned to the Tūhoe over a large area. The newly created reserve was intended to ensure permanent protection for the lands, rivers, forests, birds, the Tūhoe, and their way of life. According to the Waitangi Tribunal, "It seemed to herald a new era in Te Urewera, in which a lasting relationship between iwi and the Crown would be founded on mutual recognition of their rights and responsibilities."

Unfortunately the promise of a new relationship was short-lived. The government violated the intent and the letter of the new law by continuing to acquire land within the reserve through what the Waitangi Tribunal described as "unfair, predatory, and at times illegal purchases."

Because of its rugged and remote beauty, primeval forests, and blue lakes, Te Urewera was designated a national park in 1954. The park was significantly expanded in 1957. The area is home to rich biodiversity, including many threatened species like kiwi, kōkako, kaka, and the distinctive whio, or blue duck. The region's name has an unusual origin. Te Urewera is a Māori phrase meaning "the burnt penis," from the story of a Māori chief who died after rolling over in his sleep while too close to a campfire.

In 1987, the Tūhoe filed a claim with the Waitangi Tribunal, asserting more than forty treaty breaches related to Te Urewera that inflicted catastrophic hardships upon their people. Hearings were held between 2003 and 2005. The tribunal's hearings for the Urewera claims were a national *cause célèbre*, in part because they provided an outlet for the pent-up frustrations and anger of Tūhoe people responding to more than a century of unfair treatment. In one notorious incident at Ruatoki, a bare-chested Māori man named Tame Iti with an impressive *tā moko* (facial tattoo) discharged a shotgun into a Union Jack in front of the tribunal. Iti was convicted of several firearms offences, but his conviction was overturned when the Court of Appeal ruled that his actions had been foolhardy rather than harmful. Later, a massive police raid on the Te Urewera region in 2007, involving about 300 officers, was purportedly based on concerns about Māori terrorists planning a guerilla war to establish a sovereign Tūhoe state. The controversial raid, which resulted in only four convictions for minor firearms offences, further soured relations between Tūhoe and the government.

The Waitangi Tribunal eventually issued six reports spanning 3,500 pages. It was sharply critical of the government's actions in Te Urewera, concluding that the Crown had broken multiple promises. These included the pledge of self-governance, wrongful expropriation of land, and effective dispossession of the Tūhoe from their homeland. The tribunal noted that "in some Te Urewera communities, poverty, and the absence of public services to ameliorate its consequences, has almost reached Third World proportions."

Further, there had been no meaningful consultation with Tūhoe about either the creation or the expansion of the park. The new park was administered under an act that made no provision for Māori interests. In the decades since 1954, the government had "ignored, undermined, fragmented and, more recently, paid lip-service to the *kaitiaki* responsibilities of the peoples of Te Urewera."

In light of this dark history, the settlement culminating in a law called the Te Urewera Act 2014 marked a bright leap forward for reconciliation between the Tūhoe and the Pākehā, as well as legal recognition of the rights of nature. At a signing ceremony, Minister Christopher Finlayson formally apologized, saying, "The relationship between Tūhoe and the Crown—which should have been defined by honour and respect—was instead disgraced by many injustices including indiscriminate *raupatu* [confiscations], wrongful killings, and years of scorched earth warfare. The Crown apologises for its unjust and excessive behaviour and the burden carried by generations of Tūhoe who suffer greatly and carry the pain of their ancestors."

The new law recognizes that Te Urewera has intrinsic worth and possesses "all the rights, powers, duties, and liabilities of a legal person." Like the Whanganui River owning the riverbed beneath it, Te Urewera now owns itself and possesses extensive legal rights. Te Urewera is no longer a national park, although the public can continue to enjoy the trails, lakes, and campgrounds.

According to the Tūhoe *iwi*, "Te Urewera continues to be the source of inspiration for our culture, language, and identity, the two being inseparable." Te Urewera is inalienable, meaning no part of it can ever be sold.

Section 3 of the Te Urewera Act 2014 contains unexpectedly poetic language:

3. Background to this Act

Te Urewera

(1) Te Urewera is ancient and enduring, a fortress of nature, alive with history; its scenery is abundant with mystery, adventure, and remote beauty.

(2) Te Urewera is a place of spiritual value, with its own mana and mauri.

(3) Te Urewera has an identity in and of itself, inspiring people to commit to its care.

Te Urewera and Tūhoe

(4) For Tūhoe, Te Urewera is Te Manawa o te Ika a Māui; it is the heart of the great fish of Maui, its name being derived from Murakareke, the son of the ancestor Tūhoe.

(5) For Tūhoe, Te Urewera is their ewe whenua, their place of origin and return, their homeland.

(6) Te Urewera expresses and gives meaning to Tūhoe culture, language, customs, and identity. There Tūhoe hold mana by ahikāroa; they are tangata whenua and kaitiaki of Te Urewera.

Te Urewera and all New Zealanders

(7) Te Urewera is prized by other iwi and hapū who have acknowledged special associations with, and customary interests in, parts of Te Urewera.

(8) Te Urewera is also prized by all New Zealanders as a place of outstanding national value and intrinsic

worth; it is treasured by all for the distinctive natural values of its vast and rugged primeval forest, and for the integrity of those values; for its indigenous ecological systems and biodiversity, its historical and cultural heritage, its scientific importance, and as a place for outdoor recreation and spiritual reflection.

Tūhoe and the Crown: shared views and intentions

(9) Tūhoe and the Crown share the view that Te Urewera should have legal recognition in its own right, with the responsibilities for its care and conservation set out in the law of New Zealand. To this end, Tūhoe and the Crown have together taken a unique approach, as set out in this Act, to protecting Te Urewera in a way that reflects New Zealand's culture and values.

(10) The Crown and Tūhoe intend this Act to contribute to resolving the grief of Tūhoe and to strengthening and maintaining the connection between Tūhoe and Te Urewera.

Some of the concepts in the law are written only in Māori, due to concerns about the impossibility of defining them in English, and fears that they could be misinterpreted. The purpose of the act further illustrates its unique approach, wherein the interests of humanity and nature are seen as interrelated and interdependent:

4. Purpose of this Act

The purpose of this Act is to establish and preserve in perpetuity a legal identity and protected status for Te Urewera for its intrinsic worth, its distinctive natural and cultural values, the integrity of those values, for its national importance, and in particular to—

(a) strengthen and maintain the connection between Tūhoe and Te Urewera; and

(b) preserve as far as possible the natural features and beauty of Te Urewera, the integrity of its indigenous ecological systems and biodiversity, and its historical and cultural heritage; and

(c) provide for Te Urewera as a place for public use and enjoyment, for recreation, learning, and spiritual reflection, and as an inspiration for all.

Te Urewera is now managed by a board of trustees rather than the Department of Conservation. The Te Urewera Board is mandated "to act on behalf of, and in the name of, Te Urewera." Tamati Kruger, now serving as the board chair, said in a press release, "Recognizing Te Urewera has its own identity confirms Tūhoe's view that it is not something which anyone owns. Te Urewera exists in its own right, and we as Tūhoe and New Zealanders have the responsibility to recognise its *mana* and commit to its care and protection." For the first three years, the board has eight members, with half appointed by the Tūhoe and half by the government. Subsequently, the board will consist of six Tūhoe appointees and three government appointees. The board's decision-making must be guided by Tūhoe principles, including *mana me mauri* (the sensitive perception of a living and spiritual force in a place), *rāhui* (the prohibition or limitation of a use for an appropriate reason), and *tapu* (a state or condition that requires certain respectful human conduct, including raising awareness or knowledge of the spiritual qualities requiring respect). The board has issued a statement of principles that will guide the development of a unique management plan by 2017.

Whereas in its conception as a national park, there was a wilderness preservation mandate that imposed strict prohibitions on activities like hunting or harvesting native plants, in the reimagined Te Urewera, these activities are permitted in certain circumstances. For example, hunting can be authorized if there is no adverse effect on the status of a particular species, the effects on Te Urewera are minor, *iwi* and *hapū* support the application, and "the proposed activity is important for the restoration or maintenance of customary practices that are relevant to the relationship of *iwi* and *hapū* to Te Urewera." The new regime reflects the Māori worldview that human uses can form part of a flourishing natural world as long as they are properly managed.

Tamati Kruger said what most amazed him after the Te Urewera agreement was announced was the lack of opposition: "Both Crown and Tuhoe were expecting some negative response, and there was none." Dr. Nick Smith, the minister for the environment, marvelled at "how far this country and this Parliament have come when we now get to this Tūhoe settlement in respect of the treasured Te Urewera National Park. If you had told me fifteen years ago that Parliament would almost unanimously be able to agree to this bill, I would have said, 'You're dreaming, mate.'" Dr. Pita Sharples, the former Minister of Māori Affairs, said the Te Urewera Act 2014 "is a profound alternative to the human presumption of sovereignty over the natural world."

Māori law professor Jacinta Ruru of the University of Otago, who completed her Ph.D. dissertation on the potential of employing national parks for purposes of reconciliation between settlers and Indigenous peoples, wrote in the *Māori Law Review*, "The *Te Urewera Act* is undoubtedly legally revolutionary here in Aotearoa/New Zealand and on a world scale. [It] makes me immensely proud to be a New Zealander." In the same journal, Professor Rawinia Higgins of Victoria University observed, "Te Urewera existed before the people and will continue to exist long after the people. Our role is to take care of it for future generations."

Now the conversation is turning to the fate of the rest of Aotearoa/New Zealand's national parks, which comprise almost thirty percent of the country's land. Professor Ruru has suggested that the Te Urewera approach could be replicated, so that all national parks become legal persons that are owned not by the Crown or the Māori, but by themselves. According to Ruru, "they have their own heartbeat, their own place, and their own identity."

For the first time anywhere in the world, a government created laws recognizing that an area of nature is no longer subject to legal claims of human ownership. In the eyes of the law, the status of Te Urewera and the Whanganui River has undergone an unprecedented and profound shift, from property and natural resources to independence and interdependence. This legal development is as potentially transformative as British judge Lord Mansfield's decision in 1772 that James Somerset, an enslaved African, was by law a free man who could not be owned by another person. That British case was the death knell for slavery, although it took decades for the abhorrent practice to be largely eliminated, and shadows persist to this day. Could the Te Urewera and Whanganui River laws be the death knell for the human conceit that nature is nothing but mere property, to be used and exploited for our exclusive benefit?

The trailblazing legal developments emerging from Aotearoa/New Zealand underscore the essential understanding that people are part of and dependent upon nature, not separate from and dominant over it. The Whanganui River and Te Urewera laws recognize the rights of nature but also emphasize the importance of the corresponding human responsibilities. They signal that the government and entire society of Aotearoa/New Zealand have begun to embrace, or at least accept, the Māori views that regard nature from an eco-centric perspective, and as a relative, having intrinsic value and legal rights. From this perspective, nature is so much more than just an endless storehouse of exploitable resources.

From transferring title to a group of lakes to a trust fund in 2006, to recognizing the Waikato River as an indivisible physical and metaphysical being in 2010, to acknowledging that Te Urewera and the Whanganui River are legal persons that own themselves, the law has made a series of rapid evolutionary leaps, the likes of which we rarely witness. In the eloquent conclusion of a prize-winning essay published in the *Māori Law Review*, law student Laura Hardcastle speculated, "Perhaps Te Awa Tupua and its younger companion, Te Urewera, are the start of a journey towards a new set of fundamental values to underlie our law." She acknowledges that the journey may be long and difficult, but observes that "although one drop of water cannot alter a landscape, put many together and give them sufficient time and they can form caves, waterfalls, and cliffs, altering the landscape irrevocably, just as the majestic Whanganui has done."

While the focus of treaty negotiations is on reconciliation between Pākehā and Māori, a deeper rapprochement is also taking place between people and the natural world. In this regard, the legal revolution underway in New Zealand is of vital importance not only for relationships around the globe between Indigenous and colonial peoples, but for showing the path toward re-establishing a healthy, sustainable relationship between humans and the ecosystems of which we are part.

Another promising development for the rights of nature in New Zealand occurred after the government appointed a constitutional advisory panel in 2011 to gather public advice on modernizing their bill of rights. This human rights law was passed in 1990 but is widely seen as ineffective. The panel held more than 100 meetings and received over 5,000 written submissions from citizens. In 2013, the advisory panel recommended adding environmental rights to the bill of rights. This could take the form of a human right to a healthy environment, legally recognized by most countries, but not New Zealand (or the U.S. or Canada). Or, the panel suggested, another option would be to "affirm the rights of the environment itself, for example by placing obligations on the state and citizens to protect Papatūānuku, Mother Earth, Mother Nature, or the biosphere."

The
RIGHTS *of* NATURE

New Constitutional and Legal Foundations

*"The drive to recognize the rights of nature
is absolutely critical if we are to again find a balance
with the world that supports us."*

Dr. David Suzuki, scientist, broadcaster, author,
and co-founder of the David Suzuki Foundation

A RIVER GOES TO COURT

In 2007, two Americans, Eleanor (Norie) Huddle and her husband, Richard Wheeler, travelled to Ecuador for a six-week vacation. The trip not only dramatically changed the lives of the slim and active seniors, but led to a globally celebrated precedent in advancing nature's rights. One of the places Norie and Richard visited was Vilcabamba, a region in Southern Ecuador also known as the Valley of Longevity. Just a few kilometres to the east are the renowned cloud forests of Podocarpus National Park. On a whim, the couple stopped at a farm that was for sale. The property's southern border curved for more than two kilometres along the banks of the Vilcabamba River. It was a classic case of love at first sight. Norie described the experience as being "spiritually hijacked." They bought the farm and an adjacent property, naming it the Garden of Paradise. Their dream was to create a model of sustainable agriculture, including organic crops, reforestation projects, good jobs for local people, and a small retreat centre. They built a small farmhouse before flying back to the U.S.

When the couple returned in 2008, they were stunned to see that the narrow, pot-holed road that ran past their farm was being transformed into a three-lane highway. Even more shocking was the discovery that construction waste had been dumped directly into the river along the southern boundary of their farm. Thousands of tonnes of debris were bulldozed into the river, reducing its width by as much as half in some stretches. Norie began travelling to Loja, the provincial capital, to learn what was going on, stop the dumping, and have the damage repaired. In scenes straight out of Kafka, she was shuffled from one government office to another, with solicitous but unhelpful bureaucrats eventually sending her back to the office where she started. "Be patient," they repeatedly advised.

Norie learned that Ecuadorian law required an environmental impact assessment prior to major road construction projects. Despite repeated requests, nobody in a government office could produce such a document or even confirm its existence. At roughly the same time, unbeknownst to Norie and Richard, Ecuador was putting the finishing touches on a revolutionary constitution that would be the first in the world to enshrine the rights of nature.

Disaster struck the Garden of Paradise in 2009 when spring rain morphed into a massive storm. Water levels in the Vilcabamba River rose several feet above normal for an entire month. In the middle of the night, Richard and Norie woke to the sound of rushing water, terrified that their house might be swept away. The raging Vilcabamba was just steps from their door, and, according to Norie, "sounded like a train." Topsoil was flushed away from several hectares of their best farmland. An ancient stone wall, a brand-new well, fences, fish ponds, huge trees, and irrigation canals were destroyed by the flood.

Norie ran out of patience and filed a formal complaint with the federal Ministry of Environment. Inspectors visited the farm, wrote a report, and instructed the provincial government to prepare an environmental assessment and a plan to repair the damages. Provincial officials began restoring one of the worst-hit areas. Then, as suddenly as it had started, the rehabilitation work stopped. Road construction resumed. Dynamite began knocking boulders and debris into the river again.

Norie and Richard hired a lawyer, Carlos Bravo. Carlos assumed that the couple wanted money to compensate them for the damages inflicted on their property. He was wrong. By this time, Norie and Richard had heard about the pioneering provisions in Ecuador's constitution, and Carlos agreed to look into them.

Three days later, he filed a lawsuit against the provincial government. Called an "action for protection," the plaintiffs requested: (1) that the highway project immediately stop dumping debris in the Vilcabamba River; (2) that the natural course of the river be restored; and (3) that the rocks, dirt, gravel, and vegetation deposited in the river be removed.

Within weeks, the case was brought before a local judge. The hearing did not go well. The judge called the government's lawyer by his nickname, Paolito. She dismissed the lawsuit, concluding that one of the defendants had not received adequate notice. Right away, Norie turned to Carlos and said, "This is absurd. We'll appeal."

Two months later, in 2011, an appeal court overturned the trial judge's decision, and sent shockwaves across the global legal community. For the first time in the world, a court, the Provincial Court of Loja, upheld the constitutional rights of a river. The judge stated, "It is the duty of constitutional judges to immediately guard and to give effect to the constitutional rights of nature, doing what is necessary to avoid contamination or to remedy it." The judgment ordered the defendants to immediately clean up existing damage, secure environmental permits, protect against oil spills or leakage into the river and the surrounding soils caused by machinery, implement a warning system to prevent future damage to the environment, find appropriate sites for disposing of debris if construction continued, and publish an official apology in the local newspaper. The court concluded, "We cannot forget that injuries to Nature are 'generational injuries' which are such that, in their magnitude have repercussions not only in the present generation but whose effects will also impact future generations." Lawyer Bravo said, "For me it was a great opportunity to do something for nature. This is the beginning of the development of jurisprudence in favor of nature."

Norie and Richard soon learned that a victory in court is only one step in the struggle for ecological justice, rather than an ultimate solution. While the Ecuadorian judiciary interpreted the recent constitutional changes as imposing strict responsibilities on the government, enforcement has been lacking. In an episode of CBC's *The Nature of Things*, David Suzuki visited Ecuador to see whether constitutional recognition of the rights of nature was leading to improvements in environmental protection. He interviewed Huddle and Wheeler about their case. The American couple told Suzuki that the provincial government had not stopped the road construction, complied with the Court's order to clear the debris, or remedied the damage to the riverbed. A few seedlings had been planted, and some soil trucked in to rebuild one of the fields. The government also erected some large signs declaring that the riverbanks had been rehabilitated. Norie noted that there was "a big stretch between the doing and the saying," and added, "changing centuries-old mindsets doesn't happen overnight." The Vilcabamba River case is a good legal precedent, demonstrating that the rights of nature are no longer just a philosophical concept. However its lustre is tarnished by the government's delays in obeying the Court's order. To Norie and Richard's credit, their vision of transforming a weed-strewn, overgrazed farm into a verdant and productive paradise is well underway. Photos show fields of blossoming flowers and bushes as well as hundreds of fruit trees already producing copious quantities of mangoes, papayas, and other tropical fruit. The Vilcabamba River, despite the damage, looks healthy and beautiful too. As Norie concluded in her interview with David Suzuki, "Nature is worth fighting for."

Chapter 10
PACHAMAMA AND ECUADOR'S PIONEERING CONSTITUTION

"Ecuador can no longer be a beggar sitting on a sack of gold."
RAFAEL CORREA, former president of Ecuador

"President Correa does not understand the rights of nature."
ALBERTO ACOSTA, former president of
Ecuador's Constitutional Assembly

Nearly four decades after Professor Stone's pioneering article and Justice Douglas's eloquent dissenting Supreme Court judgment, the idea of the rights of nature returned to the headlines. Ecuador is among the most biologically diverse countries on Earth. A single hectare of tropical rainforest in the Ecuadorian Amazon is home to more species of trees than all of Canada and the United States combined. Yasuní National Park is the epicentre of Ecuador's megadiversity. The park holds records for the rich variety of amphibians, reptiles, bats, and trees that live there. Dr. David Romo, co-director of the Tiputini Biodiversity Research Station, said, "It teems with so much life it leaves people lost for words." One tree in Yasuní may be home to as many as ninety-six different species of orchids and bromeliads and forty-five species of ants. In a single day, you are likely to see more species of butterflies than you could see in a lifetime in Canada. And yet this biodiversity is threatened by industrial resource extraction—oil and gas, mining, logging, palm oil plantations, and more.

Humans have inhabited Ecuador for more than 11,000 years. Many Indigenous peoples were conquered by the Incan empire, which in turn was overthrown by Spanish conquistadors. Yet there are still many Indigenous people in Ecuador today, the majority of whom are Quechua. The country is also home to several remote Amazon tribes—including the Huaorani, Shuar, Achuar, and Cofán—renowned for their courageous resistance to the industrialization of their homelands.

In spite of, or perhaps because of, its natural wealth, Ecuador has been plagued by political instability. Eight different individuals served as president in the decade between 1996 and 2006. Several ex-presidents from this era were charged with criminal offences including embezzlement and corruption. The emergence of Rafael Correa on the Ecuadorian political scene led to a rare period of stability. Until 2005, Correa was a left-leaning economist and professor in the faculty of economics at the Universidad San Francisco de Quito. He had earned a doctorate in economics from the University of Illinois, where he was influenced by Nobel Prize–winning economist Joseph Stiglitz. After the overthrow of President Lucio Gutiérrez in April 2005, Correa became minister of economy and finance in President Alfredo Palacio's administration. He was young, charismatic, and bursting with patriotism. He soon acquired a reputation as a political maverick, describing President George W. Bush as "dim-witted" and attacking the neo-liberal policies of the World Bank and International Monetary Fund.

In 2006, Correa became leader of the Alianza PAIS, a movement uniting parties on the left side of the political spectrum. In a country disillusioned by corrupt politicians, Correa positioned himself as an anti-establishment figure, referring to other politicians as Mafiosos, liars, and dinosaurs headed for extinction. Twisted Sister's "We're Not Gonna Take It" was the theme song for his campaign, which promised to tackle poverty and to shift funding from international debt repayment—which consumed more than a third of the government's revenue—to spending on education and health care. Although Correa earned only 23 percent of the vote in the first stage of the 2006 presidential election, that was good enough for second place, behind wealthy businessman Álvaro Noboa (with 27 percent). The Ecuadorean system involves a run-off between the top two candidates. Noboa was one of the richest people in Ecuador. Correa mercilessly portrayed him as a puppet of the elites. Correa's ability to speak Kichwa (Quechua) and his promises to redistribute wealth to poorer citizens convinced Indigenous Ecuadoreans to support him. Correa won the runoff with 57 percent of the vote.

One of the main slogans of Correa's election campaign in 2006 was *Constituyente ya!* (Constitutional revision now!) Correa promised to develop a new constitution for Ecuador that would provide a blueprint for the type of society the country aspired to become, a foundation for what he described as "the citizens' revolution." Cynics noted that this would be Ecuador's twentieth constitution since achieving independence in 1830.

Among Correa's closest colleagues was Alberto Acosta, also an economist and university professor, who worked with Correa at the Latin American Institute for Social Research prior to entering politics. Their friendship dated back to 1991, when they co-authored a book criticizing the unfettered expansion of free trade. They had denounced the inequitable sharing of revenue from the development of Ecuador's natural wealth, as well as the environmental devastation inflicted by foreign multinationals. Acosta was also elected in 2006. Correa appointed him minister of energy and mines, a powerful position given the importance of these industries to Ecuador's economy. During his brief stint as minister, Acosta came up with the Yasuní-ITT proposal, where Ecuador promised to permanently refrain from exploiting the rich Ishpingo-Tambococha-Tiputini (ITT) oilfield beneath Yasuní National Park if the global community would donate half of the oil's value to Ecuador, or roughly $3.5 billion at the time. Ecuador could not afford to turn its back on oil revenues without the international community's support.

In 2007, Acosta was elected to lead a constituent assembly to develop Ecuador's new constitution. Correa viewed the constitution-drafting exercise as an opportunity to showcase Ecuador's rejection of the neoliberal policies that had concentrated wealth in the hands of elites and exacerbated the poverty of millions of marginalized people. The process was intense, inclusive, and strove to be genuinely democratic. More than 3,000 proposals were submitted, and the assembly conscientiously sifted through them all. As the process dragged on, President Correa rejected Acosta's requests for extensions to complete the project. Acosta resigned, on principle. Correa accused him of being "too democratic." Before his resignation, however, Acosta played a central role in championing the inclusion of rights of nature in Ecuador's new constitution.

The initial proposal advanced at the constituent assembly was narrowly focused on the rights of animals. Inspired by the concept, Acosta wrote two discussion papers called "Do Animals Have Rights?" and "Nature as a Subject of Rights." In the latter, Acosta wrote, "There is still time for our laws to recognize the right of a river to flow, prohibit acts that destabilize the Earth's climate, and impose respect for the intrinsic value of all living things. It is time to stop the rampant commodification of nature, as the buying and selling of human beings was once prohibited."

The initial debate at the constituent assembly was led by Monica Chuji, the Indigenous president of the natural resources and biodiversity roundtable. Opposition to the idea of rights for nature was strong. In fact, some members of the assembly thought the idea was nonsensical, violating the basic principle that rights are only meant for humans. Chuji, Acosta, and their allies strategically moved the discussion about the rights of nature to the fundamental rights roundtable.

The internationally renowned Uruguayan writer Eduardo Galeano weighed in with an influential article on the rights of nature, identifying the possibility that Ecuador could become the first country in the world to take such a bold step. Galeano wrote, "It sounds weird, right? This idea that nature has rights . . . Crazy. As if nature were a person! Instead, it sounds perfectly normal that large U.S. companies enjoy human rights. In 1886, the Supreme Court of the United States, a model of universal justice, extended human rights to private corporations. The law recognized them possessing the same rights as people . . . as if companies breathe."

When it was explained that corporations enjoy extensive rights as legal persons, much of the initial opposition disappeared.

To many assembly members, it made more sense to speak of the rights of nature than the rights of corporations.

Among the main proponents of including the rights of nature in Ecuador's new constitution were Indigenous people, united as part of the Confederation of Indigenous Nationalities of Ecuador (CONAIE). Since its creation in the 1980s, CONAIE had evolved into a politically powerful force, mobilizing hundreds of thousands of people in street protests that brought down several governments. The rights of nature concept dovetailed with the Indigenous aspiration of living in harmony with nature.

Even assembly members on the conservative side of the spectrum endorsed the rights of nature. As a bold idea that gave Ecuador an opportunity to demonstrate global leadership, to be part of making history, it appealed to their sense of pride. Rafael Esteves, from a right-wing party, stated, "We are trying to write a constitution that is advanced, progressive, revolutionary, [and] adds to the evolution of international constitutional rights." Humberto Guillem argued that "some will think that to recognize nature's rights is a juridical heresy, as rights are for humans, not things. This is how the ones opposing the rights of slaves in the nineteenth century would have thought." Sofia Espin cited Eduardo Galeano and said, "Because we are part of nature, to speak of nature's rights is to speak of the rights of communities, the rights of the Huaorani, the rights of the uncontacted tribes, because they live from nature."

Natalia Greene is a leading Ecuadorean environmentalist. Petite but persuasive, she lobbied for recognition of the rights of nature, drawing on the intellectual arguments made by Latin American scholars as well as Professor Stone. Thanks to a serendipitous connection between Greene and American environmental activist Randy Hayes (founder of the Rainforest Action Network), the Community Environmental Legal Defense Fund was invited to Ecuador to inform the assembly about the work they were doing with American communities to protect the rights of nature. CELDF's Thomas Linzey and Mari Margil twice travelled to Quito and Montecristi (home of the assembly) to meet with delegates and offer input about drafting specific provisions.

The constitution that emerged is extraordinary. At its heart is an Indigenous concept called *sumak kawsay* (*buen vivir* in Spanish), a phrase which roughly translates as "good living" or, more accurately, as "harmonious coexistence," referring to relations between people, nature, and society. According to Alberto Acosta, the ideal envisioned by *buen vivir* opposes industrial capitalism, the subjugation of nature, the pursuit of endless economic growth, and the corrosive influence of consumerism. *Buen vivir* promotes organic agriculture, renewable energy, ecotourism, and recycling as the basis for an economy in which people, communities, and nature can flourish.

The preamble of the 2008 constitution states, "We women and men, the sovereign people of Ecuador . . . celebrating nature, the Pachamama (Mother Earth), of which we are a part and which is vital to our existence . . . hereby decide to build a new form of public coexistence, in diversity and in harmony with nature, to achieve the good way of living, the *Sumak Kawsay*." Pachamama, a goddess whose creative power sustains life on Earth, is at the heart of Indigenous worldviews in the Andean region. As Catherine Walsh, a professor at the Universidad Andina Simón Bolívar in Ecuador, describes it: "She is the mother that protects her children and provides the spaces, sustenance, and elements—cosmic, physical, affective, spiritual, cultural, and existential—necessary to live. She is the body of nature that receives and gives the seed of life in its infinite manifestations. Human beings are an expression of nature, her children. As such, there is no division between humans and nature."

From this perspective, nature cannot be reduced to mere "natural resources." According to Quechua leader and Ecuador's former minister of foreign affairs, Nina Pacari, "All beings of nature are invested with an energy that we call *samai* and, as a consequence, they are living beings: a rock, a river (water), a mountain, the sun, the plants, that is, all beings are alive." As is the case for the Māori, all of nature is worthy of respect and preservation for its intrinsic value.

The sections of the constitution articulating the rights of nature (as follows) are part of a comprehensive set of provisions intended to ensure the protection of Pachamama. The constitution states that both humans and nature have rights, that none of these rights is superior to the other, and that the state's "supreme duty" is to respect and enforce respect for these rights. Individuals have the right to live in an environment that is pollution-free, healthy, and ecologically balanced. They have a corresponding obligation, along with the government, to "respect the rights of nature, preserve a healthy environment and use natural resources sustainably." Even the constitutional provisions related to economic development make repeated references to the rights of nature and "living in harmony with nature."

~

Article 71. Nature, or Pachamama, where life is reproduced and occurs, has the right to integral respect for its existence and the maintenance and regeneration of its life cycles, structure, functions, and evolutionary processes. All persons, communities, peoples, and nations can call upon public authorities to enforce the rights of nature. To enforce and interpret these rights, the principles set forth in the Constitution shall be observed, as appropriate. The State shall give incentives to natural persons and legal entities and to communities to protect nature and to promote respect for all the elements comprising an ecosystem.

Article 72. Nature has the right to be restored. This restoration shall be apart from the obligation of the State and natural persons or legal entities to compensate individuals and communities that depend on affected natural systems. In those cases of severe or permanent environmental impact, including those caused by the exploitation of non-renewable natural resources, the State shall establish the most effective mechanisms to achieve restoration and shall adopt adequate measures to eliminate or mitigate harmful environmental consequences.

Article 73. The State shall apply preventive and restrictive measures on activities that might lead to the extinction of species, the destruction of ecosystems and the permanent alteration of natural cycles. The introduction of organisms and organic and inorganic material that might definitively alter the nation's genetic assets is forbidden.

Article 74. Persons, communities, peoples, and nations shall have the right to benefit from the environment and the natural wealth enabling them to enjoy the good way of living. Environmental services shall not be subject to appropriation; their production, delivery, use and development shall be regulated by the State.

~

The provisions laid out in the constitution reflect a game-changing cultural and legal shift from an anthropocentric view of the world to an eco-centric perspective that reflects the interdependence of all species and the ecosystems that make life on Earth possible. Ecuador's 2008 constitution also includes extremely detailed provisions about the environmental laws, policies, and programs needed to fulfill these ambitious goals. For example, the constitution prohibits genetically modified organisms (GMOs) from being used in agriculture, clarifies that access to safe drinking water is a fundamental human right, and emphasizes the importance of sustainable modes of transportation, going so far as to mandate that bicycle lanes be given priority in urban areas.

There are, however, troubling contradictions within Ecuador's constitution. For example, while nature's rights are recognized, elements of nature, such as water, biodiversity, and hydrocarbons, are defined as strategic resources of the state. Article 407 bans the extraction of non-renewable resources in national parks and protected areas, but allows the president to lift this ban with the consent of the National Assembly. Sadly, this is the fate that eventually befell Yasuní National Park.

The majority of Ecuadorian citizens (65 percent) approved the new constitution in a referendum. President Correa acknowledged the referendum's success, saying, "Today Ecuador has decided on a new nation. The old structures are defeated. This confirms the citizens' revolution." Alberto Acosta claimed that it rejects the "perpetual accumulation of material goods as an index of development and progress, a road that leads nowhere but to humanity's self-destruction."

Unfortunately, Ecuador has not yet realized the ambitions and ideals embodied in its new constitution. Many Indigenous people and environmentalists anticipated the end of such destructive practices as open-pit mining, palm oil plantations, shrimp farming in mangrove ecosystems, and oil and gas extraction in tropical rainforests. Of course, a constitution is not a magic wand. Even Acosta acknowledged the magnitude of the challenges ahead and expected that it would take decades for his country to achieve the intended social, economic, and environmental transformation.

Natural resource extraction, despite causing extensive environmental damage and harming the health of many Indigenous people, is still the backbone of Ecuador's economy. In 2009, a new mining law authorized open-pit mines that had been halted for two decades by social and environmental protests. President Correa claimed that environmental impacts would be mitigated through strong laws and best practices and argued that "mining is central to the modern era. Without it we go back to being like cavemen." The industry-friendly law was controversial, and tens of thousands of people took to the streets in protest. The government charged hundreds of environmentalists and Indigenous leaders with terrorism and shut down major organizations, including the Pachamama Foundation.

In 2013, President Correa announced that Ecuador was abandoning the Yasuní-ITT proposal because only $300 million had been pledged and just $13 million deposited. He bluntly stated,

"The world has failed us." The government then began auctioning oil and gas rights in large blocks of the Yasuní region, threatening the Indigenous cultures of the Huaorani, Tagaeri, and Taromenane peoples. The decision to exploit the Yasuní's oil reserves provoked intense public protests as well as a vicious war of words between former allies Rafael Correa and Alberto Acosta. Acosta questioned the president's commitment to the constitutional rights of Indigenous people and nature, even accusing him of treason. Correa responded by accusing anyone blocking Ecuador's economic development of being a terrorist.

President Correa claimed that fulfilling the extensive list of human rights in the new constitution—including water, food, health care, employment, and housing—required Ecuador to rely on natural resource extraction. He redirected funds away from paying off Ecuador's foreign debt and boosted spending on education, health care, and poverty reduction. The results are impressive. There have been substantial improvements in education outcomes and access to health care, as well as decreases in poverty. This progress is reflected in Ecuador's higher ranking on the UN Human Development Index and the Happy Planet Index. But much of this progress has been achieved through environmentally destructive activities such as large-scale mining and oil and gas extraction from the upper Amazon. Ecuador's challenge is to fulfill its commitment to human rights through economic development that relies less heavily on exploiting natural resources.

Correa's government was criticized for being slow to enact and implement many of the laws and policies needed to make the constitutional rights of nature effective. New water and mining laws actually weakened existing environmental protections. However, in 2014, Ecuador revised its criminal code to include crimes against Pachamama, among them mistreatment of animals and harm to biodiversity, soil, water, and air. In 2016, a new environmental code was enacted that includes extensive provisions intended to strengthen protection for both the rights of animals and the rights of nature.

While legislators have moved slowly, lawyers have not. Many lawsuits have already attempted to define and defend nature's rights. These cases have produced mixed results—some promising outcomes, some disappointing decisions, and one disturbing example of the rights of nature being exploited by government for ulterior motives.

The first lawsuit asserting that nature's rights were being violated was filed against the new mining law by CONAIE (representing fourteen Indigenous groups) and several community water councils. These groups asked the Constitutional Court to strike down the mining law and prohibit mining in parks and ecologically sensitive areas. The court ruled that environmental safeguards embedded in both the mining law and the constitution were sufficient to ensure that the rights of nature would be respected rather than violated.

The first successful case was, in fact, the lawsuit brought on behalf of the Vilcabamba River by Norie Huddle and Richard Wheeler. Two other precedent-setting cases were decided in 2011. In one, the Correa government used nature's rights as a pretext for cracking down on thousands of impoverished people who were eking out a living in the Amazon jungle by illegally mining gold. The Ministry of Interior applied to the Twenty-Second Criminal Court of Pichincha for permission to forcibly evict miners in

Esmeraldas province. Government lawyers argued that the illegal mining caused mercury and other toxic substances to contaminate freshwater ecosystems, violating the rights of nature. After the Court agreed, President Correa declared a state of emergency in the region. He ordered the military to seize and destroy all mining equipment. A force of nearly 600 soldiers carried out the mission. This process was replicated in three other provinces. Even opponents of mining were taken aback at the government's exploitation of the rights of nature as a rationale for carrying out such dramatic actions.

The other 2011 case also involved an illegal activity: shrimp farming in coastal mangrove forests. The Ministry of Environment initiated a crackdown on these businesses. Manuel de los Santos Meza Macías, owner of the Marmeza shrimp company, responded by filing a lawsuit asserting that his constitutional rights to property and work were being violated. The trial court ruled in favour of Marmeza and prohibited the Ministry of Environment from removing the company's equipment from the Cayapas ecological reserve. The government appealed and lost. The final appeal, to the Constitutional Court, was successful. The court ruled that private rights, such as property rights, should not trump nature's rights.

The rights of nature were again invoked in a sequel to the unsuccessful litigation against the 2009 Mining Act. In 2012, the government approved a massive open-pit mine in an Amazonian biodiversity hotspot called Mirador Cóndor. The project was proposed by EcuaCorriente, a Chinese company. A broad coalition of Indigenous, environmental, and community organizations filed a lawsuit arguing that the inevitable loss of biodiversity and contamination of water would violate the rights of nature. The company's own report anticipated the extinction of four endemic species, including three amphibians and one reptile. A court rejected the lawsuit, but its decision was fraught with errors. In a contorted decision, the judge concluded that the public interest in economic development outweighed the private interest in protecting nature. The judge also suggested that nature's rights were limited to areas designated for environmental protection, such as national parks or ecological reserves, and determined that no protected areas would be harmed by the mine. This was directly contradicted by the government's environmental assessment. The plaintiffs appealed but lost again.

It subsequently came to light that President Correa had circulated a memo to all judges, criticizing "the illegitimate use of protective actions provided for in the constitution." Citing the potentially enormous economic costs inflicted on Ecuador, the memo warned that judges would have to personally reimburse the government for "damages and harm" incurred as a result of court orders delaying or halting proposed resource extraction projects. This extraordinary violation of the judiciary's independence would never be tolerated in Canada or the U.S., yet provoked little uproar in Ecuador. A complaint was lodged with the Inter-American Commission on Human Rights, but that international tribunal proceeds at a glacial pace and, in 2017, the complaint is still under consideration. The Mirador mine is already fully constructed and operating.

On several occasions, judges themselves raised the constitutional rights of nature in lawsuits where the litigants did not. For example, in a 2009 case where local communities argued that their human right to a clean and healthy environment was being violated by massive pig farms and pork-processing facilities, the judge observed that the rights of nature were also being violated. In 2012, a judge ruled that the rights of nature could be enforced not only against the government, but also against private entities. This case was started by a group of businesses in the Galapagos Islands concerned that road construction at the peak of tourist season would harm their income. The legal basis of their case was that the municipal government lacked an environmental licence for the construction. Judge Pineda Cordero noted the construction area included endangered species habitat, and the road crossed a migratory path for marine iguanas and other species. Invoking the constitutional rights of nature and the precedent of the Vilcabamba case, the judge ordered that construction be suspended until the municipality obtained an environmental licence that guaranteed the protection of species habitat. In issuing a preliminary injunction against the municipal government of Santa Cruz, the judge noted that the rights of nature enjoy "constitutional rank and due to their hierarchical superiority, directly bind everyone, whether they are public entities or private persons."

Another important case involved illegal shark fishing in Galapagos National Park and Marine Reserve. On July 19, 2011, the Ecuadorian Coast Guard and rangers from the park boarded the fishing boat *Fer Mary I*. It turned out to be their biggest shark bust ever. There were almost 400 dead sharks onboard, including 286 bigeye threshers, 22 blue sharks, 40 Galapagos sharks, 40 scalloped hammerheads, 2 tiger sharks, and 1 mako shark. Many of the sharks had been beheaded and gutted. All were species listed by the International Union for the Conservation of Nature as vulnerable or threatened. The rangers found 1,335 fishing hooks on a long line that extended fifty kilometres. University of North

Carolina marine sciences professor John Bruno was at a nearby research station. He got permission to board the ship to look at the sharks, and the next day wrote on his blog, "This is what a marine massacre looks like. It was one of the most depressing and intense days of my life. I felt like we were unearthing a mass grave in a war zone." Every shark was missing its dorsal fin. These fins are sold at a high price to Chinese restaurants for shark fin soup.

Criminal charges were laid against the captain and crew for fishing in a marine protected area. Hugo Echeverria, a lawyer with an environmental organization called the Sea Shepherd Conservation Society, filed a submission putting forward the interests of the sharks. Echeverria argued that he was legally entitled to do so on the basis of protecting the constitutional rights of nature, and the Court agreed.

Despite the global attention this horrific case received, in December 2011 a local judge in the Galapagos cancelled all the charges. Apparently he found it impossible to prioritize "fish over a human's ability to feed his family and continue a career he has been doing over a lifetime." After an international outcry, the judge was suspended. The criminal charges were reinstated, and the case was moved to a court on the mainland. Ultimately the fishermen were found guilty of poaching in a national park. The captain was sentenced to two years in jail while nine crew members were sent to prison for a year. The *Fer Mary I* was scuttled. Judge Franco Fernando specifically referred to the importance of the rights of nature provisions in the constitution as guiding his decision. In November 2015, an appeal court unanimously confirmed the guilty verdict and prison sentences.

In 2014, a young people's environmental organization in Ecuador, YASunidos, filed a lawsuit in the local court of Chimborazo in response to a large pine tree plantation authorized in the fragile *páramo* ecosystem of Tangabana. YASunidos alleged that the constitutional rights of the *páramo* ecosystem were violated by the plantation and sought the removal of the pine trees and the restoration of the *páramo*. The first judge rejected the lawsuit on the grounds that the claimants failed to prove they owned the land in question, an unnecessary requirement in cases asserting the rights of nature. On appeal, the decision was upheld. YASunidos has appealed to the constitutional court, but the case had not yet been decided in early 2017.

In 2016, a local agricultural association challenged the establishment of a new protected area in Quimsacocha. The constitutional court upheld the new park as necessary for the conservation of biodiversity. The court noted that Ecuador's new constitution represents "a departure from the classic anthropocentric conception, by which the human is the centre and aim of all things, and brings us closer to an eco-centric vision that acknowledges our interdependence with nature." This passage echoes the Asiatic lion and wild buffalo decisions of India's Supreme Court. The rights of nature provisions in Ecuador's constitution, according to the Court, are an important innovation, "rupturing the traditional paradigm of considering nature a mere object of law, to consider it as a subject like a living person."

From India to Ecuador, courts are beginning to acknowledge a revolution in the legal system, emphasizing the importance of recognizing nature's rights to address today's environmental woes.

Whether those in power were Incan emperors, Spanish conquistadors, American multinationals, Chinese state-owned enterprises, Ecuadorean elites, or even a socialist government, Indigenous peoples and nature in Ecuador continue to be exploited. Whether the country's constitutional recognition of the rights of nature has the ability to change this narrative remains an open question. But at least the question is being discussed.

In a world where virtually all legal systems define nature as property and natural resources as intended for human use and exploitation, Ecuador's groundbreaking 2008 constitution suggests that hundreds of years of conventional legal, judicial, and political wisdom need to be reconsidered. The constitution emphasizes the fundamental importance of humans living in harmony with nature, and takes the unprecedented step of describing the rights of Pachamama, or Mother Earth. The vision represented by the 2008 constitution challenges centuries of law, the dominant economic paradigm, and the deeply entrenched inequalities of twenty-first-century Ecuador.

Nobody realistically expected Ecuador to change overnight. Ecuador's experience illustrates that even when a society recognizes the rights of nature in its highest and strongest law, there will still be tremendous challenges when these rights confront entrenched interests. The opponents of the revolutionary changes envisioned by Ecuador's constitution are wealthy and powerful. Carlos Zorrilla, executive director of the environmental group Ecological Defence and Conservation, said, "As exciting as these developments were, it was inevitable that the people in power would, and will, find ways to circumvent, undermine, and ignore those rights."

To be fair, President Correa's administration improved infra-structure, hospitals, and education. But this socio-economic progress was financed in the age-old way—by the exploitation and environmental destruction of the Amazon. A sign beside a Chinese-funded road blasted through Indigenous territory in the upper Amazon to access oil fields ironically reads, "The Citizens' Revolution is achieved through public works." According to his old ally Alberto Acosta, Rafael Correa was trapped by an economic model that exploits nature to pay for social programs and poverty reduction.

Acosta, Natalia Greene, and many others are still fighting to accelerate the process of change within Ecuador. They are working to have the rights of nature incorporated into laws, institutions, and processes to ensure that they are implemented and enforced. As Professor Marc Becker concluded, "It is not sufficient to draft new legislation; social movements need to remain ever vigilant to ensure that the government follows through on its promises and implements its progressive policies." Despite the daunting implementation challenges, Ecuador serves as an inspiration to those around the world who are working to secure recognition of the rights of nature in their own communities, countries, and at the global level.

AN UNLIKELY PRESIDENT
AND CHAMPION FOR NATURE'S RIGHTS

One of the world's most vocal advocates for recognizing and honouring the rights of nature is Evo Morales. A member of Bolivia's Indigenous Aymara community, Morales grew up in extreme poverty. His family farmed and raised llamas, but their home had no electricity or running water. Four of his seven siblings died as young children because they lacked access to health care. He remembers the first time he ate an orange, when he was nine or ten. He was about to eat the peel when his mother yelled at him to save it so she could brew tea. Morales also says that he did not have a shower until he was fifteen.

After working in a variety of trades, from baker to brickmaker, Morales returned to farming and began to grow coca. He became involved with trade unions, initially as a secretary of sport, organizing soccer games. Eventually Morales became leader of Bolivia's powerful coca union. He passionately defends coca for its traditional and medicinal uses, and created a huge stir by demonstrating how to chew it at the United Nations. Morales told world leaders and diplomats, "This is a coca leaf. This is not cocaine. This represents the culture of Indigenous people of the Andean region."

Entering politics in the mid-1990s, Morales was elected to the National Congress, now known as the Plurinational Legislative

Assembly, and became a vocal critic of the government. He was a leader in a series of prominent protests against the privatization of drinking water services and the natural gas industry. Despite being arrested several times, and criticized by the U.S. ambassador, his popularity grew.

In 2005, Evo Morales was elected as Bolivia's first Indigenous president. Like Rafael Correa, Morales surfed to power on a wave of antipathy toward neoliberalism. Known for his fiery anti-capitalist rhetoric, Morales articulated a distinctive socialist vision in which Bolivia tackles poverty and inequality, but does so in harmony with nature. It is this latter aspect that differentiated Bolivia from other socialist Latin nations like Cuba and Venezuela. When Morales was elected, one of his first actions was to immediately reduce both his own presidential wage and that of his ministers by 57 percent to $1,875 a month.

Morales often wears a modified Nehru jacket, embroidered with Bolivian colours, and a white dress shirt. He has a dark, sun-wizened face, the product of years of walking under the harsh sun in the Bolivian highlands. Every day, Morales rises before dawn and endures a punishing schedule of meetings and trips. He relishes the adulation heaped upon him by poor and Indigenous Bolivian citizens, who often greet him with showers of flower petals. In many communities, he joins in soccer matches, maintaining a high level of fitness that serves him well as president.

President Morales is a vocal critic of the United States. He expelled the U.S. ambassador to Bolivia, forced the U.S. to close a military base, and sent the Drug Enforcement Agency away. His anti-American actions and rhetoric led President Obama to shun him at international meetings, including the Paris Summit on climate change.

Despite cutting many ties with the U.S., World Bank, and International Monetary Fund, Bolivia enjoys the fastest-growing economy in Latin America. Prior to 2006, oil and gas corporations paid 18 percent of their profits to the Bolivian state, but Morales reversed this, so that now 82 percent of profits go to the state. Oil and gas companies threatened to file lawsuits or leave the country, but ultimately relented. Thus, where Bolivia had received $173 million in revenue from hydrocarbon extraction in 2002, by 2006, they received $1.3 billion and by 2014, close to $7 billion. This revenue enabled Morales to invest heavily in public infrastructure (roads, electricity supply, water, and sanitation). He has raised the minimum wage and implemented a variety of monthly payments to parents, the elderly, and pregnant women. The World Bank reports that the proportion of people living in poverty in Bolivia has dropped from 66 percent in 2000 to 38 percent today. A report by the International Monetary Fund concluded that the policies of the Morales government over the past decade "dramatically reduced inequality and poverty even compared to peers in Latin America." According to the *New York Times*, "Inflation has been kept in check. The budget is balanced, and once-crippling government debt has been slashed. And the country has a rainy-day fund of foreign reserves so large—for the size of its economy—that it could be the envy of nearly every other country in the world." Morales was handily re-elected in 2009 and 2014. Writing in the *Guardian*, Ellie Mae O'Hagan attributed his enduring popularity not to anti-imperialist rhetoric, but to his "extraordinary socio-economic reforms."

Morales has some powerful ideas, such as diverting the majority of the world's military budgets to eradicating poverty and restoring nature. He also has some absurd notions, such as his claim that European men are bald because of their diet, and that eating chicken can undermine masculinity.

After the dismal failure of UN climate negotiations in Copenhagen in 2009, President Morales hosted a summit in Cochabamba the following spring. More than 30,000 attended the World People's Conference on Climate Change and the Rights of Mother Earth. Morales argued that the wealthy nations were essentially fiddling while the planet burned. He said, "It's easy for people in an air-conditioned room to continue with the policies of destruction of Mother Earth. We need instead to put ourselves in the shoes of families in Bolivia and worldwide that lack water and food and suffer misery and hunger." The rich countries' feeble proposals, according to Morales, "are not solutions, but ways to cook all of humanity."

Instead, Morales is advocating for a Universal Declaration of the Rights of Mother Earth and the incorporation of the rights of nature into every country's legal system. He persuaded the United Nations to rename Earth Day as International Mother Earth Day. He presided over the passage of Bolivia's Law on the Rights of Mother Earth and continues to promote recognition of the rights of nature both in Bolivia and internationally. He has repeatedly stated, "Sooner or later, we will have to recognise that the Earth has rights, too, to live without pollution. What mankind must know is that human beings cannot live without Mother Earth, but the planet can live without humans."

Chapter 11
BOLIVIA AND THE RIGHTS OF MOTHER EARTH

"You never change things by fighting the existing reality. To change something, build a new model that makes the existing model obsolete."
R. BUCKMINSTER FULLER,
writer, engineer, and architect

Like their Andean neighbours in Ecuador, Bolivia's advocacy of the rights of Mother Earth is powered by Indigenous worldviews. It is an effort to construct a compelling alternative to capitalism, and reflects a desperate sense that climate change must be tackled before its impacts are irreversible. About 55 percent of the nation's population is Indigenous, mainly Quechua and Aymara. As in Ecuador, there is a deep connection with Pachamama, the goddess of fertility. Although Bolivia's 2009 constitution does not include detailed rights for nature, in a section called Environmental Rights, it does state, "Everyone has the right to a healthy, protected, and balanced environment. The exercise of this right must be granted to individuals and collectives of present and future generations, *as well as to other living things*" (emphasis added). This final phrase suggests that non-human animals, plants, and possibly ecosystems have constitutional rights in Bolivia.

Bolivia's constitution parallels Ecuador's in terms of its

overarching focus on *sumaj kamaña* (*sumak kawsay*), or *buen vivir*. *Buen vivir* recognizes the intimate human relationship with nature and implicitly condemns the excessive exploitation of natural resources taking place under current conceptions of development and progress.

Along with small island states, Bolivia is one of the countries facing the most immediate impacts of climate change. There have been devastating floods in the Amazonian region, while drought is wreaking havoc in other parts of the country. Alarmingly, the glaciers that provide fresh water to the majority of Bolivia's population have decreased 50 percent in the past fifty years, and scientists warn that all of the country's glaciers could be completely gone as early as 2030.

The second-largest lake in Bolivia, Lake Poopó, dried up completely in 2016, becoming a salt desert. "I don't think we'll be seeing the azure mirror of Poopó again," said Milton Perez, a Universidad Técnica researcher, to the *Guardian*. "I think we've lost it." During the twentieth century, the global average temperature rose by 0.8°C, but in the Lake Poopó region the increase was 2.5°C. Bolivia's former ambassador to the UN, Pablo Solon, observed in a blog post that the lake's disappearance left in its wake "thousands of dead fish, dead flamingos, fishing boats anchored to the ground, and hundreds of Indigenous people, who for centuries were devoted to fishing, that now roam for help thinking of a very uncertain future. That is the true face of climate change that expands like a cancer throughout the world."

Florida Institute of Technology biologist Mark B. Bush warns that the long-term trend of warming and drying threatens the entire Andean highlands. A 2010 study he co-authored in the journal *Global Change Biology* says that La Paz, Bolivia's capital, could face catastrophic drought this century. The resulting water shortages would create an agricultural crisis and eventually turn the region into an uninhabitable wasteland. The study predicted that "inhospitable arid climates" would decrease the availability of food and water for more than three million Bolivians.

In light of these threats, it's not surprising that Bolivia has become one of the world's leading voices on the rights of nature, the human right to water, and the need for faster and stronger action on climate change. To Bolivians, there is no difference between protecting nature's rights and protecting human rights. The Bolivian government's critique of capitalism is succinctly summarized in the following paragraph from its national commitment to implement the Paris climate accord of 2015: "The capitalist system seeks profit without limits, strengthens the divorce between human beings and nature, establishes a logic of domination of men against nature and among human beings, and transforms water, earth, the environment, the human genome, ancestral cultures, biodiversity, justice, and ethics into goods. In this regard, the economic system of capitalism privatizes the common good, commodifies life, exploits human beings, plunders natural resources, and destroys the material and spiritual wealth of the people."

Bolivia's proposals for addressing the global climate crisis include recognizing the rights of Mother Earth, replacing capitalism and consumerism with healthy communities living in harmony with nature, and redirecting money from military spending to poverty alleviation and clean technology.

Bolivia garnered world acclaim in 2010 for its groundbreaking Law on the Rights of Mother Earth. This law is the first to set out in detail the rights of nature and the corresponding responsibilities of governments and people. It is based on a draft prepared by the Pact of Unity, a coalition of Indigenous and campesino (small farmer) organizations. The law was rushed through the legislature so that President Morales could present it at the 2010 UN climate change negotiations in Cancún, Mexico. Referring to the new law, Bolivian vice-president Álvaro García Linera said, "It makes world history. Earth is the mother of all." He added that "it establishes a new relationship between man and nature, the harmony of which must be preserved as a guarantee of nature's regeneration." As explained by Pablo Solon in a 2011 Earth Day panel, "To speak about Mother Earth's rights challenges the entire legal system on which capitalism is based. This is why we insist on talking about rights. Someone who kills someone else goes to jail, but if you pollute a river, nothing happens to you. We have to be accountable. The key issue is to make us accountable in relation to our Earth system."

The Law on the Rights of Mother Earth identifies nature's rights and clarifies the responsibilities of government and society for ensuring these rights are respected. Its governing principles include achieving harmony between humans and nature, promoting the collective good, restoring ecosystems, defending Mother Earth, and refusing to commercialize nature or treat it as private property. Mother Earth is defined as a dynamic living system that is indivisible, interrelated, and interdependent. The law articulates seven broad rights of Mother Earth:

> 1. To life: The right to maintain the integrity of living systems and the natural processes that sustain them, and the capacities and conditions for regeneration.

2. To the diversity of life: The right to preserve the variety of beings that make up Mother Earth, without being genetically altered or structurally modified in an artificial way, so that their existence, functioning or future potential would be threatened.

3. To water: The right to preserve the functionality of the water cycle, its existence in the quantity and quality needed to sustain living systems, and its protection from pollution for the reproduction of the life of Mother Earth and all its components.

4. To clean air: The right to preserve the quality and composition of air for sustaining living systems and its protection from pollution, for the reproduction of the life of Mother Earth and all its components.

5. To equilibrium: The right to maintain or restore the interrelationship, interdependence, complementarity, and functionality of the components of Mother Earth in a balanced way for the continuation of their cycles and reproduction of their vital processes.

6. To restoration: The right to timely and effective restoration of living systems directly or indirectly affected by human activities.

7. To pollution-free living: The right to preserve Mother Earth's components from contamination, as well as toxic and radioactive waste generated by human activities.

The details and consequences of the rights of Mother Earth will depend upon the specific facts of a particular situation. Human rights may, in some situations, be constrained by nature's rights. For example, a river may need some minimum level of water flow to maintain its ecological functions, which will prevent humans from taking too much water at certain times of the year. Any conflict between human rights and the rights of Mother Earth must be resolved in ways that do not irreversibly affect the viability of living systems.

The Law on the Rights of Mother Earth clearly identifies the government's responsibilities, including preventing the extinction of species and the disruption of natural cycles, creating patterns of production and consumption that enable Bolivians to live well but in balance with nature, preventing the commodification of living systems, addressing the structural causes of climate change, developing a clean and efficient energy system, promoting peace and eliminating weapons of mass destruction, and demanding international recognition that today's environmental debt obligates wealthy countries to finance and transfer clean technologies to poorer countries.

The duties of individual Bolivians and corporations include respecting the rights of Mother Earth, promoting harmony with nature, generating proposals designed to improve environmental protection, and reporting any act that violates the rights of Mother Earth. All citizens are empowered to take legal action to defend Mother Earth's rights.

The original Law on the Rights of Mother Earth was only five pages long. In 2012, Bolivia enacted a complementary law that is far more detailed, called the Framework Law on Mother Earth and Holistic Development for Living Well. This second Mother Earth law provides additional detail about the ecological restructuring of Bolivia's economy and society, requiring all existing and future laws to respect the rights of Mother Earth and accept the ecological limits inherent in living on a finite planet. It echoes the constitution by requiring public policy to strive for the goal of living well in harmony with nature and people, rather than the conventional approach of unlimited economic growth.

The explicit objective of this second law is to "establish the vision and fundamentals of holistic development in harmony and balance with Mother Earth to live well, guaranteeing the continued capacity of Mother Earth to regenerate natural systems, recuperating and strengthening local and ancestral practices, within a framework of rights, obligations and responsibilities." Living well in harmony with Mother Earth is at the heart of the law and is defined as "a civilizational and cultural alternative to capitalism, based on the Indigenous worldview."

The law requires the government to: transition from non-renewable to renewable energy; develop new economic indicators that assess the ecological impact of all development; carry out ecological audits of all private and state companies; regulate and reduce greenhouse gas emissions; become self-sufficient for food, water, and energy; research and invest resources in energy efficiency, ecological practices, and organic agriculture; and require all companies and individuals to be held accountable for environmental damage and pollution. The law also emphasizes the rights and knowledge of Bolivia's Indigenous population.

The Framework Law on Mother Earth and Holistic Development for Living Well includes extensive provisions related to climate change. It articulates the concept of "climate justice," meaning that some countries, because of their historical contributions to the problem and high levels of wealth, have a responsibility to be leaders in responding to climate change. President Evo Morales has called for climate reparations—essentially, payments from the rich nations that have caused the climate crisis to the poor nations that are suffering the consequences. The law also makes it clear that all policies and programs related to reducing greenhouse gas emissions must not involve the commodification of nature. For example, Bolivia criticizes the programs in which wealthy nations pay poorer nations to protect the latter's forests in exchange for carbon credits that enable ongoing pollution in the rich countries.

A study published by the London School of Economics described the passage of Bolivia's two Mother Earth laws as "a sweeping overhaul" of environmental and natural resource law, including a "novel approach to climate change." Undarico Pinto, leader of the 3.5-million-strong campesino movement that helped draft these laws, believed they represented a turning point in Bolivian history.

Unfortunately, this second Mother Earth law is fraught with contradictions. It endorses the resource extraction–focused economic agenda of President Morales, explicitly promoting the agriculture, oil and gas, and mining sectors, saying that the government must "promote the industrialization of the components of Mother Earth."

This seems diametrically opposed to recognizing nature's rights. Bolivia attempts to distinguish between selling nature's goods (resources), which it encourages, and selling nature's functions (ecosystem services), which it prohibits. The logic behind this distinction is unclear. The law purports to require that clean technology be used in the extraction of oil, gas, and minerals, in a manner consistent with living in harmony with nature, but reports from Bolivia indicate that so far, these are empty promises.

As has been the case in Ecuador, Bolivia's implementation of the rights of Mother Earth has been at best inconsistent, with minor progress offset by major failures. Bolivia shares with Ecuador the need to juggle the conflicting priorities of reducing poverty and protecting nature.

On the positive side, a new institution called the Plurinational Mother Earth Authority was established in 2013. The original director of that unit, Benecio Quispe, began the onerous process of developing strong environmental policies and overseeing their effective implementation. Quispe, a former deputy minister of clean water and sanitation, launched a campaign called Mi Madre Tierra, Mi Futuro (My Mother Earth, My Future) in 2015. Targeting the general public, it focused on protecting forests, conserving water, and managing waste. Initial activities included planting trees, limiting the use of plastic bags, boosting recycling, and recognizing water as a human right. Over six million trees were planted between October 2015 and March 2016. The agency also played a leading role in developing Bolivia's ambitious climate change strategy. In its plan to implement the 2015 Paris climate accord, Bolivia commits to rapidly increasing renewable energy, from 39 percent currently to 81 percent by 2030, and to carry out reforestation of six million hectares of land.

Local governments are also working to realize the commitments made by the federal government. For example, the municipal government in Cochabamba created a special Mother Earth Protection Office, with a particular focus on cleaning up the

Rocha River, which runs through the city. More than fifty factories dump industrial pollution into the Rocha, so the Mother Earth Protection Office is implementing a comprehensive watershed management plan. The plan is making progress in reducing the dumping of solid waste into the river, and some polluters have been fined.

On the other hand, the ombudsperson intended to promote and protect nature's rights has not yet been appointed, even though more than six years have passed since the law was enacted. A major obstacle to the implementation of the laws is Bolivia's dependence on oil, gas, and mining. Since the Spanish conquistadors discovered silver in the sixteenth century, Bolivia's people and ecosystems have been exploited, transferring billions of dollars to other countries. Almost three-quarters of Bolivia's exports are still minerals, gas, and oil. This structural dependence on resource extraction will be very difficult to unravel.

Like Ecuador's Rafael Correa, Evo Morales oversaw the passage of a new mining law that was heavily criticized. Indigenous leader Mama Nilda Rojas claimed that the new law was created without adequate input from Indigenous peoples or the communities most likely to be impacted by mining. Rojas was particularly angry that the law threatened criminal penalties against protesters, saying, "It was the same Evo Morales who [used to] participate in marches and road blockades. And so how is it that he is taking away the right to protest?"

In 2011, the government of Bolivia tried to begin building a new highway through a national park and Indigenous lands (the Isiboro Ségure National Park and Indigenous Territory, or TIPNIS in Spanish). The project provoked a massive backlash among Indigenous people, environmentalists, and many other Bolivians. Tens of thousands of people marched from the Bolivian lowlands to La Paz in protests that were violently suppressed by police. In 2014, the government backed down and cancelled the construction of the highway.

Pablo Solon, one of the world's most high-profile advocates for the rights of nature, resigned his post as Bolivia's ambassador to the United Nations in 2011. Solon was frustrated by Bolivia's increasing dependence on the mining and fossil fuel industries. "There must be coherence between what we say and what we do," he wrote in a letter to President Morales. Solon recognized that "it will be a process. It won't be something that will be approved and implemented immediately." But he obviously felt that Bolivia was moving in the wrong direction.

In 2015, President Morales signed a presidential decree that allowed exploration for oil and gas in national parks and Indigenous territories. According to Morales, exploiting these hydrocarbons will benefit the common good of the nation by combatting poverty. Popular support for Morales and his government has begun to waver. A constitutional referendum that would have allowed him to run for a fourth term as president was defeated. Despite this, Morales insists he will run again in 2019, ignoring both the constitution and the referendum results.

Despite the setbacks, there are promising signs that Bolivia does intend to chart a new course. One involves lithium, an essential element of the lightweight batteries that power everything from cell phones to electric vehicles. Bolivia has the world's largest lithium deposits—roughly half the global supply—worth tens of billions of dollars. President Morales calls lithium "hope for humanity" and has refused corporate offers to extract and export the lithium. Instead he proposes to mine it, process it, and manufacture batteries within Bolivia. Then the country will export the finished product, rather than just the raw materials. The lithium reserves are located in the vast Salar de Uyuni salt flat, where mining could potentially be accomplished without adversely affecting the country's Indigenous peoples or biodiversity. Bolivia recently signed a contract with a German firm to develop a local lithium processing plant.

Bolivia's social movements—especially the Pact of Unity that was a key force behind the Mother Earth laws—understood that the existence of new laws alone would not prompt immediate and dramatic changes in the country's economy. Raúl Prada, a Pact of Unity leader, concluded that, even with ongoing pressure from Bolivia's powerful social movements, the transition from resource extraction to a new economy based on *buen vivir* would be difficult. Prada acknowledged, "We clearly can't close mines straight away, but we can develop a model where this economy has less and less weight. . . . It will need redirection of investment and policies towards different ecological models of development. It will need the co-operation of the international community." Ultimately, this is a global challenge, said Prada: "Our ecological and social crisis is not just a problem for Bolivia or Ecuador; it is a problem for all of us."

The Bolivian approach, based on Indigenous worldviews, represents a radically different vision of the pathway to a sustainable future than the approach employed by industrialized countries. *Buen vivir* weaves together the fulfillment of human rights and the rights of Mother Earth, promising an interdependent community of all living beings and life systems. In 2010, the president of the UN General Assembly, Miguel d'Escoto Brockmann, declared Bolivian president Evo Morales a "world hero for Mother Earth."

A VOICE FOR THE GREAT BARRIER REEF

It takes imagination to attempt to speak on behalf of nature, especially to the Western-trained mind. Dr. Michelle Maloney, an Australian environmental lawyer, was struck by this challenge when she served as a witness in a case about damage to the renowned Great Barrier Reef, off the east coast of Australia. Maloney, an articulate person with a soft Aussie accent, is worried about the fact that environmental law has won many victories but still fails to address the root causes of the global ecological crisis. As she says, "At the heart of our society is the idea that humans can do whatever they want."

Maloney serves as coordinator for the Australian Earth Law Alliance and has written about the emergence of wild law, a new direction for environmental law that puts nature's needs first. To Maloney, focusing on the rights of nature is "a means of giving legal recognition to nature's inherent worth by recognizing what is already there. In operational terms, it is a means of redressing the imbalance between humans and nature."

Maloney testified on behalf of the Great Barrier Reef in 2014 in a case heard by the International Rights of Nature Tribunal. The tribunal was brought into existence by an alliance of individuals and organizations in 2014. In situations where there are allegations that nature's rights are being violated, lawyers, prosecutors, and judges are appointed, evidence is put forward, and verdicts are reached. The tribunal's decisions are not legally binding as it is not formally a part of any legal system. However, the tribunal brings important cases to world attention.

Because of its extraordinary coral ecosystems that provide a home to a tremendous diversity and abundance of marine life, the Great Barrier Reef is a World Heritage Site. However, the reef is deteriorating because of climate change, pollution from land- and marine-based human activities, shipping, and excessive tourist traffic. In 2012, the United Nations Educational, Scientific, and Cultural Organization (UNESCO) warned the Australian government that the reef was under threat, and its World Heritage status could be downgraded to "at risk" unless immediate steps were taken to reduce these pressures.

Prosecutors before the first hearing of the International Rights of Nature Tribunal on the reef's case argued that human activities are violating the Great Barrier Reef's rights by disrupting its ability to continue its vital cycles and processes. They called upon the tribunal to hold the Australian and Queensland governments accountable for allowing the types of coastal development that threaten the reef, and to set limits on human activities in the region to prevent further violations of the reef's rights. Dr. Maloney's testimony on behalf of the reef included the following statements:

> I am a colourful, vibrant network of connected coral
> villages, made by the collective effort of millions of
> coral polyps over millions of years. Free swimming
> coral babies float about until they find a place to settle,

and they normally settle on the comforting skeletons of their ancestors. They have made walls and mounds and hills of coral that, in turn, are the home for others in our community: algae, sponges, starfish, mollusks, sea snakes, fish. . . . Without the Reef, there is no home, no cosy place to play, nowhere to hide from predators, nowhere to lay their eggs. If the Reef dissolves and disappears, so will all of the thousands of species of life that call the Reef home. If the Reef disappears, there is nowhere else for these communities of life. . . .

For thousands of years people would visit us at the Reef: pop in and out with their little boats, take some fish with great respect, then go home. But now the ships have gotten bigger. And there are many more of them. We watch the coastline with fear when there are great rains, as the rivers fill up with sediment, garbage and litter that comes to our Reef. . . .

So in conclusion, how might the Reef feel? I would imagine the Reef feels the same way that people who love and care about the Reef feel. We are frightened. We are frightened that something precious and irreplaceable and ancient will die.

Maloney was in tears as she finished her presentation. She later wrote in a law review article, "It was deeply disturbing to imagine the world from the point of view of the Great Barrier Reef." One of the innovative aspects of the tribunal is that it allows and even encourages this radically different type of testimony, giving a voice to the voiceless.

The next stage in the Great Barrier Reef case was the convening of Australia's first regional Rights of Nature Tribunal in Brisbane, Queensland, in October 2014. Five judges—including three scientists, an Indigenous leader, and a youth representative—heard evidence from local prosecutors, witnesses (including Michelle Maloney), and a lawyer for the defence. At the end of the hearing, the tribunal criticized the Australian and Queensland governments for permitting several of the rights of the Great Barrier Reef to be violated, including the rights to existence, to integrity, and to regeneration. They cited evidence that it was not too late for the reef, but that steps needed to be taken immediately to ensure its long-term sustainability. Finally, the judges echoed the Supreme Court of India in concluding that "given the overwhelming impacts from the ongoing growth in current modes of production and consumption, a new eco-centric ethic and legal system is needed." The case was continued in Quito, Ecuador, in 2014, where the tribunal demanded a range of actions be undertaken to reduce human pressures on the reef and petitioned the governments to implement the recommendations made by UNESCO.

The Australian and Queensland governments subsequently submitted a Reef 2050 Long-Term Sustainability Plan to UNESCO that was intended to address at least some of the pressing environmental challenges, although it has been criticized as weak on climate change, the biggest threat to the reef. In 2017, new studies revealed a massive die-off of the Great Barrier Reef due to rising ocean temperatures.

Chapter 12
GLOBAL GAME CHANGERS

"The earth does not belong to humans."

ARNE NÆSS, Norwegian philosopher

Laws evolve to reflect changes in societies' attitudes and values. People in the U.S., New Zealand, Ecuador, and Bolivia have enacted laws, filed lawsuits, and even amended constitutions to reshape our relationship with other species and the ecosystems within which we all live. These local and national changes to the legal system can have direct impacts and also reinforce the shift in values that is taking place. But there are also efforts underway to establish global rules and institutions that will accelerate the spread of the idea that nature has rights.

One of these initiatives is the Universal Declaration of the Rights of Mother Earth, spearheaded by Bolivia, Ecuador, and other nations, and intended to complement the 1948 Universal Declaration of Human Rights. Because it is led by the Andean nations, the declaration is currently phrased in language that reflects Indigenous thought, and the underlying focus is on protecting nature.

The campaign is gathering momentum, and the idea is gaining increased recognition at the United Nations and across the world. In 2009, the UN General Assembly adopted a resolution, proposed by Bolivia, proclaiming April 22 each year International Mother Earth Day. The General Assembly acknowledged that "Mother Earth is a common expression for the planet Earth in a number of countries and regions, which reflects the interdependence that exists among human beings, other living species and the planet we all inhabit." Evo Morales expressed the hope that, just as the twentieth century has been called the century of human rights, the twenty-first century will become the century of Earth's rights. At the 2010 People's Congress on Climate Change and the Rights of Mother Earth, over 30,000 people from more than 100 countries visited Cochabamba. During this grassroots event, a group led by South African lawyer Cormac Cullinan drafted the Universal Declaration of the Rights of Mother Earth (see below).

~

The Universal Declaration of the Rights of Mother Earth

Preamble
We, the peoples and nations of Earth:

- *considering that we are all part of Mother Earth, an indivisible, living community of interrelated and interdependent beings with a common destiny;*
- *gratefully acknowledging that Mother Earth is the source of life, nourishment and learning and provides everything we need to live well;*
- *recognizing that the capitalist system and all forms of depredation, exploitation, abuse and contamination have*

caused great destruction, degradation and disruption of Mother Earth, putting life as we know it today at risk through phenomena such as climate change;

- convinced that in an interdependent living community it is not possible to recognize the rights of only human beings without causing an imbalance within Mother Earth;

- affirming that to guarantee human rights it is necessary to recognize and defend the rights of Mother Earth and all beings in her and that there are existing cultures, practices and laws that do so;

- conscious of the urgency of taking decisive, collective action to transform structures and systems that cause climate change and other threats to Mother Earth;

proclaim this Universal Declaration of the Rights of Mother Earth, and call on the General Assembly of the United Nations to adopt it, as a common standard of achievement for all peoples and all nations of the world, and to the end that every individual and institution takes responsibility for promoting through teaching, education, and consciousness raising, respect for the rights recognized in this Declaration and ensure through prompt and progressive measures and mechanisms, national and international, their universal and effective recognition and observance among all peoples and States in the world.

Article 1. Mother Earth
(1) Mother Earth is a living being.
(2) Mother Earth is a unique, indivisible, self-regulating community of interrelated beings that sustains, contains and reproduces all beings.

(3) Each being is defined by its relationships as an integral part of Mother Earth.

(4) The inherent rights of Mother Earth are inalienable in that they arise from the same source as existence.

(5) Mother Earth and all beings are entitled to all the inherent rights recognized in this Declaration without distinction of any kind, such as may be made between organic and inorganic beings, species, origin, use to human beings, or any other status.

(6) Just as human beings have human rights, all other beings also have rights which are specific to their species or kind and appropriate for their role and function within the communities within which they exist.

(7) The rights of each being are limited by the rights of other beings and any conflict between their rights must be resolved in a way that maintains the integrity, balance and health of Mother Earth.

Article 2. Inherent Rights of Mother Earth

(1) Mother Earth and all beings of which she is composed have the following inherent rights:

> *(a) the right to life and to exist;*
>
> *(b) the right to be respected;*
>
> *(c) the right to continue their vital cycles and processes free from human disruptions;*
>
> *(d) the right to maintain its identity and integrity as a distinct, self-regulating and interrelated being;*
>
> *(e) the right to water as a source of life;*
>
> *(f) the right to clean air;*
>
> *(g) the right to integral health;*
>
> *(h) the right to be free from contamination, pollution and toxic or radioactive waste;*

(i) the right to not have its genetic structure modified or disrupted in a manner that threatens it integrity or vital and healthy functioning;

(j) the right to full and prompt restoration for the violation of the rights recognized in this Declaration caused by human activities;

(2) Each being has the right to a place and to play its role in Mother Earth for her harmonious functioning.

(3) Every being has the right to well-being and to live free from torture or cruel treatment by human beings.

Article 3. Obligations of Human Beings to Mother Earth

(1) Every human being is responsible for respecting and living in harmony with Mother Earth.

(2) Human beings, all States, and all public and private institutions must:

(a) act in accordance with the rights and obligations recognized in this Declaration;

(b) recognize and promote the full implementation and enforcement of the rights and obligations recognized in this Declaration;

(c) promote and participate in learning, analysis, interpretation and communication about how to live in harmony with Mother Earth in accordance with this Declaration;

(d) ensure that the pursuit of human well-being contributes to the well-being of Mother Earth, now and in the future;

(e) establish and apply effective norms and laws for the defence, protection and conservation of the rights of

Mother Earth;

(f) respect, protect, conserve and, where necessary, restore the integrity of the vital ecological cycles, processes and balances of Mother Earth;

~

This document obviously represents a profound challenge to conventional thinking about sustainable development. It repositions humans as part of nature, emphasizes our dependence on ecosystems for survival and well-being, takes aim at prevailing economic models, and posits that all beings have rights that are specific to their species. Thus humans have human rights, and while there is some overlap (such as rights to life, water, clean air, and respect), the rights of bees, trees, manatees, and chimpanzees will be differentiated on the basis of their unique needs, functions, and communities. The declaration rejects human dominion and promotes an ethical, egalitarian vision of life on Earth.

In 2011, at Bolivia's request, the UN General Assembly held a debate about the proposed Universal Declaration of the Rights of Mother Earth. Since then, each year the UN has adopted a resolution and hosted an ongoing dialogue about living in harmony with nature, in which nature's rights are a central topic of conversation. At the Rio+20 Earth Summit in Johannesburg, South Africa, in 2012, a group of Latin American nations, led by Bolivia, Ecuador, Costa Rica, and Paraguay, called on the UN to endorse the rights of nature in the final agreement. The final report of the conference, called *The Future We Want*, stated:

39. We recognize that planet Earth and its ecosystems are our home and that "Mother Earth" is a common expression in a number of countries and regions, and we note that some countries recognize the rights of nature in the context of the promotion of sustainable development.

40. We call for holistic and integrated approaches to sustainable development that will guide humanity to live in harmony with nature and lead to efforts to restore the health and integrity of the Earth's ecosystem.

In 2014, leaders from the Group of 77 (a coalition of developing countries) and China met in Bolivia and adopted the Declaration and Plan of Action of Santa Cruz de la Sierra—"Towards a New World Order for Living Well." The declaration repeatedly calls for "living well in harmony with nature," highlights the need to respect the Earth, and refers to recognition of the "rights of nature" in some countries.

In addition to spearheading the campaign for a universal declaration on the rights of nature, Evo Morales and Rafael Correa have called for the establishment of an International Court of Climate Justice to hold countries accountable for fulfilling their climate change commitments. The creation of a new international court may take years or even decades to achieve, but the global rights of nature movement is working to make these concepts more familiar to a broader range of people, overcoming their initial strangeness in Western thought and ultimately pushing the ideas forward.

One of the leading organizations advocating the Universal Declaration for the Rights of Mother Earth is the Global Alliance for the Rights of Nature. The Global Alliance also created the International Rights of Nature Tribunal, which heard the Great Barrier Reef case described earlier. The tribunal was formally established in 2013 to respond to the concern that existing environmental laws—national and international—were not just ignoring the damages being inflicted on the natural world, but facilitating and legitimizing them. The tribunal was also created in response to the perception among Ecuadorians that President Correa's government was failing to enforce the pioneering rights of nature provisions of Ecuador's constitution.

The tribunal is comprised of lawyers and leaders from Indigenous, social justice, and environmental communities around the world, and it works within a codified set of rules, much as government-mandated courts operate. Its mandate is to hear cases, determine whether violations of the rights of nature have occurred, identify who should be held responsible, and prescribe the actions required to prevent further harm and to restore damaged ecosystems and communities.

Regional rights of nature tribunals are also being established around the world, such as the Australian one that heard the Great Barrier Reef case. The founders of these tribunals hope to shine a spotlight on acts that violate the rights of nature, even where the activities causing these harms are legal under today's laws. More broadly, by critiquing the current legal system, participants seek to illustrate the structural flaws and weaknesses in the obsessive pursuit of economic growth and today's anthropocentric laws. One of the key reasons for creating the tribunal was to give a voice to the voiceless—to allow human defenders to speak for nature and challenge the destructive practices prevalent across the planet in the twenty-first century. By framing the discussion in this way—that environmental destruction violates the rights of nature and is therefore morally unacceptable—the tribunal could play a key role in advancing the movement toward a more eco-centric steward-ship of the Earth.

One specific crime that the tribunal can address is ecocide, meaning the act of seriously damaging or destroying an ecosystem. At least ten countries, including Guatemala, the Ukraine, Russia, and Vietnam, have designated ecocide as a crime under their criminal legislation. For example, Article 278 of Vietnam's Penal Code states that "destroying the natural environment, whether committed in time of peace or war, constitutes a crime against humanity." Similarly, Article 441 of the Ukraine's Criminal Code states, "Mass destruction of flora and fauna, poisoning of air or water resources, and also any other actions that may cause an envi-ronmental disaster,—shall be punishable by imprisonment for a term of eight to fifteen years." Unfortunately, many of the coun-tries with national ecocide laws are ranked high for corruption and low for respect for the rule of law by Transparency International.

An international effort led by UK lawyer Polly Higgins seeks to add ecocide to the Rome Statute that currently covers genocide, war crimes, and crimes against humanity. This would enable seri-ous environmental crimes to be brought before the International Criminal Court. The ICC announced in 2016 that it will con-sider prosecuting international crimes that cause environmental destruction.

The International Rights of Nature Tribunal was inspired, in part, by the International War Crimes Tribunal created in 1966 by Nobel Prize winner Bertrand Russell to investigate alleged human rights abuses committed against the Vietnamese peoples by the U.S. military. Representatives from eighteen countries participated in two sessions of this tribunal, held in Sweden and Denmark. The tribunal consisted of twenty-five well-known people, predominantly from the left wing of the political spectrum. The International War Crimes Tribunal led to the creation of similar bodies, including the Russell Tribunal and the Permanent Peoples' Tribunal. The Russell Tribunal reported on human rights violations perpetrated by dictatorships in Argentina, Brazil, and Chile in the 1970s. The Permanent Peoples' Tribunal held sessions on human rights violations in Eritrea, East Timor, Guatemala, and Zaire. More recently there was a World Tribunal on Iraq, which reported on human rights violations inflicted by the invasion and subsequent occupation by the United States.

Critics accused these tribunals of bias and one-sidedness, with predetermined outcomes and no attention paid to procedural fairness. Tribunal judges were accused of lacking appropriate expertise and experience. While these tribunals contributed to public education, raising the profile of human rights abuses, they had no authority to impose sanctions or hold anyone accountable. However, one could argue that these tribunals set a precedent for the eventual establishment of the International Criminal Court in 2002.

The first cases brought to the International Rights of Nature Tribunal were heard in 2014, in Quito, Ecuador. Alberto Acosta presided over the hearings. Prosecutors and judges were appointed by the Global Alliance for the Rights of Nature, but no lawyers appeared on behalf of the defendants. The first cases presented to the tribunal involved British Petroleum's oil pollution in the Gulf of Mexico; fracking for oil and gas in the U.S.; the Chevron/ Texaco oil pollution case in Ecuador; the case of the failed attempt to protect Yasuní-ITT in Ecuador; the Mirador Mine in Ecuador; and damage to Australia's Great Barrier Reef. Two additional issues were presented to the tribunal—the danger to life on earth allegedly posed by genetically modified organisms (GMOs) and the persecution of 'defenders of nature' by the Ecuadorian government. The tribunal decided to hear additional evidence in each of these cases.

In December 2014, the second tribunal session was held in Lima, Peru, under the direction of renowned global activist Vandana Shiva. For two days, a panel of thirteen judges heard evidence in twelve cases. The tribunal ordered BP to abstain from any future deepwater exploration. Chevron was found guilty of ecocide and ordered to pay the $9 billion in damages previously ordered by an Ecuador court as a result of devastating oil pollution in the Amazon River basin. The tribunal recommended that the government of Ecuador suspend the operation of the Mirador open-pit mine, require the mining company to restore the Cordillera del Cóndor, increase protection for the region's ecosystems, compensate the affected people, and ensure that this type of industrial exploitation was not repeated in any other area of Ecuador. The tribunal announced that future cases would put Monsanto and Exxon on trial for violating the rights of nature and for committing ecocide.

In 2015, the tribunal convened for a third time, concurrently with ongoing UN climate change negotiations in Paris. Cormac

Cullinan supervised the proceedings. On his blog, Cullinan explained his vision for the tribunal: "Imagine if legal systems were designed to ensure that people contributed to the health of ecological systems instead of authorizing their degradation. Imagine a system that empowers defenders of nature to take action against those that seek to destroy and manipulate communities or the environment for their own commercial interests. Imagine a system that acknowledges that ecosystems have the right to exist, persist, maintain and regenerate their vital cycles and have legal standing in a court of law." Additional hearings are scheduled for 2017.

Prosecutors have included Ramiro Avila, an Ecuadorian lawyer and professor, and Linda Sheehan, an American attorney. Judges have included Alberto Acosta; Cormac Cullinan; Vandana Shiva; Tom Goldtooth of the Indigenous Environmental Network; Osprey Orielle Lake from the Women's Earth & Climate Action Network; Atossa Soltani, founder of Amazon Watch; Nnimmo Bassey from Friends of the Earth; Ruth Nyambura of the African Biodiversity Network; Blanca Chancoso, a Kichwa leader from Ecuador; Verónika Mendoza, a Peruvian congresswoman; Raúl Prada Alcoreza, former member of the Bolivian Constituent Assembly; Julio César Trujillo, a constitutional lawyer from Ecuador; Tantoo Cardinal, an actress and activist from Canada; and Professor Dominique Bourg from the University of Lausanne, Switzerland. Although the judges represent an impressive diversity of backgrounds, few if any have judicial training or experience.

Critics argue, with reason, that the tribunal lacks legitimacy because it was not created by democratically elected governments, is not established by any law, and does not ensure that defendants are represented. Many of the countries in which alleged violations of the rights of nature are occurring do not legally recognize these rights. Most judges are activists drawn from within the international rights for nature movement. Therefore it is not surprising that, in every case decided to date, the judges determined that the rights of nature had been violated. Given its lack of authority, there are no legal consequences for the perpetrators "found guilty" of violating nature's rights.

Education is likely the tribunal's greatest strength. It provides a framework for educating civil society, governments, the media, and the public about the rights of nature. It offers a forum where legal experts, scientists, and Indigenous leaders can gain practical experience in articulating the rights of nature and the ways in which human activities violate these rights. Like the people's tribunals that preceded and inspired it, the International Rights of Nature Tribunal offers an alternative narrative to the stories offered by the mainstream legal system regarding environmental destruction. As Australian lawyer Michelle Maloney concluded in "Finally Being Heard," the tribunal is "pregnant with the promise of transforming existing law."

Conclusion
RIGHT PLANET, RIGHTS TIME

"There is still time to make our laws recognize the right of rivers to flow, prohibit acts that destabilize the Earth's climate, and impose respect for the inherent worth of every living being."

ALBERTO ACOSTA

The hour is late. Human actions have unleashed a tsunami of death and destruction upon the planet, killing tens of billions of animals annually, causing the worst mass extinction in 65 million years, and eroding the integrity of ecosystems and natural cycles that support all life on Earth. Animal welfare laws, endangered species laws, and other environmental laws have put the brakes on some types of harm, but the train is still headed for a cliff. Not only our laws, but also our cultures require a fundamental reorientation, transforming humans from conquerors of nature to members of the planet's community of life.

Perhaps in the nick of time, a global movement has emerged, calling for acknowledgement of the fact that individual animals, wild species, and nature have rights that humans are morally obligated to respect and protect. The Global Alliance for the Rights of Nature unites organizations from across the planet, including groups from Australia, Bolivia, Canada, Ecuador, India, Italy, Romania, South

Africa, Switzerland, the UK, and the U.S. Almost one million people from around the world have signed a petition calling for the adoption of the Universal Declaration of the Rights of Mother Earth. *Shift* magazine recently described the rights of nature movement as one of the top ten grassroots efforts in the world. The growing calls to recognize nature's rights are a direct and revolutionary response to the ecological crises of the twenty-first century.

In the predominant western frame of thought, non-human animals and ecosystems have always been treated as things, property intended for human use and exploitation. In dramatic developments spanning the globe, these entities are being recognized as legitimate, rights-bearing subjects. The fundamental values and laws that have governed society for hundreds of years are in the early stages of the most radical transformation in history. To some extent, this is a revitalization of long-suppressed Indigenous cosmologies that offer a different, and many would say far healthier, vision of humanity's relationship with the rest of the natural world. Recognizing that other animals and other species have rights rejects anthropocentrism, challenging the global predominance of a single species. Recognizing that nature itself has rights goes even further, undermining the idea of property, and bringing into question our wholesale and accelerating appropriation of the planet.

Throughout history, the expansion of rights to previously rightless entities has always begun as unthinkable. Abolitionists fought to transform slaves from property into rights-holders. Suffragettes struggled to transform women from property into rights-holders. Today, Indigenous people, scientists, and activists are struggling to transform animals and nature from property into rights-holders. Professor Roderick Nash, in his classic book on the topic, said the rights of nature constituted "arguably the most dramatic expansion of moral theory" ever contemplated. Writing in 1989, Nash noted that the idea of rights for non-humans struck many as kooky. Yet as a historian, he was "aware that the same incredulity met the first proposals for granting independence to American colonists, freeing the slaves, respecting Indian rights, integrating schools, and adding an Equal Rights Amendment to the Constitution." According to philosopher John Stuart Mill, "every great movement must experience three stages: ridicule, discussion, and adoption."

The rights of nature are advancing rapidly through these stages. As Professor Cristina Espinosa observed, "Advocates for the Universal Declaration on the Rights of Mother Earth are pursuing a previously inconceivable cause." The idea first gained prominence in the late 1960s and early 1970s, in response to emerging concerns about the global environment. In those early years, the rights of nature were often ridiculed. Examples include the poems written by lawyers and judges, and the people who barked at animal lawyer Steven Wise. Critics continue to attack the premise of extending rights to non-human entities. Several years ago, I wrote an article about the rights of nature for Canada's *National Post* newspaper. In the online comments, I was attacked as "anti-Christian, anti-human, anti-freedom, and anti-capitalism." I was called a "commie tree-hugger lunatic." Canadian media commentator Rex Murphy was alarmed by Bolivia's Law on the Rights of Mother Earth, writing, "What does the new Bolivian law mean? It means ticks that suck the blood, the choking sulphur pits of volcanic vents, the indestructible cockroach, the arid desert wastes, and the bleak frigid spaces of the planet's poles—everything from the locusts that despoil, to the great mountain ranges, the earth and all that is in it, are to have . . . rights. . . . The proposal combines the decayed anti-capitalism of Marxism with a veritable litany of new-age twaddle and camp spiritualism—paganism in the age of bluetooth and Twitter."

Others have described the rights of nature as "a catastrophe for the Roman-French legal tradition," "conceptual gibberish," and a "patchouli-soaked Gaia fantasy translated into legalese."

Wesley J. Smith from the right-wing Discovery Institute warned that "deep ecologists, global warming alarmists, and other assorted green radicals want to accord legally enforceable 'rights' to 'nature,' thereby subverting human exceptionalism by demoting us, in effect, to just another species in the forest." Smith expressed grave concern that recognizing nature's rights would "open the courtroom doors to radical environmentalist lawyers who would surely fire a continual barrage of lawsuits seeking to uphold the rights of their animal and vegetable clients." In the past, critics used similar arguments to reject the human right to live in a healthy environment, claiming that this would water down existing human rights and give rise to a blizzard of litigation. Now the human right to a healthy environment is legally recognized in more than 150 countries around the world, including Norway, Finland, Sweden, France, South Africa, Brazil, and Costa Rica. None of the critics' fears have materialized.

Today, what was considered unthinkable just a few decades ago has entered the mainstream and enjoys surprisingly strong support. According to an Angus Reid poll conducted in 2012, 80 percent of Canadians support including the rights of nature in the constitution, alongside human rights.

The revolutionary idea that nature has rights is gaining momentum. Countries are passing laws that acknowledge great apes, cetaceans, and elephants have the fundamental right to freedom, to live in wild habitat. Rules regarding animal research have been dramatically strengthened, reflecting a right to be free from torture or cruel and unusual punishment. In Argentina, courts have recognized that chimpanzees and orangutans are legal persons with enforceable rights. A chimpanzee named Cecilia became the first non-human animal in the world freed from a zoo thanks to a court decision based on her rights. In American courtrooms, lawyers are seeking similar breakthroughs. Germany added animal rights to its constitution. The rights of nature gained constitutional recognition in Ecuador, leading a judge to uphold the Vilcabamba River's right to be restored after it was damaged by highway construction. Nature's rights are protected by law in New Zealand, Bolivia, and dozens of American communities, from Santa Monica to Pittsburgh. In New Zealand, the Whanganui River and Te Urewera (previously a national park) not only have the rights of legal persons, but also were granted title to themselves, meaning they're no longer subject to human ownership. Courts in the U.S., Costa Rica, and India have made extraordinary decisions about endangered species. These courts halted harmful human activities to save the snail darter, palila, northern spotted owl, Asiatic lion, and Asiatic buffalo. These judicial decisions share a common logic: all of life has intrinsic and incalculable value, and humans have a moral responsibility to avoid causing extinctions.

One of the consequences of today's hyperconnected world is that ideas can spread with incredible speed. Nothing can stop their dispersal. In addition to the precedents in the U.S., Ecuador, Bolivia, and New Zealand, recognition of the rights of nature is progressing in countries across the globe, including Belize, the Philippines, Mexico, and Colombia. Additional efforts to gain protection for nature's rights are underway in India, Romania, Indonesia, Nepal, and Cameroon. Even Pope Francis, in his 2015 address to the United Nations, said, "It must be stated that a true 'right of the environment' does exist."

In early 2009, a large cargo ship called the *Westerhaven* crashed into the Mesoamerican Reef off the coast of Belize. An estimated 225 million years old, it's the largest coral reef in the Atlantic Ocean and home to more than 500 species of fish. The shipping company was charged with violating Belize law. In evidence produced at the trial, experts from both the prosecution and the defence agreed that it was more accurate to describe the damage to the reef as an "injury" because it's a living organism. In 2010, the Chief Justice of the Supreme Court of Belize ruled that the reef is a living being, a site of outstanding natural value whose ecological value is inestimable. Because of these attributes, the Court acknowledged that it is "difficult to comprehend it within the concept of 'property' as that word is ordinarily understood." Ultimately the Court found the shipping company liable and imposed a fine of $11 million Belize dollars (roughly U.S.$5.5 million) to reflect the substantial environmental injuries and the cost of rehabilitating the ecosystem.

In the Philippines, the Supreme Court Rules of Procedure for Environmental Cases established a new type of remedy called a writ of *kalikasan* (nature), a court order intended to protect nature's intrinsic value without the traditional legal requirement of proving injury to human interests. Successful cases using this innovative writ have forced a company to repair a pipeline, required restoration of forests damaged by mining, and stopped field testing of genetically modified eggplants.

Two Mexican states recently granted legal recognition to the rights of nature. In 2013, the Federal District of Mexico amended its main environmental law to be called the Environmental Law for the Protection of the Earth. Inspired by the legal innovations in Ecuador and Bolivia, the new law recognized the Earth as a living being and included extensive provisions related to the rights of nature. The state of Guerrero amended its constitution in 2014 to "guarantee and protect the rights of nature." Respect for life in all its forms is mentioned as a fundamental value along with freedom, democracy, equality, and social justice. It is fascinating to see human rights and the rights of nature accorded equal value, indicating that they are perceived as complementary rather than contradictory. How this will play out in Guerrero remains to be seen.

The Constitutional Court of Colombia has extended constitutional protection to the rights of nature. In 2015, the Court ordered the government to develop a long-term plan for restoring the ecological health of Tayrona National Park, and suspended all fishing activity in the area. Ecological deterioration was robbing fishers of their livelihoods. In its decision, the Court stated that society has "the duty to respect and guarantee the rights of nature." The Court observed that rivers, mountains, forests, and the atmosphere must be protected, not because of their utility to humans but because of their own rights to exist. Recognizing nature's rights and corresponding human responsibilities, the Court explained, is imperative for transforming humanity's relationship with the rest of the natural world. Like India's Supreme

Court, Colombia's highest court explicitly rejected anthropocentrism and applied an eco-centric perspective, citing the World Charter for Nature that recognized the intrinsic value of every form of life on Earth. Finally, the Court emphasized that society "must develop new values, norms, legal techniques and principles" to successfully shift from today's ecologically destructive practices to the sustainable approaches of the future.

In a more recent decision, Colombia's Constitutional Court issued an historic judgment recognizing the rights of the Rio Atrato to protection, conservation, and restoration. The Court ordered the government to create a guardian for the river comprised of one state representative and one Indigenous representative, similar to the one established for the Whanganui River in New Zealand. The government was given one year to develop a comprehensive plan to end the pollution and damage being inflicted on the Rio Atrato watershed by activities such as deforestation and illegal mining. The decision, in the words of the court, was based on "the relationship of profound unity between nature and humans."

Advocates in Australia are seeking recognition of the rights of the Great Barrier Reef, the World Heritage Site in dire straits because of human activities. In Nepal, a grassroots group is working to have the rights of nature incorporated into a new constitution, with assistance from Pennsylvania's Community Environmental Legal Defense Fund. The African nation Benin enacted a sacred forest law inspired by the rights of nature. Turkey's Green Party is championing a constitutional amendment that would recognize nature's rights. "We are just starting a campaign calling for an ecological constitution," said Turkey's Green Party spokesperson Ümit Şahin.

In Indonesia, home to the world's largest Muslim population, the leading Muslim clerical body issued a *fatwa*, or edict, against illegal wildlife trafficking. The Indonesian Council of Ulama declared illegal hunting and trading of endangered species to be *haram* (forbidden). Many people will recall the word *fatwa* from Ayatollah Khomeini's death threat against Salman Rushdie for blasphemy in his novel *The Satanic Verses* back in 1989. However this unprecedented wildlife *fatwa* requires Indonesia's 200 million Muslims to take an active role in protecting and conserving endangered species, including tigers, rhinos, elephants, and orangutans. Hayu Prabowo, chair of the Council of Ulama's environment and natural resources body, said, "People can escape government regulation, but they cannot escape the word of God."

In India, a broad coalition is campaigning for a law to recognize the legal rights of the sacred Ganga River. The Ganga (also known as the Ganges) supports roughly 500 million people. Despite its central importance to the Hindu religion, the Ganga is treated more like an open sewer than a cultural and ecological treasure. An estimated three billion litres of wastewater are dumped into the river daily, and species like the Ganga River dolphin are gravely endangered.

Advocates believe that a transformative approach to governance, based on nature's rights, is required to protect and restore this damaged ecosystem. Swami Chidanand Saraswatiji of the Ganga Action Parivar stated in the *Times of India*, "Her rights are being violated, and in turn, our rights to clean water are being violated. People are getting sick. Children are dying. It's time we say no more. Ganga has the right to flow in a clean, pristine form." The proposed Ganga Rights Act would:

- Recognize the river's right to exist, thrive, regenerate, and evolve;
- Establish the rights of people, ecosystems, and natural communities to a healthy watershed;
- Prohibit any activity that interferes with the river's rights;
- Establish enforcement mechanisms and government institutions to protect and defend the watershed's rights;
- Empower people, communities, civil society, and governments within India to protect and defend the watershed's rights; and
- Provide that any damages awarded for violations of the watershed's rights must be used to restore the ecosystem to its pre-damaged state.

Sadhvi Bhagwati of the Ganga Action Parivar said, "If Ganga dies, India dies. If Ganga thrives, India thrives. In violating her rights, we are also violating basic human rights, and we are putting at risk the bright futures our children so greatly deserve." India's minister for water resources, Harish Rawat, expressed his support for the rights of nature approach, stating, "Through the Ganga Rights Act, we can change the direction of our society and protect future generations." This campaign received a major boost in 2017 when the High Court of Uttarakhand issued a decision ordering governments to recognize that the Ganga and Yamuna Rivers have the rights of legal persons, which must be respected and protected. The court instructed governments to set up a management board to advocate for the best interests of the Ganga. Shortly thereafter, the same court extended legal rights to glaciers, lakes, forests, meadows, waterfalls, and other natural entities in the Himalayan region of India, with the goal of stopping environmental destruction.

This catalogue of examples could go on and on. A major rights of nature campaign is being launched in the European Union in 2017. Organizers are planning to gather one million signatures for an official citizens' initiative, which calls on the European Commission to draft a legislative proposal on the rights of nature. A similar citizen-led initiative on the right to water was successful, leading to changes that strengthened the EU's legislation for safe drinking water. In Uganda, local communities and organizations are developing a rights of nature initiative to defend Lake Albert from mining. In Brazil, Councillor Eduardo Tuma proposed an amendment in 2015 to the constitution of the city of São Paolo to recognize the rights of nature.

Global initiatives are also seeking recognition for nature's rights. In 2012, the International Union for the Conservation of Nature, one of the world's most venerable global environmental organizations, decided to make the rights of nature "the fundamental and absolute key element for planning, action, and assessment at all levels and in all areas of assessment in all decisions taken with regard to IUCN's plans, programmes, and projects." Inspired by Bolivia and Ecuador, the IUCN called for the development of a "Universal Declaration of the Rights of Nature, as a first step towards reconciliation between human beings and the Earth." The United Nations continues to host discussions about the creation of such an international declaration and published an experts' report on living in harmony with nature in 2016.

To move from exploiting nature to respecting nature requires a massive transformation of law, education, economics, philosophy, religion, and culture. The shift is underway but will take years, probably decades, to be implemented. And yet it is a scientific fact that all living things share common ancestors, and all depend on air, water, earth, and sunlight to survive. Humans must acknowledge that we are related to millions of other amazing species. We must increase our understanding of and appreciation for their intelligence, abilities, and communities.

Rights for nature impose responsibilities on humans to modify our behaviour in ways that will re-establish a mutually beneficial relationship. Recognizing and respecting nature's rights does not put an end to all human activities, but requires eliminating or modifying those which inflict suffering on animals, threaten the survival of species, or undermine the ecological systems that all life depends on. The precise meaning and effects of recognizing the rights of nature will be worked out through community conversations, scholarly dialogue, public and political debates, negotiation, and, where necessary, litigation, just as all novel legal concepts evolve.

It should be obvious that nature's rights cannot be reconciled with endless economic growth, consumerism, unconstrained globalization, or laissez-faire capitalism. We cannot continue to prioritize property rights and corporate rights, burn fossil fuels at current rates, or perpetuate today's linear economy that treats nature as a commodity rather than a community. Actions needed to respect, protect, and fulfill nature's rights include treating all animals (human and non-human) with greater empathy and respect; rapidly shifting to 100 percent renewable energy;

protecting vital natural cycles of life, such as water, carbon, and nitrogen; focusing on local production and consumption; and redesigning the economy to acknowledge ecological limits and emulate nature's circular approach. In a circular economy, all inputs, outputs, and byproducts must be non-toxic, reusable, recyclable, or compostable. By redesigning products, processes, and supply chains, we could create a restorative economy that benefits both people and the planet.

Perhaps the most critical missing piece of the puzzle is an informed public willing and able to close the gap between their actions and their professed love of animals, endangered species, and nature. We need to place ecological literacy on par with reading, writing, and arithmetic as foundational learning in our education systems. People need to speak out about the rights of nature and elect politicians who are willing to do the same. People need to rethink their own priorities so as to leave a lighter footprint on the Earth and cause less suffering to animals, using renewable energy, eating less meat and dairy (and shifting to ethical sources), reducing consumption, and shifting purchases toward services and cradle-to-cradle products.

Many questions remain regarding the impact of recognizing nature's rights. Yet there is a widespread and growing sense that treating nature as a mere warehouse of resources for our use, and a repository for our pollution and garbage, is fundamentally wrong. Cormac Cullinan believes that "the day will come when the failure of our laws to recognize the right of a river to flow, to prohibit acts that destabilize Earth's climate, or to impose a duty to respect the intrinsic value and right to exist of all life will be as reprehensible as allowing people to be bought and sold."

Propelled by the global environmental crisis, the rights of nature movement has the potential to create a world where people live in genuine harmony with nature. It forces us to reflect upon the fact that we live on the only planet in the universe known to support life. Our evolution, and the evolution of the millions of other species both different from and similar to humans, have combined to form an interdependent fabric that makes this planet a natural miracle, a one-in-a-billion long shot.

Returning to the Southern Resident killer whales that were a catalyst for this book, we can imagine what it means to acknowledge that they have the right to live and flourish in their native habitat. To recognize this right would force us to change our behaviour in specific ways. The easiest step, already taken in a growing number of countries, is to end the practice of capturing killer whales and holding them in captivity to entertain us. To fulfill the orca's right to a sufficient quantity of Chinook salmon to survive and recover their population would require reallocating quota from the commercial and sports fisheries to the whales and taking action to restore salmon habitat. These steps could eventually bolster salmon populations, to the benefit of multiple species, ours included. To fulfill the orca's right to a healthy environment would require decreasing levels of pollution, waste, and ship noise, which would benefit not only the whales but all species in this region. If we change our behaviour so that the orcas can recover and flourish, then humans, whales, and myriad other species can carry on living in the Salish Sea for eons to come. Respecting the rights of nature will not harm humans, but will enable us to grow as a species, to achieve harmony with the rest of this wild and wonderful world.

In the words of Patricia Siemen, executive director of the Center for Earth Jurisprudence, "It has to happen. We have to be able to give legal protection and consideration to the rest of nature. It's in the human best interest, as well as the larger natural world's."

SELECTED BIBLIOGRAPHY

The following sources provide much of the background information for this book. For details regarding specific passages, please contact the author at drdavidboyd@gmail.com.

Introduction

Barnosky, Anthony D., Nicholas Matzke, Susumu Tomiya, et al. (2011). "Has the Sixth Mass Extinction Already Arrived?" *Nature* 471: 51–57.

Bentham, Jeremy. (1789). *An Introduction to the Principles of Morals and Legislation.* Amherst: Prometheus Books.

Berry, Thomas. (1999). *The Great Work: Our Way into the Future.* New York: Three Rivers Press.

Berry, Thomas. (2011). "Rights of the Earth: We Need a New Legal Framework Which Recognises the Rights of All Living Beings," in Peter Burdon, ed., *Exploring Wild Law: The Philosophy of Earth Jurisprudence.* Adelaide, Australia: Wakefield Press.

Cullinan, Cormac. (2011). *Wild Law: A Manifesto for Earth Justice.* 2nd ed. White River Junction, Vermont: Chelsea Green Books.

Dershowitz, Alan. (2005). *Rights from Wrongs: A Secular Theory of the Origins of Rights.* New York: Basic Books.

Ehrenfeld, David. (1981). *The Arrogance of Humanism.* Oxford: Oxford University Press.

Food and Agriculture Organization. (2017). *Global Livestock Production and Health Atlas*. http://kids.fao.org/glipha/

International Union for the Conservation of Nature. (2017). *Red List of Threatened Species*. http://iucnredlist.com

Kolbert, Elizabeth. (2014). *The Sixth Extinction: An Unnatural History*. New York: Henry Holt.

Laytner, Anson, and Dan Bridge, trans. (2005). *The Animals' Lawsuit against Humanity: An Illustrated 10th Century Iraqi Fable*. Louisville, KY: Fons Vitae.

Leopold, Aldo. (1949). *A Sand County Almanac*. New York: Ballantine Books.

Millennium Ecosystem Assessment. (2005). *Ecosystems and Human Well-Being: Synthesis*. Washington, DC: Island Press.

Mohawk, John. (1988, Summer). "The Rights of Animal Nations to Survive." *Daybreak Magazine*.

Nash, Roderick F. (1989). *The Rights of Nature: A History of Environmental Ethics*. Madison, WI: University of Wisconsin Press.

Pavlik, Steve. (2015). "Should Trees Have Standing in Indian Country?" *Wicazo Sa Review* 30 (1): 7–28.

Quammen, David. (1996). *The Song of the Dodo: Island Biogeography in an Age of Extinctions*. New York: Scribner.

Rockstrom, Johan, Will Steffen, Kevin Noone, et al. (2009). "Planetary Boundaries: Exploring the Safe Operating Space for Humanity." *Ecology and Society* 14(2): 32.

Steffen, Will, Paul J. Crutzen, and John R. McNeill. (2011). "The Anthropocene: Are Humans Now Overwhelming the Great Forces of Nature?" *Ambio* 36 (8): 614–621.

WWF. (2016). *Living Planet Report*. https://wnf.n./custom/LPR_2016_fullreport/

1. Breakthroughs in Understanding Animal Minds

Ackerman, Jennifer. (2016). *The Genius of Birds*. New York: Penguin.

Balcombe, Jonathan. (2016). *What a Fish Knows: The Inner Lives of Our Underwater Cousins*. New York: Farrar, Straus and Giroux.

Casey, Susan. (2015). *Voices in the Ocean: A Journey into the Wild and Haunting World of Dolphins*. New York: Doubleday.

Chamovitz, Daniel. (2012). *What a Plant Knows: A Field Guide to the Senses*. New York: Farrar, Straus and Giroux.

Cheney, Dorothy L., and Robert M. Seyfarth. (1990). *How Monkeys See the World: Inside the Mind of Another Species*. Chicago: University of Chicago Press.

de Waal, Franz. (2016). *Are We Smart Enough to Know How Smart Animals Are?* New York: W.W. Norton.

Emery, Nathan. (2016). *Bird Brain: An Exploration of Animal Intelligence*. Princeton: Princeton University Press.

Griffin, Donald R. (1976). *The Question of Animal Awareness: Evolutionary Continuity of Mental Experience*. New York: Rockefeller University Press.

Griffin, Donald R. (2001). *Animal Minds: Beyond Cognition to Consciousness*. Chicago: University of Chicago Press.

King, Barbara J. (2013). *How Animals Grieve*. Chicago: University of Chicago Press.

Linden, Eugene. (1999). *The Parrot's Lament: And Other True Tales of Animal Intrigue, Intelligence, and Ingenuity*. New York: Penguin.

Loukola, Olli J., Clint J. Perry, Louie Coscos, and Lars Chittka. (2017). "Bumblebees Show Cognitive Flexibility by Improving on an Observed Complex Behavior." *Science* 355 (6327): 833–836.

Mancuso, Stefano, and Alessandra Viola. (2015). *Brilliant Green: The Surprising History and Science of Plant Intelligence*. Washington, DC:

Island Press.

Marino, Lori. (2011). "Brain Structure and Intelligence in Cetaceans," in P. Brakes and M.P. Simmonds, eds., *Whales and Dolphins: Cognition, Culture, Conservation, and Human Perceptions*. London: Earthscan.

Mather, Jennifer A., Roland C. Anderson, and James B. Wood. (2010). *Octopus: The Ocean's Intelligent Invertebrate*. Portland: Timber Press.

Montgomery, Sy. (2015). *The Soul of an Octopus: A Surprising Exploration into the Wonder of Consciousness*. New York: Atria Books.

Morell, Virginia. (2014). *Animal Wise: How We Know Animals Think and Feel*. New York: Broadway Books.

Peterson, Dale. (2011). *The Moral Lives of Animals*. New York: Bloomsbury.

Pitman, Robert L., Volcker B. Deecke, Christine M. Gabriele, et al. (2017). "Humpback Whales Interfering When Mammal-Eating Killer Whales Attack Other Species: Mobbing Behavior and Inter-species Altruism?" *Marine Mammal Research* 33 (1): 7–58.

Quinn, Tom, ed. (2017). "The Forum: Animal Minds." *The Philosopher's Magazine* (76).

Reece v. Edmonton (City). 2011 Alberta Court of Appeal Judgment 238.

Safina, Carl. (2015). *Beyond Words: What Animals Think and Feel*. New York: Picador.

Wohlleben, Peter. (2016). *The Hidden Lives of Trees: What They Feel, How They Communicate—Discoveries from a Secret World*. Vancouver: Greystone.

2. The Evolution of Animal Welfare

Campbell, Kathryn M. (2013). "Zoos as Prisons: The Role of Law and the Case for Abolition." *Mid-Atlantic Journal on Law and Public*

Policy 2 (53).

Cao, Deborah, and Steven White, eds. (2016). *Animal Law and Welfare: International Perspectives*. Switzerland: Springer.

Francione, Gary. (2008). *Animals as Persons: Essays on the Abolition of Animal Exploitation*. New York: Columbia University Press.

Kalof, Linda, ed. (2017). *The Oxford Handbook of Animal Studies*. Oxford: Oxford University Press.

Regan, Tom. (2004). *The Case for Animal Rights*. Berkeley: University of California Press.

SaveLucy.ca.

Singer, Peter. (1975). *Animal Liberation: A New Ethic for Our Treatment of Animals*. New York: Harper.

Totten, Tyler. (2015). "Should Elephants Have Standing?" *Western Journal of Legal Studies*. 6 (1).

3. Can a Chimpanzee Be a Legal Person?

A.F.A.D.A, on behalf of Cecilia v. Province of Mendoza (2016, November 3). File No. P-72.245/15. Third Court of Guarantees, Judge Maria Alejandra Mauricio.

Cavalieri, Paola, and Peter Singer, eds. (1993). *The Great Ape Project: Equality Beyond Humanity*. New York: St. Martin's Press.

Mitani, John C., Josep Call, Peter M. Kappeler, Ryne A. Palombit, and Joan B. Silk, eds. (2012). *The Evolution of Primate Societies*. Chicago: University of Chicago Press.

Siebert, Charles. (2014, April 27). "The Rights of Man and Beast." *New York Times Magazine*.

The Nonhuman Rights Project, on Behalf of Hercules and Leo v. Samuel L. Stanley Jr and State University of New York at Stony Brook. (2013). In the Matter of a Proceeding Under Article 70 of the CPLR for a

Writ of Habeas Corpus.

The Nonhuman Rights Project, on Behalf of Kiko v. Carmen Presti, Christie E. Presti, and the Primate Sanctuary, Inc. (2013). In the Matter of a Proceeding Under Article 70 of the CPLR for a Writ of Habeas Corpus.

The Nonhuman Rights Project, on Behalf of Tommy v. Patrick Lavery, Diane Lavery, and Circle L. Trailer Sales, Inc. (2013). In the Matter of a Proceeding Under Article 70 of the CPLR for a Writ of Habeas Corpus.

Wise, Steven M. (2007). *Drawing the Line: Science and the Case for Animal Rights*. New York: Basic Books.

Wise, Steven M. (2009). *Rattling the Cage: Toward Legal Rights for Animals*. Cambridge: Da Capo Press.

4. The Expansion of Animal Rights

Bisgould, Lesli. (2011). *Animals and the Law*. Toronto: Irwin Law.

California Orca Protection Act, A.B. 1453. (2016, September 14).

Declaration of Rights for Cetaceans: Whales and Dolphins. Cetaceanrights.org.

Donaldson, Sue, and Will Kymlicka. (2011). *Zoopolis: A Political Theory of Animal Rights*. Oxford: Oxford University Press.

Ending the Captivity of Whales and Dolphins Act, Bill S-203, 42nd Parliament, 1st Session. Senate of Canada.

Francione, Gary L. (1995). *Animals, Property and the Law: Ethics and Action*. Philadelphia: Temple University Press.

Francione, Gary L. (2008). *Animals as Persons: Essays on the Abolition of Animal Exploitation*. New York: Columbia University Press.

New Zealand Animal Welfare Act 1999. Public Act No. 142. (1999, October 14).

Ontario Society for the Prevention of Cruelty to Animals Amendment Act, 2015. S.O. 2015, c. 10.

Orca Responsibility and Care Advancement Act of 2015, House of Representatives 4019, 114th Congress.

Regan, Tom. (2004). *The Case for Animal Rights*. Berkeley: University of California Press.

Singer, Peter. (1975). *Animal Liberation: A New Ethic for Our Treatment of Animals*. New York: Harper.

Taylor, Rowan. (2001). "A Step at a Time: New Zealand's Progress Toward Hominid Rights." *Animal Law Review* 7 (37): 35–43.

5. *Saving Endangered Species*

Carson, Rachel. (1962). *Silent Spring*. New York: Houghton Mifflin.

Convention on International Trade in Endangered Species of Wild Fauna and Flora. (1973). 12 I.L.M. 1085.

Endangered Species Act of 1973, 16 U.S.C. 1531 et seq.

Huffman, James L. (1992). "Do Species and Nature Have Rights?" *Public Land and Resources Law Review* 13 (51): 51–76.

Northern Spotted Owl v. Hodel, 716 F. Supp. 479 (W.D. Wash. 1988).

Northern Spotted Owl v. Lujan, 758 F. Supp. 621 (W.D. Wash. 1991).

Palila et al. v. Hawaii Department of Land and Natural Resources, 639 F. 2d 495 (9th Circuit, 1991).

Plater, Zygmunt J.B. (2013). *The Snail Darter and the Dam: How Pork-Barrel Politics Endangered a Little Fish and Killed a River*. New Haven: Yale University Press.

Suckling, Kieran, Noah Greenwald, and Tierra Curry. (2012). *On Time, On Target: How the Endangered Species Act Is Saving America's Wildlife*. Center for Biological Diversity.

Tennessee Valley Authority v. Hiram Hill et al., 437 U.S. 153 (1978).

United Nations Educational, Scientific, and Cultural Organization. (1978). Universal Declaration of Animal Rights.

6. *Endangered Species Laws Go Global*

Boyd, David R. (2012). *The Environmental Rights Revolution: Constitutions, Human Rights and the Environment.* Vancouver: UBC Press.

Center for Environment Law and WWF-India v. Union of India (2013). I.A. No. 100 in Writ Petition No. 337 of 1995, Supreme Court of India (Asiatic lion case).

Dinerstein, Eric, David Olson, Anup Joshi, et al. (2017). "An Eco-Region Based Approach to Protecting Half the Terrestrial Realm." *Bioscience* 1: 1–12.

Earth Charter Initiative. (2000). The Earth Charter. http://earthcharter.org/discover/the-earth-charter/

Google Constitute. Constituteproject.org.

International Union for Conservation of Nature. (1980). *World Conservation Strategy: Living Resource Conservation for Sustainable Development.* IUCN–UNEP–WWF.

International Union for Conservation of Nature. (1991). *Caring for the Earth: A Strategy for Sustainable Living.* IUCN/WWF.

Pope Francis. (2015). *Laudato Si': On Care for Our Common Home* (encyclical).

Shadbolt, Tanya, Ernest W.T. Cooper, and Peter J. Ewins. (2015). *Breaking the Ice: International Trade in Narwhals, in the Context of a Changing Arctic.* TRAFFIC and WWF-Canada.

Species at Risk Act, S.C. 2002, c. 29.

T.N. Godavarman Thirumulpad v. Union of India et al. (2012). I.A. Nos. 1433 and 1477 of 2995 in Writ Petition No. 202 of 1995, Supreme

Court of India (Asiatic buffalo case).

United Nations Convention on Biological Diversity. (1992, June 5). 31 I.L.M. 818.

United Nations General Assembly. (1982, October 28). World Charter for Nature. UNGA Res. 37/7. A/Res/37/7.

Wilson, Edward O. (2016). *Half-Earth: Our Planet's Fight for Life.* New York: Liveright.

7. *Watershed Moments*

Byram River v. Village of Port Chester, No. 74 Civ. 4054 (S.D.N.Y. January 8, 1976).

Cullinan, Cormac. (2008, January/February). "If Nature Had Rights." *Orion Magazine.*

Douglas, William O. (1965). *A Wilderness Bill of Rights.* New York: Little, Brown.

Leopold, Aldo. (1949). *A Sand County Almanac.* New York: Ballantine Books.

Linzey, Thomas, and Anneke Campbell. (2016). *We the People: Stories from the Community Rights Movement in the United States.* Oakland, California: PM Press.

Margil, Mari. (2014). "Building an International Rights of Nature Movement," in M. Maloney and P. Burdon, eds., *Wild Law in Practice.* New York: Routledge.

Muir, John. (1916). *Thousand-Mile Walk to the Gulf.* Boston: Houghton-Mifflin.

Naff, John. (1972). "Rejoinder." *American Bar Association Journal* 58: 727.

Pennsylvania General Energy (PGE) v. Grant Township (U.S. District Court, W.D., Pennsylvania).

Resident Marine Mammals of the Protected Seascape of Tanon Strait et al. v. Angelo Reyes in His Capacity as Secretary of the Department of Energy (2015), G.R. No. 180771 (Supreme Court of the Philippines).

Sierra Club v. Morton, 405 U.S. 727 (1972).

Stone, Christopher D. (1987). *Earth and Other Ethics: The Case for Moral Pluralism.* New York: Harper & Row.

Stone, Christopher D. (1972). "Should Trees Have Standing? Law, Morality and the Environment." *Southern California Law Review* 45: 450.

8. A River Becomes a Legal Person

Hsiao, Elaine C. (2013). "Whanganui River Agreement—Indigenous Rights and Rights of Nature." *Environmental Policy and Law* 42 (6): 371–375.

Hutchison, Abigail. (2014). "The Whanganui River as a Legal Person," *Alternative Law Journal* 39 (3): 179–182.

Jones, Carwyn. (2016). *New Treaty, New Tradition: Reconciling New Zealand and Maori Law.* Wellington: Victoria University Press.

Iorns Magallanes, Catherine. (2015). "Maori Cultural Rights in Aotearoa New Zealand: Protecting the Cosmology that Protects the Environment." *Widener Law Review* 21 (2): 273–327.

Iorns Magallanes, Catherine. (2015, September). "Nature as an Ancestor: Two Examples of Legal Personality for Nature in New Zealand." *Vertigo* 22.

Morris, James D.K., and Jacinta Ruru. (2010). "Giving Voice to Rivers: Legal Personality as a Vehicle for Recognising Indigenous Peoples' Relationships to Water?" *Aboriginal and Indigenous Law Reporter* 14 (49).

New Zealand Parliament. (Various dates.) *Hansard Reports.*

Ngati Rangi Trust v. Manawatu Wanganui Regional Council. (2004, May

18). New Zealand Environment Court, Auckland A 67/04.

Strack, Mick. (2017). "Land and Rivers Can Own Themselves."
International Journal of Law in the Built Environment 9 (1).

Te Awa Tupua (Whanganui River Claims Settlement) Act 2017. (2017,
March 20). New Zealand Public Act No. 7.

Waitangi Tribunal. (1999). *The Whanganui River Report*. WAI 167.

9. *Te Urewera*

Arif, Arisha. (2015, April). "New Zealand's Te Urewera Act 2014."
Native Title Newsletter 14–15.

Constitutional Advisory Panel. (2013). *New Zealand's Constitution: A
Report on a Conversation*.

Higgins, Rawinia. (2014, October). "Tuhoe-Crown Settlement: Te
Wharehou o Tuhoe, the House that 'We' Built." *Maori Law Review* 7.

New Zealand Parliament. (Various dates.) *Hansard Reports*.

Ruru, Jacinta. (2014, October). "Tuhoe-Crown Settlement: Te Urewera
Act 2014." *Maori Law Review* 7.

Ruru, Jacinta. (2017). "A Treaty in Another Context: Creating
Reimagined Treaty Relationships in Aotearoa New Zealand," in
J. Borrows and M. Coyle, eds., *The Right Relationship: Reimagining
the Implementation of Historical Treaties* (305–324). Toronto:
University of Toronto Press.

Te Urewera Act 2014, New Zealand Public Act No. 51.

Te Urewera Board. (2016). *Te Kawa o Te Urewera: Final Statement of
Priorities*.

Tuhoe Claims Settlement Act 2014, New Zealand Public Act No. 50.
(2014, July 27).

Waitangi Tribunal. (Various dates). Te Urewera (Parts I-VI). WAI 894.

10. Pachamama and Ecuador's Pioneering Constitution

Acosta, Alberto. (2010). "Toward the Universal Declaration of Rights of Nature: Thoughts for Action." *Revista de la Asociación de Funcionarios y Empleados del Servicio Exterior Ecuatoriano.*

Acosta, Alberto, and Esperanza Martínez, eds. (2009). *Derechos de la Naturaleza—El Futuro Es Ahora (Rights of Nature: The Future Is Now).* Quito: Abya-Yala.

Aguirre, Jessica C., and Elizabeth S. Cooper. (2010). "Evo Morales, Climate Change, and the Paradoxes of a Social-Movement Presidency." *Latin American Perspectives* 37 (4): 238–244.

Becker, Marc. (2011). "Correa, Indigenous Movements, and the Writing of a New Constitution in Ecuador." *Latin American Perspectives* 38 (1): 47–62.

Becker, Marc. (2013). "The Stormy Relations between Rafael Correa and Social Movements in Ecuador." *Latin American Perspectives* 40 (3): 43–62.

Colon-Rios, Joel I. (2015). "On the Theory and Practice of the Rights of Nature," in P. Martin, S.Z. Bigdeli, T. Daya-Winterbottom, et al., eds. *The Search for Environmental Justice* (120–134). Cheltenham, UK: Edward Elgar.

Constitution of Ecuador. (2008.)

Daly, Erin. (2012). "The Ecuadorian Exemplar: The First Ever Vindications of Constitutional Rights of Nature." *Review of European Community and International Environmental Law (RECIEL)* 21 (1): 63–66.

Galeano, Eduardo. (2008, April 27). "La Naturaleza No Es Muda," (Nature Is Not Mute). *Página 12.*

Gudynas, Eduardo. (2011). "Buen Vivir: Today's Tomorrow." *Development* 54 (4): 441–447.

Huddle, Norie. (2013). "World's First Successful Rights of Nature Lawsuit." *Kosmos Journal.*

Humphreys, David. (2015). "Know Your Rights: Earth Jurisprudence and Environmental Politics." *International Journal of Sustainability Policy and Practice* 10 (3–4): 1–14.

Kauffman, Craig M., and Pamela L. Martin. (2017). "Can Rights of Nature Make Development More Sustainable? Why Some Ecuadorian Lawsuits Succeed and Others Fail." *World Development* 92: 130–142.

Kotzé, Louis, and Paola Villavicencio Calzadilla. (2017). "Somewhere between Rhetoric and Reality: Environmental Constitutionalism and the Rights of Nature in Ecuador." *Transnational Environmental Law* 1–33.

R.F. Wheeler and E.G. Huddle v. Attorney General of the State of Loja (2011) Judgment No. 11121-2011-0010. (2011, March 30). Loja Provincial Court of Justice.

Ruhs, Nathalie, and Aled Jones. (2016). "The Implementation of Earth Jurisprudence through Substantive Constitutional Rights for Nature." *Sustainability* 8 (2): 174.

Suarez, Sofia. (2013). "Defending Nature: Challenges and Obstacles in Defending the Rights of Nature. The Case of the Vilcabamba River." Centro Ecuatoriano de Derecho.

Tanasescu, Mihnea. (2016). *Environment, Political Representation and the Challenge of Rights: Speaking for Nature.* London: Palgrave Macmillan.

Tanasescu, Mihnea. (2013). "The Rights of Nature in Ecuador: The Making of an Idea," *International Journal of Environmental Studies* 70 (6): 846–861.

Whittemore, Mary Elizabeth. (2011). "The Problem of Enforcing Nature's Rights under Ecuador's Constitution: Why the 2008

Environmental Amendments Have No Bite." *Pacific Rim Law and Policy Journal* 20 (3): 659–691.

11. Bolivia and the Rights of Mother Earth

Associated Press. (2016, January 23). "A Lake in Bolivia Evaporates and with It a Way of Life." *New York Times.*

Bush, Mark B., J.A. Hanselman, and W.D. Gosling. (2010). "Non-Linear Climate Change and Andean Feedbacks: An Imminent Turning Point?" *Global Change Biology* 16 (12): 3223–3232.

Framework Law on Mother Earth and Holistic Development for Living Well, Law. No. 300 of 2012.

Grantham Research Institute on Climate Change and Environment. (2015). *The 2015 Global Climate Legislation Study: A Review of Climate Change Legislation in 99 Countries.*

Hernandez, Anna. (2017). "Defending Mother Earth in Bolivia." *Indigenous Policy Journal* 27 (3).

Hill, David. (2015, February 24). "Is Bolivia Going to Frack 'Mother Earth'?" *The Guardian.*

Law on the Rights of Mother Earth, Law No. 71 of December 2010.

Morales Ayma, Evo, Maude Barlow, Nnimmo Bassey, et al. (2011). *The Rights of Nature: The Case for a Universal Declaration of the Rights of Mother Earth.* Council of Canadians, Fundación Pachamama, and Global Exchange.

O'Hagan, Ellie Mae. (2014, October 14). "Evo Morales Has Proved that Socialism Doesn't Damage Economies." *The Guardian.*

Oikonomakis, Leonidas, and Fran Espinoza. (2014). "Bolivia: MAS and the Movements that Brought It to State Power," in Richard Stahler-Sholk, Harry E. Vanden, Marc Becker, eds., *Rethinking Latin American Social Movements from Below* (285–305). Lanham,

Maryland: Rowman & Littlefield.

Sivak, Martin. (2008). *Evo Morales: The Extraordinary Rise of the First Indigenous President of Bolivia*. New York: Palgrave Macmillan.

Solon, Pablo. (2017). *Systemic Alternatives*. La Paz: Fundacion Solon.

Vidal, J. (2011, April 10). "Bolivia Enshrines Natural World's Rights with Equal Status for Mother Earth." *The Guardian*.

Villalba, Unai. (2013). "Buen Vivir vs. Development: A Paradigm Shift in the Andes?" *Third World Quarterly* 34 (8): 1427–1442.

12. Global Game Changers

Cullinan, Cormac. (2010). *The Legal Case for the Universal Declaration of the Rights of Mother Earth*.

Espinosa, Cristina. (2014). "The Advocacy of the Previously Inconceivable: A Discourse Analysis of the Universal Declaration of the Rights of Mother Earth at Rio+20." *J. Environ Dev.* 23 (4): 391.

Higgins, Polly. (2010). *Eradicating Ecocide: Exposing the Corporate and Political Practices Destroying the Planet and Proposing the Laws Needed to Eradicate Ecocide*. London: Shepheard-Walwyn.

Maloney, Michelle. (2015). "Finally Being Heard: The Great Barrier Reef and the International Rights of Nature Tribunal." *Griffith Journal of Law & Human Dignity* 3 (1): 40–58.

Maloney, Michelle. (2016). "Building an Alternative Jurisprudence for the Earth: The International Rights of Nature Tribunal." *Vermont Law Review* 41: 129–142.

Maloney, Michelle, and Patricia Siemen. (2015). "Responding to the Great Work: The Role of Earth Jurisprudence and Wild Law in the 21st Century." *Environmental and Earth Law Journal* 5: 6–22.

United Nations General Assembly. (2012, July 27). *The Future We Want*. UNGA Res. 66/288.

Conclusion

Attorney General of Belize v. MS Westerhaven et al. (2009). Supreme Court of Belize, April 26, 2010.

Boyd, David R. (2013, January 26). "Make It the Law." *National Post.*

Burdon, Peter, ed. (2011). *Exploring Wild Law: The Philosophy of Earth Jurisprudence.* Adelaide, Australia: Wakefield Press.

Constitutional Court of Columbia. (2016). Rio Atrato Case. Decision T-622/16.

Constitutional Court of Colombia. (2015). Tayrona National Park Case. Decision T-606/15.

Cullinan, Cormac. (2003). *Wild Law: A Manifesto for Earth Justice.* White River Junction, Vermont: Chelsea Green Books.

Foer, Jonathan Safran. (2010). *Eating Animals.* New York: Back Bay Books.

Keim, Brandon. (2011, April 18). "Nature to Get Legal Rights in Bolivia." *Wired.*

Maloney, Michelle, and Peter Burdon, eds. (2014). *Wild Law in Practice.* London: Routledge.

Murphy, Rex. (2011, April 16). "Excuse Me Sir, That Cockroach Has Rights." *National Post.*

Smith Wesley J. (2011, December 30). "Beware the Rights of Nature." *The Daily Caller.*

Solon, Pablo. (2017). *Systemic Alternatives.* La Paz: Fundacion Solon.

Suzuki, David. (1997). *The Sacred Balance: Rediscovering Our Place in Nature.* Vancouver: Greystone.

Wilson, Edward O. (2016). *Half-Earth: Our Planet's Fight for Life.* New York: Liveright.

ACKNOWLEDGEMENTS

The seeds of this book were planted by Maude Barlow and Susan Renouf, a dynamic duo to whom I am deeply grateful for their ongoing support and encouragement. I drew inspiration from the work of the Global Alliance for the Rights of Nature, the Nonhuman Rights Project, the Community Environmental Legal Defense Fund, the Great Ape Project, People for the Ethical Treatment of Animals, Earthjustice, Ecojustice, Animal Justice, Argentina's Association of Officials and Lawyers for Animal Rights, and the Earth Law Center.

Individuals who provided assistance, served as a sounding board, or whose words sparked insights include Alberto Acosta, Maude Barlow, Shannon Biggs, Peter Burdon, Lynda Collins, Cormac Cullinan, Erin Daly, Gary Francione, Jane Goodall, Polly Higgins, Catherine Iorns Magallanes, Mumta Ito, Thomas Lindzey, Michelle Maloney, Mari Margil, Louis Kotze, Tamati Kruger, Pamela Martin, Zygmunt Plater, Rachel Plotkin, Lynda Prince, Paul Richardson, Jacinta Ruru, Linda Sheehan, Peter Singer, Pablo Solon, Christopher Stone, David Suzuki, Terri-Lynn Williams-Davidson, Edward O. Wilson, and Steven Wise.

The folks at ECW Press were again delightful to work with, including Susannah Ames, David Caron, Samantha Dobson, Chelsea Humphries, Jen Knoch, Stephanie Strain, and a posse of others beavering away behind the scenes.

INDEX

Buddy (dog), 32
Buenos Aires Zoo, 50–51
buffalo, 69
  see also Asiatic wild buffalo
Building an Ark: 101 Solutions to Animal Suffering, 21
bulls, 55
Buompadre, Pablo, 50–51
Bureau of Land Management (United States), 75
Burger, Warren, 64–65
Bush, George H.W., 75
Bush, Mark B., 190–191

Cajete, Gregory, xxx
California
  elephant sanctuaries in, 23–24
  lawsuits on behalf of orcas in, 52–54
  lawsuits over corporate and property rights in, 128–129
  local laws recognizing nature's rights in, 114, 127
  Mendocino County fracking ban, 127
  Mineral King Valley lawsuit, 102–105, 108
  protection of cetaceans in, xix, 46
California condors, 71, 77–78
Cambridge Declaration on Consciousness, 20
Canada
  animal cruelty sentences in, 31
  animal welfare laws in, 27
  evaluation of animal welfare laws in, 28
  intrinsic value of nature in laws of, 88
  rights of Indigenous people in, 49
  rights of women in, 48–49
  see also individual provinces
Canadian legislation
  Act to Improve the Legal Situation of Animals of 2015 (Quebec), 29
  Animal Protection Act (Alberta), 23
  animal welfare laws, 27
  Criminal Code animal cruelty sections, 31
  Ending the Captivity of Whales and

Dolphins Act (S-203), 46–47
  Fisheries Act (Manitoba), xxviii
  Species at Risk Act of 2002, xvii, 87, 90, 98
  Wild Animal and Plant Protection and Regulation of International and Interprovincial Trade Act (WAP-PRIITA), 81–84, 89–90
  Wildlife Act (British Columbia), xxviii
  Wildlife Act of 2013 (Northwest Territories), 88
capitalism
  alternative to, 189, 195
  Bolivia's critique of, 191–192
  vs. nature's rights, 230
  vs. *sumak kawsay (buen vivir)*, 171
captivity
  of chimpanzees, 38–39, 52, 223
  of dolphins, 46
  of great apes, 50–51
  of killer whales, xvii, 232
  lawsuits re, xxxv, 38
Cardinal, Tantoo, 217
Carson, Rachel, 70
Carter, Jimmy, 60, 67
The Case for Animal Rights, 45
Cayapas ecological reserve (Ecuador), 178
Cecilia (chimpanzee), 51–52
Center for Biological Diversity (United States), 75–76, 78
Center for Constitutional Rights (United States), 40
Center for Earth Jurisprudence (United States), 233
cetaceans
  Cetacean Community v. Bush, 77
  conversations among, xiii
  focus on, 48
  protection of, 45, 46
  see also dolphins; orcas/killer whales
Chancoso, Blanca, 217
Charles (octopus), 5
Chellam, Ravi, 95–96
Chevron/Texas oil pollution case, 216
Chilliwack Cattle Sales, 33–34

Heaton, Jeremiah, xxvii
Hercules (chimpanzee), 38, 41, 43
Hiasl (chimpanzee), 49–50
hierarchical ladder of existence, xxiii, 8
Higgins, Polly, 214
Higgins, Rawinia, 155
high seas, as global commons, xxvii
Hill, Hiram (Hank), 61
Ho-Chunk Nation, xxxi–xxxii
home rule municipalities, 120–121
Hominidae, xxxiv
homo sapiens, xxii, xxvi, 9, 131
    see also humans
How Animals Grieve, 11
Hsiao, Elaine, 139
Huddle, Eleanor (Norie), 160–164, 177
Huffman, James L., 74
Human Development Index (United
    Nations), 176
Humane Society (United States), 26
humans
    as animals, 7
    arrogance of, xxviii–xxix
    colonization of Earth by, xxii
    environmental impact of, xxii
    hallmarks of humanity, 8
    as interdependent, xxx, xxxiv–xxxv
    myth of superiority of, xxv, 8, 20–21
    obligations to Mother Earth of, 210–211
    relationship with other animals, xxi
    right to healthy environment, 222
    see also homo sapiens
humpback whales, 12–13, 19
hyenas, co-operation amongst, 17

Independent Petroleum Association of
    New Mexico, 126
India
    Animal Welfare Board, 55
    Biodiversity Conservation Trust of
        India, 95
    case re treatment of circus animals in, 55
    constitutional duty to animals in, 55
    Ganga (Ganges) River, 92, 227–228
    legal protection of rights of nature

in, 95
    Ministry of Environment and Forests,
        46, 96–97
    National Wildlife Action Plan, 95
    progressive environmental judgments
        in, 91–92
    protection of Asiatic buffalo in, 92–93
    protection of Asiatic lions in, 93–95
    protection of dolphins in, 46
    rights of Indigenous people in, 97
    rights of nature in, 229
    Supreme Court biodiversity decisions,
        92
    Supreme Court decision re *jallikattu*, 55
India's Wandering Lions, 94
Indigenous Environmental Network, 217
Indigenous peoples
    concept of *sumak kawsay (buen vivir)*,
        171, 190
    exploitation of, 183
    importance of legal revolution to, 156
    influence on Wildlife Act, 88
    lawsuits in Ecuador, 177
    legal systems of, xxx
    national parks and, 154–155
    as proponents of Ecuador's constitu-
        tion, 170
    protection of lands of, 97
    rights of, 49, 176, 195
    on rights of animals, xxx
    worldview of, xxvii–xxx, 131–132, 154,
        171–172, 195, 200
Indonesia, 224, 227
Inky (octopus), 4
intelligence
    brain size and, 8–9
    brain-to-body weight ratio and, 9
    memory and, 14–15
Inter-American Commission on Human
    Rights, 179
International Court of Climate Justice, 212
International Criminal Court (ICC), envi-
    ronmental crimes before, 214–215
International Marine Mammal Project, 46
International Monetary Fund, 166, 187

Dr. David R. Boyd is an environmental lawyer and associate professor at the Institute for Resources, Environment, and Sustainability at the University of British Columbia. Boyd is the award-winning author of over 100 articles and eight books including *The Optimistic Environmentalist: Progress Towards a Greener Future* (ECW Press) and *Cleaner, Greener, Healthier: A Prescription for Stronger Canadian Environmental Laws and Policies* (UBC Press). He lives on Pender Island, B.C., and is the reigning world record holder (22 hours, 55 minutes) in the Barnacleman triathlon. For further information, visit www.davidrichardboyd.com

Published by ECW Press
665 Gerrard Street East, Toronto, ON M4M 1Y2
416-694-3348 / info@ecwpress.com

MIX
Paper from
responsible sources
FSC
www.fsc.org   FSC® C016245

Editor for the press: Susan Renouf
Cover design: Michel Vrana
Cover image: Antelopes running across flooded
    grasslands, by Grodza / Shutterstock
Interior image: "Lake Waikaremoana, Urewera,
    New Zealand" by Phillip Capper used under
    CC by 2.0 / Desaturated from original
Author photo: Davy Rippner
Type: Rachel Ironstone

Library and Archives Canada
Cataloguing in Publication

Boyd, David R. (David Richard), 1964–, author
Rights of nature : a legal revolution that could save
the world / David R. Boyd.

Issued in print and electronic formats.
ISBN 978-1-77041-239-2 (softcover)
ISBN 978-1-77090-965-6 (PDF)
ISBN 978-1-77090-966-3 (epub)

1. Environmental law. 2. Animal rights. I. Title.

K3585.B69 2017   344.04'6   C2017-902400-0
C2017-902979-7

The publication of The Rights of Nature has been generously supported by the Canada Council for the Arts, which last year invested $153 million to bring the arts to Canadians throughout the country, and by the Government of Canada through the Canada Book Fund. Nous remercions le Conseil des arts du Canada de son soutien. L'an dernier, le Conseil a investi 153 millions de dollars pour mettre de l'art dans la vie des Canadiennes et des Canadiens de tout le pays. Ce livre est financé en partie par le gouvernement du Canada. We also acknowledge the support of the Ontario Arts Council (OAC), an agency of the Government of Ontario, which last year funded 1,737 individual artists and 1,095 organizations in 223 communities across Ontario for a total of $52.1 million, and the contribution of the Government of Ontario through the Ontario Book Publishing Tax Credit and the Ontario Media Development Corporation.

Ontario
Ontario Media Development
Corporation

ONTARIO ARTS COUNCIL
CONSEIL DES ARTS DE L'ONTARIO
an Ontario government agency
un organisme du gouvernement de l'Ontario

Canada Council
for the Arts

Conseil des Arts
du Canada

Canada

Printed and bound in Canada
by Friesens   5   4   3   2   1

GET THE EBOOK FREE!

At ECW Press, we want you to enjoy this book in
whatever format you like, whenever you like.
Leave your print book at home and take the eBook to go!
Purchase the print edition and receive the eBook free.
Just send an email to ebook@ecwpress.com and include:

- the book title
- the name of the store where you purchased it
- your receipt number
- your preference of file type: PDF or ePub?

A real person will respond to your email with
your eBook attached. Thank you for supporting
an independently owned Canadian publisher with
your purchase!